PENNSYLVANIA CAVES
& OTHER ROCKY ROADSIDE WONDERS

PENNSYLVANIA CAVES

& OTHER ROCKY ROADSIDE WONDERS

KEVIN PATRICK

STACKPOLE
BOOKS

Copyright © 2004 by Stackpole Books

Published by
STACKPOLE BOOKS
5067 Ritter Road
Mechanicsburg, PA 17055
www.stackpolebooks.com

Printed in the United States of America

10 9 8 7 6 5 4 3 2

FIRST EDITION

Cover photo of Indian Echo Caverns by Alan Wycheck
Cover design by Wendy Reynolds
Photographs by the author unless otherwise noted

Library of Congress Cataloging-in-Publication Data

Patrick, Kevin Joseph.
    Pennsylvania caves and other rocky roadside wonders / Kevin Patrick.–
1st ed.
          p.   cm.
    Includes bibliographical references and index.
    ISBN 0-8117-2632-0 (pbk.)
    1. Caves–Pennsylvania–Guidebooks.   2. Geology–Pennsylvania–
Guidebooks.   3. Pennsylvania–Guidebooks.   I. Title.
GB605.P4 P38   2004
557.48–dc22
                                            2003026228

ISBN 978-0-8117-2632-0

CONTENTS

ACKNOWLEDGMENTS

This book could not have been written without the kindness and cooperation of the proprietors, families, and staff who maintain the stewardship of Pennsylvania's current and former show caves. I offer my sincerest thanks for the time, energy, and enthusiasm they have put into this project. I am equally indebted to the community of recreational cavers and cave enthusiasts whose passion for the subject provided the research foundation for this book. My eternal gratitude goes to Tom and Kim Metzgar who introduced me to much of this research and supported this project in many ways. Thanks also to Dean Snyder, resident expert on the show caves of eastern Pennsylvania, who provided many of the historic images used in this book.

Indiana University of Pennsylvania played an important role as well, providing a Senate Fellowship Grant and support through the Geography and Regional Planning Department. Special thanks to the dedicated Geography graduate students who helped collect and organize cave information.

On my many trips to rocky roadside wonders far from home, I could always count on a good meal and a place to stay from Ted and Chris Angst, and especially my parents, Ernest and Gloria Patrick, the people who picked up the tab for my first cave trip back in 1972. Thanks to my own family, Theresa, Katie, and Veronica, for indulging my desire to bend our trips to take in another show cave or to hunt out some obscure rock city.

Finally, a heartfelt thanks to Brian Butko who was with me inside Tennessee's Ruby Falls Cavern when the idea for this book was hatched, and editor Kyle Weaver, whose unwavering work and guidance brought the idea to light.

I

Pennsylvania Geology, Caves, and the Grand Staircase

Like many Pennsylvania houses, my Indiana home is stuffed into a hillside. The driveway to my semisubterranean attached garage is bordered by a steep slope that happens to be the shortest path between the driveway and the front door. This is not the proscribed path, as dictated by a walkway, but the shortest, and therefore the one inevitably taken. Because friends and family were risking life and limb on my front-yard hill climb, I decided to build some steps. Normally I would have accepted the hill climb as a fact of life, just part of getting into the house, rather than undertake such a tedious task as step building. But I became inspired: I would turn this household chore into a quest by building steps made of rocks representing each geologic period that outcropped in Pennsylvania. I would scour the state for stone and arrange the rocky ages of the past chronologically as treadles from the ancient Precambrian bottom step up to the relatively recent Quaternary top step. My construction-savvy colleague, Whit Watts, assured me that such a thing was possible, and that was all I needed. I immediately began reading three different books on Pennsylvania geology—and none on how to build steps.

Geologic maps in hand, I canvassed the countryside, foraging into the farthest corners of the state in search of the perfect road cut from which I could pry my step-size stones. The rock collecting was not a random thing, but revealed the pattern of Pennsylvania geology, something that could not be deciphered until I first learned the cadence of geologic time. Rock ages are subdivided into periods of variable lengths and titled with names that have evolved relative to changing interpretations of historical geology. The Precambrian Era covers the first 4 billion years, a mind-bending seven-eighths of all geologic time. These ancient rocks are so old and altered that it's nearly impossible to develop a reliable system of differentiation within the strata. The rock record of the last half billion years or so is a little easier to chronicle, beginning with the four-hundred-million-year-long Paleozoic Era, which is subdivided into the Cambrian, Ordovician, Silurian, Devonian, Mississippian, Pennsylvanian, and Permian Periods. The Mesozoic "Age of the Dinosaurs" followed and included the Triassic, Jurassic, and Cretaceous Periods, lasting to about 65 million years ago. The most recent era, the Cenozoic, has been divided into the Tertiary and Quaternary Periods, ending with the dawn of humanity.

The tune of this geologic rock song was more easily remembered with a mnemonic device taught to me by University of Illinois professor Don Johnson. Going forward in time from Cambrian to Quaternary, the weird wording goes: Can Ollie Stick (his hands) Down My Pants Pockets To Jingle Change Tightly and Quietly? Regardless of the questionable meaning, Dr. Johnson promised I would never forget it. I never did, and I recited that silly ditty—never aloud—dozens of times to remind myself what rocks I had in the trunk, and what rocks I still needed to get.

The map of Pennsylvania surface geology is a swirl of colors that could easily pass as vividly hued abstract art. There is nonetheless a method to this madness. The highly generalized pattern, with some exceptions, has the oldest rocks in the east-southeast part of Pennsylvania trending toward younger rocks in the west-southwest. Ancient Precambrian Era rocks, my bottom step, make up the low, hilly Piedmont in the southeastern corner of the state, bounded to the west by South Mountain—Pennsylvania's piece of the Blue Ridge—and on the north by the Reading Prong, a rocky ridge of New England Upland that extends across New Jersey and along the southern margin of the Lehigh Valley to the city of Reading.

The folded Appalachian Ridge and Valley section of central and northeast Pennsylvania is mostly underlain by the oldest Paleozoic Cambrian *(Can)*, Ordovician *(Ollie)*, Silurian *(Stick)*, and Devonian *(Down)* rocks, in addition to several synclinal basins containing younger Paleozoic Mississippian *(My)* and Pennsylvanian *(Pants)* age rocks. Northeast Pennsylvania's Pocono Plateau is Devonian, and the northern Allegheny Plateau west from the Wyoming Valley is Devonian and younger Mississippian. Nearly all of western Pennsylvania's Allegheny Plateau is underlain by rocks from the coal-forming Pennsylvanian Period, which trend younger toward the southwest until finally becoming Permian

(Pockets)—the most recent Paleozoic period—in Greene, Washington, and Fayette Counties.

The bulk of Pennsylvania's rocks were laid down millions of years before the existence of dinosaurs. The relatively small portion of Mesozoic rocks that outcrop in the state buck the east-west, oldest-to-youngest surface trend. The youngest Triassic *(To)* and Jurassic *(Jingle)* rocks are hard up against the oldest Precambrian metamorphics in a broad band that borders the Piedmont from Bucks County southwest through Gettysburg. The 400-million-year gap resulted from a rift valley that dropped the older erosion surface downward during the Triassic, when the Atlantic Ocean was opening between Africa/Europe and North America. Reddish sandstones and shales were deposited in the basin along with igneous inclusions resulting from volcanic activity stimulated by the rifting. Pennsylvania has no Cretaceous *(Change)* rocks. They were either eroded away or never deposited in the first place. Cenozoic Era Tertiary *(Tightly)* and Quaternary *(Quietly)* deposits are so recent as to still be in an unconsolidated state, being expressed primarily as coastal plain sands and gravels, alluvium, and glacial outwash laid down in the state's river valleys, as well as glacial drift mantling the mountains and plateaus of northeastern and northwestern Pennsylvania.

Pennsylvania's sedimentary rocks were laid down one on top of the other as sediments deposited by some medium like water, wind, or glaciers. Time and the weight of overlying sediments compressed the sand of ancient beaches and floodplains into sandstone. A mixture of pebbles and sand became conglomerate. Shale originated as the mud of prehistoric coastal swamps, and the partially decayed and buried vegetation of such swamps became coal. The same process could convert the billions of calcium-rich, microscopic sea creatures, shells, and crustaceans that littered the mucky bottoms of shallow seas into limestone, the rock most associated with cave formation. These rocks were stacked with the youngest always on top, like a multitiered layer cake, recording the state's ever-changing environments through the ages, the rise and fall of ancient oceans, the expansion and contraction of tropical marshes and desert sands, even the fickle movement of long-gone rivers.

The earth is a dynamic place. Even inert rock deeply buried for eons is not immune to radical transformation. The rocks of Pennsylvania have experienced the heat and pressure of no less than four separate orogenies, mountain-building periods that have bent, broken, and in places physically altered the rock into metamorphic equivalents. Erosion-resistant sandstones and conglomerates have been converted into even tougher quartzites, shale into slate, limestone into marble, and soft bituminous coal into harder, more concentrated anthracite.

Pennsylvania's distinctive geography of rolling hills, dissected plateaus, and long, sharp back ridges separated by broad valleys resulted from the most recent Alleghenian Orogeny, which brought Africa into collision with North America during the assemblage of a supercontinent known as Pangaea. This titanic Pennsylvanian-age continental collision faulted and compressed the state's Paleozoic rock package into a series of great upturned and downturned folds, like a rug pushed from its end to one side of a room. The folds were greatest to the east and southeast, closer to the zone of contact. Here a sole thrust fault 20,000 feet beneath the surface split horizontally through Cambrian beds, allowing the entire rock package above the fault to be shoved northwestward at the same time that it was being folded into the Appalachian Mountains. Farther west, the sole thrust fault ramped upward through 75 million years worth of rock, then split horizontally again through weak Silurian shales. Because the rock package above this part of the thrust fault was thinner, it offered less resistance to the compression of continental collision, and therefore the folds under what is now the Allegheny Plateau are shallower.

While being compressed over the course of millions of years, these 10- and 20-mile-wide folds were also being planed down by the forces of erosion. In places, 10,000 vertical feet of rock have been eroded away. Because some rocks are harder than others, they erode at different rates and therefore create different topographies. Shales and limestones are

Huntingdon county's Thousand Steps, where quarry workers built their own grand staircase in 1936 using slabs of Tuscarora quartzite.

more easily eroded; sandstones, conglomerates, and quartzites are more resistant. Where these weaker rocks outcrop adjacent to more resistant beds, the shales and limestones erode faster, resulting in valleys. The more slowly eroding sandstones, conglomerates, and quartzites are left standing as ridges. Silurian-age Tuscarora quartzite, Mississippian Pocono sandstone and conglomerate, and Pennsylvanian-age Pottsville sandstone and conglomerate are the three dominant ridge-forming rock strata in Pennsylvania's Appalachian Mountains.

The best way to appreciate these ridge forms is to visit Thousand Steps in Jacks Narrows just north of Mt. Union. Thousand Steps was built by quarry workers in 1936 to access the Tuscarora quartzite, used in the manufacture of silica bricks, at the top of Jacks Mountain. The stiff climb up 900 vertical feet can still be made today.

A layered, sedimentary rock package that has been bent upward into an anticline will have older rocks toward the core. Sedimentary rocks that have been bent downward into a syncline will have younger rocks toward the core. In Pennsylvania, the older rocks outcropping at the surface of anticlinal valleys include cave-bearing Ordovician and Devonian limestones. The younger rocks cupped within the synclinal basins contain mine-studded, Pennsylvanian age coal seams.

Months of rock hunting fetched me a yard full of stones that no mason in his right mind would assemble together. Silvery Wissahickon schist was wrested from the hills of Philadelphia's Manayunk for the bottom step. The origins of Wissahickon schist are shrouded in the mystery and metamorphic change of geologic time. Some geologists assign it to the Precambrian Era; others have pegged it to the Lower Paleozoic. Either way, I could not resist the precious-metal appearance of this silver-streaked, mica-studded stone. Cambrian quartz chunks and dolostone from Lancaster County were set for the second step. Slabs of Ordovician limestone from Morrison Cove in Bedford County were acquired for the third. Silurian Tuscarora quartzite was chosen for the fourth step after being pried from the crest of Tussey Mountain west of Saxton. Sandstones and shales of the Devonian Catskill Formation, the hardened record of a massive delta that once nearly covered the state, were plucked from the banks of the Juniata River in Blair County. Anthracite (hard coal) was collected from the eviscerated bowels of Schuylkill County for the all-important Pennsylvanian step and joined with a piece of Pottsville conglomerate taken from the top of Mount Davis, highest peak in the state. Permian shales were pulled from a ditch along the National Road in Washington County. Igneous diabase from the same Jurassic-Triassic volcanic dike that forms the boulders of Gettysburg's famous Devil's Den was included into the second highest step. As the Cretaceous skipped Pennsylvania, so I skipped it, as well as the pebble, sand, and clay-cloaked Tertiary. For the top step, I used wave-washed cobbles deposited by Quaternary glaciers and scavenged from a Lake Erie beach on Presque Isle Peninsula. The rocks having been assembled, it was time to dig.

I strolled into the yard one sunny Sunday in May, blissfully ignorant of the fact that the step project would not be completed until the *following* May. Originally I had labeled the project "Geologic Steps," but after six months of labor, I wanted a new name that reflected the effort—if not the end product—and rechristened it "Grand Staircase." Apparently my wife, Theresa, thought the project would be completed by suppertime. Although by then I had not yet begun to fight, I had nonetheless hacked a great gash into our hillside. Theresa stared down into it and asked, somewhat stupefied, "Why are you digging?"

Why are you digging? It wasn't the first time I had been asked that. My mother said the same thing when I was digging that hole to China in the backyard. I figured if I was up to my knees by lunchtime, I was halfway there. Years later, the wonders of latitude and longitude taught me that contrary to popular belief, China was *not* on the opposite side of the planet from my house—the Indian Ocean was. Imagine if I had made that connection. Mom really would have been pissed to find the backyard flooded with Indian Ocean water. I suppose it was not China I was after anyway, but the sense of discovery. The New Jersey housing development I grew up in was scorched earth, scraped clean by the bulldozers that prepared the lots. That, however, did not prevent me from finding Indian arrowheads (any triangular rock or hunk of concrete), colonial farm implements (broken, rusted, and lost yard tools), and even pirate loot (shards of glass and ceramic). Each bit of booty represented the manifestation of discovery and was cherished like the riches foretold by a treasure map.

The drive to experience that sense of discovery permeated the stories of Pennsylvania's caves. Within the first few years of operation, "new discoveries" were found at Lost River Caverns, Indian Echo Cavern, Indian Caverns, and Lincoln Caverns. In all cases, proprietors responsible for finding the new chambers added them to the tour by blasting tunnels through solid rock. Cavers who explore the depths of Pennsylvania's wild caves dream of discovering a "virgin passage," a yet-to-be-plumbed hole leading to a subterranean world that has never been entered by another human being. Some have forfeited their lives in the quest. Some, like William Wilson, the Pennsylvania Hermit, have entered caves in search of self-discoveries. Embracing subterranean exile after the loss of a sister he could not save, Wilson lived in Hummelstown Cave for nineteen years and eventually found peace in solitude that allowed an undistracted communion with God.

As for me and the Grand Staircase dig, I discovered the electrical wire that ran to the front-yard coach lamp. Apparently it had to be sacrificed for the project. I also discovered the rainwater runoff pipe that drained my gutters into the sewer. That one forced a redesign. More significantly, however, the digging, the rocks, and the running around the state reawakened a fascination I have always had for the human perception, interpretation, and reordering of nature as an extension of the cultural landscape.

The simple naming of nature gives it a human dimension that can be explored for meaning. Take, for example, Balanced Rock in Huntingdon County's Trough Creek State Park. As a huge block of sandstone poised on the edge of a cliff, it is nature, the product of normal erosive processes that will eventually drop it into the valley below. As Balanced Rock, it takes on the anthropomorphic meaning of implied action, as if it were actually balanced by some being. It ceases to be just another rock and becomes a tourist attraction, requiring an infrastructure of trails, fencing, and signs that allow visitors to experience the curiosity from the proper perspective. In addition to Balanced Rocks, the state is filled with Pulpit Rocks, Devil's Racecourses, and Indian Profiles. Most of these features were given labels by early European settlers reflecting their cultural legacy and perspective of the frontier. Some reference God in nature, some echo the primordial, demon-filled fear of a chaotic wilderness, and many others reaffirm the eternal link between the land and its aboriginal inhabitants. All of this assumes some sort of human point of view. This was the *real* quest brought on by the step project. Bound within these layered pages is the human side of Pennsylvania's geology, highlighting the netherworld where our powers of perception, interpretation, and manipulation have been particularly ingenious.

Lincoln Caverns was the first cave I was ever in. Like most people's initial experiences with caves, mine was with my parents while on a family vacation. The average parent does very little comparison shopping when it comes to caves. Lincoln Caverns was chosen because it was on the way to my grandparents' house in Clearfield County. There were six of us kids crammed into the back of a Pontiac Tempest station wagon getting more excited with every "Lincoln Caverns" billboard passed. Having at last arrived, we kids wandered around the gift shop while Dad came to the realization that in order for him to see the inside of a cave he would just as soon skip, he would have to pay the admission

The original door to Lincoln Carverns's underground world was located just a few feet away from busy U.S. Route 22. DEAN SNYDER

price times eight, less the child discounts, of course. After this scary moment of parental second thought passed, we got our tickets and made the mad dash across busy U.S. Route 22 from the old gift shop to the cave entrance on the other side of the road.

Contrary to my expectations of what a cave entrance would look like, Lincoln Caverns lay behind a wooden, fairytale-like door placed in the side of a mountain. Once inside, other cavey expectations were instantly shattered. I anticipated the three Ds—dirty, dark, and dank—and possibly smelly. Having grown up in New Jersey, I must have thought caves were akin to sewers. The cave was actually well lit, reasonably dry, and astoundingly colorful. It was a subterranean world of enchantment. Although the stalactites, stalagmites, and other speleothems stole the show, I was equally fascinated with the intimidating flight of concrete steps mounted to view the Frozen Niagara, the seemingly incomprehensible labyrinth of paths, the semihidden system of colored lights, and the intriguing names given to the formations. I had no idea what Bath of Nymphs meant, but it sounded magical. The Devil's Den gave me the creeps. The implication that it was the gateway to hell was further accentuated by its being backlit with a reddish glow. The cave guide seemed all-knowledgeable, like a wise old sage from some magic kingdom. I asked him how those steps got in the cave. I was a little surprised when he acted like he had never heard such a question before but forgave him for his weak answer.

Back in the gift shop, I was drawn to the black and white photographs that hung on the wall showing happy cave visitors from the past standing next to their dark, bulbous cars. Men in sport coats and ties. Hatted women wearing dresses and high-heeled shoes. They looked more like they were going to church than into a cave. It gave me the sense that Lincoln Caverns was not just a my-time thing. The cave had operated as a tourist attraction for a long time, since when my *parents* were kids, which I had always assumed was a time of poverty and want, when the possibility of frivolous cave visits could not have existed. I rifled the racks for a book that could explain it to me, tossing aside books on bats and spelunking. They did not hold the answers. I wanted to know how Lincoln Caverns was formed geologically, as well as how it was developed. I wanted to know who those people were in the old photographs, and who painted the billboards, and how they affixed a door to a mountain. I wanted to know how someone came up with such a name as Bath of Nymphs, and I wanted a book that could tell me how those steps got in the cave. In a way, this is that book.

Although the National Speleological Society has recorded more than 1,220 caves in Pennsylvania, only nine are currently operating tours. All nine of these show caves resulted from the dissolution of limestone laid down in the Cambrian, Ordovician, Devonian, or Mississippian Periods, times when large sections of Pennsylvania lay submerged beneath shallow seas. The three eastern caves—Lost River, Crystal, and Indian Echo—are part of the Great Valley Cave Belt that stretches between southeastern Pennsylvania and eastern Tennessee. The Great Valley is more commonly known by a number of different regional names, such as the Lehigh, Lebanon, and Cumberland Valleys in Pennsylvania and the Shenandoah Valley in Virginia. The entire length is underlain by Cambrian and Ordovician limestones pockmarked with caves. Lost

The central stalactite drips onto Lincoln Caverns's Bath of Nymphs in the Palace of Splendor, later reinterpreted as the cave's Wishing Well.
DEAN SNYDER

River Caverns is on the fringe of the Lehigh Valley just south of Bethlehem. Crystal Cave is in the Schuylkill Valley to the southwest, and Indian Echo Caverns is in the western part of the Lebanon Valley between Hershey and Harrisburg. Two more Great Valley show caves have since closed. Onyx Cave operated in Berks County until the 1980s, and in southern Cumberland Valley, Baker Caverns closed in 1954. Maryland's Crystal Grottoes and the famous caves of Virginia's Shenandoah Valley—Luray, Skyline, Shenandoah, Endless, and Grand—are part of this same cave belt.

Five show caves are scattered about the limestone valleys of central Pennsylvania. Woodward Cave and Penn's Cave are in Centre County, Indian Caverns and Lincoln Caverns are in Huntingdon County, and Coral Caverns is in Bedford County. The first three are in Ordovician limestones, the last two are Devonian. Five other central Pennsylvania show caves failed decades ago. The entrance to Laurel Caverns, western Pennsylvania's only show cave, is perched high on Chestnut Ridge in Fayette County where the Mississippian Loyalhanna limestone outcrops.

These operating show caves are familiar to most Pennsylvanians, who have at least seen their colorful billboards along the highway, if not actually been in one or more of them. The closed caves, however, have for the most part fallen off the average resident's mental map of the state. To be sure, the caves still exist, their walkways and steps slowly crumbling and silting over, their handrails and hardware gradually becoming entombed in growing calcite formations.

The commercial cave tour is a blend of natural history and human history; of myth, imagination, legend, and science; of pristine nature and profitable tourism. Each tour is unique not only because of nature's infinite variety, but also because of the management style of the entrepreneur. Show caves are the final bastion of the individual family-run, owner-operated roadside attraction. Caves cannot be manufactured, or set down in more profitable locations, and it would be difficult if not impossible to manage them as standardized corporate chains with name-brand recognition. By their very geologic nature, they have resisted the corporate capitalism that has come to overwhelm modern tourism with a proliferation of theme parks, infotainment museums, and synergic crossovers. Like the family farm, a show cave is as much a lifestyle choice as a business, characterized by long-term stewardship and inheritance, with caves being passed down through family dynasties. Coral Caverns is the only show cave in Pennsylvania run by first-generation proprietors. Five others are in their second generation, and three are in their third. Penn's Cave has started to employ its fourth generation.

Although each show cave is unique, all have historic ties to romantic landscape tourism of the Victorian era. This was a time when few but the wealthy, educated elite had the means and leisure time to travel for the purpose of self-fulfillment. Tourism was a passive experience emphasizing the contemplation of visual scenery. Landscape appreciation was taught, and environments were manipulated and ordered to reflect certain values and ideals. Through literature, art, and landscape architecture, the romantic aesthetic could be applied to even the grandest of America's scenic wonders. Niagara Falls, Natural Bridge, and Mammoth Cave became significant stops on America's Grand Tour, and the landscape aesthetic became the blueprint for arranging natural tourist attractions great and small. Natural wonders were experienced by strolling circuitous paths lined with rustic benches, bridges, and gazebos to view scenic tableaux further enhanced by myth, legend, or local history. The trend was firmly established by the age of mass middle-class tourism in the twentieth century. Other aesthetics would follow, including an infatuation with all that was modern, as well as a growing emphasis on active tourism and recreation. The romantic landscape aesthetic nonetheless provided the foundation on which the others would rest, and while subsequently de-emphasized, neglected, or even abandoned, it can still be discerned.

The Grand Staircase on the day of its grand opening.

Indiana, Pennsylvania, witnessed the grand opening of my Grand Staircase on May 5, 2000. All the neighbors were there for the ribbon cutting and trooped up through the geologic ages. I made refrigerator magnets proclaiming it the "Eighth Street Wonder of the World." Some weeks later, I was admiring the new bluestone fireplace wall of my friends Chuck and Suzanne Yula when the subject of Grand Staircase came up. They had yet to see it, and Suzanne assumed that with all those different rocks, the steps must look nice. Nice? It was the first time I had ever considered the term. Nice implies appearance rather than experience, and craftsmanship over concept. Does Grand Staircase look nice? Well, it's not a matter of what it *looks* like, but what it *is*.

2

Pennsylvania Rocks and How They Got That Way

I had a rock collection when I was younger. I thought it was pretty impressive at the time, but in reality it wasn't much. After all, I lived on the coastal plain and could collect rocks only within walking distance of my house. Basically, my collection consisted of quartz pebbles and some broken bits of brick and concrete. What it lacked in quality, however, it made up for in quantity. My rock collection filled a shopping bag. After acquiring the rocks, I rolled up the top of the shopping bag and put it in a corner of the utility room. Months passed, maybe years, and the bag moldered away beneath a pile of winter boots, backyard balls, and baseball bats, until one day it was unearthed by my mother. As she picked up the bag, the bottom ripped out, releasing an avalanche of sand and stone onto the utility room floor. Yeah, my rock collection. I returned the rocks from whence they came for some other kid to find.

My rocks, like any others, were physical evidence of the environment that existed when they were deposited. Essentially, my neighborhood was a beach at the edge of the Atlantic Ocean when those wave-washed pebbles were laid down in the Cretaceous. Seeing as how the seashore is now only about 50 miles away from my old neighborhood, things have not changed all that much in the last 100 million years or so.

Pennsylvania's environments have changed radically in the last 600 million years since the Precambrian, and these changes are expressed not only underground, but aboveground as well. A mere blink ago, geologically speaking, Pennsylvania settlers began quarrying stone that it had taken nature millions of years to put in the ground. They used the stone for their vernacular buildings—barns, houses, and whatnot—creating an aboveground cultural geology that mirrors the rocks underground.

The early nineteenth-century furnace stacks scattered across the western part of the state are inevitably made of the nearly ubiquitous buff-to-brown-colored Pennsylvanian-age sandstone. Bank barn foundations and farmhouses in Lancaster and York Counties and the Great Valley are the grayish white of local Cambro-Ordovician limestones and dolomites. In the narrow Triassic lowland that separates these two regions, the stone buildings turn ruddy with red bed sandstones. Even the geologic boundary is represented in the red sandstone quoined, white limestone buildings found along the southern margin of the Lebanon Valley. Many miles of roads in northeastern Pennsylvania cast a reddish hue from the Mauch Chunk red bed used as aggregate in the paving asphalt. The walls of Philadelphia's Manayunk shimmer in the sunlight with the silvery sheen of Wissahickon schist, a building stone that is virtually absent from the brick-row-home-crowded Coastal Plain streets of South Philly not five miles away. Just west of Philadelphia, the surprisingly green buildings of West Chester University and the old Chester County Courthouse are the dressed version of locally quarried serpentine.

And finally, there is the Bucks County stone house located a stone's throw away from the Monroe Border Fault in Riegelsville. The fault

The geology of Schaefferstown, a Great Valley village, is reflected in its buildings. The building on the right is made of Lebanon Valley limestone; the Triassic red sandstone of the other building comes from the Furnace Hills to the south.

marks the plane of slippage for the Triassic half-graben, putting some of the state's youngest red sandstones and shales against the oldest Precambrian granites and gneiss of the Reading Prong. The Precambrian rocks have been thrust over younger Cambrian dolomites and quartzites, which also outcrop in the vicinity of the fault. The house is a multihued geologic sampler of local rocks containing granites, red rocks, dolomite, and other stones, reflecting the underground complexity. The rocks of Pennsylvania are wonderfully varied, each a souvenir of the environment that created it cached away in a subterranean treasure chest for millions of years.

If All of Time Were the Pennsylvania Turnpike

Time is an important factor in cave formation. One of the most commonly asked questions on any cave tour is "How old is this cave?" The same sense of astonishment is inevitably vocalized whether the answer comes back 500,000 or 500 million years. Relative to a human life span, both are a long, long time, even though there is a considerable difference between the two, and it can be difficult to conceptualize the relative difference. Both numbers may also answer the question, the older time referring to the age of the rock, and the younger being the age of the hole. And that's your basic cave: rock and absence of rock. The rock was laid down as an oozy, calcium-rich sediment at the bottom of the sea hundreds of millions of years ago, and then dissolved away to form a cavity hundreds of thousands of years ago.

To put this into perspective, let's assume the Pennsylvania Turnpike represents time since the Precambrian. The turnpike's Main Line stretches for 360 miles from Ohio to New Jersey. That would put the Gateway Toll Plaza on the Ohio border at the beginning of the Cambrian Period, about 600 million years ago. From then to the end of the Ordovician Period, most of Pennsylvania was underwater most of the time. The equivalent distance on our turnpike timeline would cover the first 100 miles (28 percent) from the Ohio border to a point nine miles west of Interchange 91 at Donegal.

Pennsylvania was on the continental shelf submerged by the landward extension of the Octoraro Sea. Off the coast to the southeast were fragments of the continent, known as the Baltimore and Brandywine microcontinents. Beyond them was a volcanic island arc, something like the modern-day Aleutians, created by a subduction zone that ran along the east coast of an ancient North America. Beyond the island arc stretched the Iapetus Ocean, the Proto-Atlantic that separated North America from Europe. The Cambrian and Ordovician seas teemed with life, including

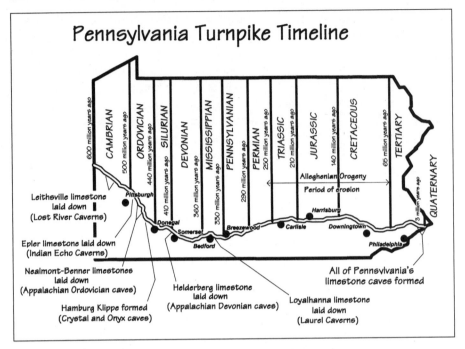

Pennsylvania Turnpike Timeline

600 million years ago
CAMBRIAN
500 million years ago
ORDOVICIAN
440 million years ago
SILURIAN
410 million years ago
DEVONIAN
360 million years ago
MISSISSIPPIAN
330 million years ago
PENNSYLVANIAN
290 million years ago
PERMIAN
250 million years ago
TRIASSIC
210 million years ago
JURASSIC
140 million years ago
CRETACEOUS
65 million years ago
TERTIARY
3 million years ago
QUATERNARY

Alleghenian Orogeny
Period of erosion

Pittsburgh
Donegal
Somerset
Bedford
Breezewood
Carlisle
Harrisburg
Downingtown
Philadelphia

Leithsville limestone laid down
(Lost River Caverns)

Epler limestone laid down
(Indian Echo Caverns)

Nealmont-Benner limestones laid down
(Appalachian Ordovician caves)

Hamburg Klippe formed
(Crystal and Onyx caves)

Helderberg limestone laid down
(Appalachian Devonian caves)

Loyalhanna limestone laid down
(Laurel Caverns)

All of Pennsylvania's limestone caves formed

trilobites, nautiloid cephalopods (invertebrate squid creatures), jellyfish, sponges, corals, and mollusklike brachiopods. Life on land, however, was still 250 million years away. This was the time and environment in which most of the dolomite and limestone beds throughout Lancaster County, the Great Valley, and the Appalachian Ridge and Valley sections formed. (Dolomite and limestone form in similar shallow sea environments, but dolomite contains more magnesium and tends to occur in shallower waters, whereas limestone contains more calcium and tends to occur in deeper water.) There were periods, however, when terrestrial sediments eroding in from the west displaced the shallow Octoraro Sea, creating future sandstone and shale layers that separated the older limestone beds from newer ones deposited in subsequent submersions.

The subduction zone to the east was bringing North America, and its offshore microcontinents, into collision with Europe. The microcontinents plowed into the island arc during the late Ordovician, an event known as the Taconic Orogeny. A massive mountain range was thrown up in what are now New England and the Maritime Provinces of Canada. The collision caused the continental shelf at Pennsylvania's location to warp downward into a foredeep basin known as the Appalachian geosyncline. This basin received sediments eroding from eastern mountains for the next 180 million years. The eastern part of the continental shelf broke in several places and was stacked northwestward along overthrust faults. This included a huge chunk of limestone that came to rest on a younger surface of Martinsburg shales and was subsequently buried by mud that would become more Martinsburg shales. Eons later, the forces of erosion exposed this isolated chunk of seafloor as the Hamburg klippe, a cave-studded section of the Great Valley that extends from Kutztown to Carlisle. Even deeper-seated Precambrian metamorphics were broken and thrust northwestward to one day be exposed as the hard rocks of the Reading Prong, Pennsylvania's extension of the New England Upland.

The Taconic Orogeny falls between Interchanges 67 (Irwin) and 110 (Somerset) on the turnpike timeline, and marks a geologic transition from marine to terrestrial environments as the shallow sea over Pennsylvania was gradually displaced by an expansive delta of sediments being shed from the mountains to the east. Called the Queenston Delta, this late Ordovician depositional feature contains numerous red beds, which resulted from the oxidation of minute iron compounds in sediments deposited in an arid environment. Pennsylvania at this time looked more like the current deserts of the American Southwest. During the early Silurian, the delta was capped by a stream-dropped stratum of sand and gravel. The heavier pebbles were dropped first, as stream velocity decreased on the eastern landward end of the delta. Finer sands were carried beyond the shoreline to the west. The pebbly stratum lithified into what would become the ridge-forming Shawangunk conglomerate that outcrops in Blue Mountain east of Harrisburg. The western sandstone was metamorphosed in the later Alleghenian Orogeny to become the Tuscarora quartzite that holds up many of the ridges in the central part of the state.

As the Taconian Mountains eroded away, the inland sea to the west made repeated incursions over future Pennsylvania, depositing limestones that included the upper Silurian Keyser Formation and lower Devonian Helderberg beds. Cavities dissolved from Helderberg limestones were destined to be commercialized as Lincoln Caverns, Coral Caverns, and Seawra Cave. This period of tectonic quiet did not last long, and thus the Silurian-Devonian limestones are not nearly as thick as the Cambro-Ordovician carbonates. The equivalent distance on the turnpike timeline is a mere 15 miles or so, from the Somerset Exit to the Allegheny Tunnel. A widespread volcanic ashfall during the middle Devonian signaled the onset of the Acadian Orogeny, an even more massive and long-lived mountain-building period resulting from the mega-collision of Europe into North America.

The mountainous suture for this new continent of Laurentia was at least as high as the present Andes and lay east of the worn-down Taconian Mountains. The Piedmont was the only part of the state to experience metamorphism and deformation as a result of the collision. The rest of the state was influenced by the replication of geologic events that occurred during the Taconic Orogeny. The down-warping of the Appalachian geosyncline was renewed, burying the Onondaga limestone deposited by an inland sea with flysch, a fine mud found in deeper waters. The flysch became the black shales of the Marcellus Formation and was itself buried by the sediments washed westward from the new Acadian Mountain range. This sedimentary wedge was the Catskill Delta, a larger version of the previous Queenston Delta that then lay buried beneath it. Sandstones, shales, and desert red beds spread westward across Pennsylvania throughout the rest of the Devonian.

It was at this time, in the late Devonian, that dual-mode sea creatures first crawled out of the water to exploit ecological niches on dry land. More than one-third of the time since the end of the Precambrian had already passed by. This is the equivalent turnpike distance from Ohio to Bedford County.

Like the Queenston Delta, the Catskill Delta was capped by a quartzitic sandstone laid down by streams flowing westward toward the inland sea. This is the Pocono sandstone and conglomerate that support all the ridges surrounding the hard coal-bearing synclinal basins of northeastern Pennsylvania, as well as the Broad Top coal basin in southern Huntingdon and northeastern Bedford Counties. The Pocono's finer-grained equivalent in the western part of the state is Burgoon sandstone, a resistant cliff rock found along the Allegheny Front and at the crests of Laurel and Chestnut Ridges.

The Pocono/Burgoon Formation belongs to the lower part of the Mississippian Period, a 30-million-year span of time that would cover the section of the Pennsylvania Turnpike between Bedford (Exit 146) and Breezewood (Exit 161). The Mississippian and Pennsylvanian are collectively known as the Carboniferous Period, a time when vast, tropical, coastal swamps repeatedly formed, were buried, and formed again throughout a prehistoric world where much of the landmass was near the equator. These coastal swamps provided the partially decayed plant matter necessary for virtually all of the planet's coal seams. On the turnpike timeline, the Pennsylvanian portion of the Carboniferous Period would extend from Breezewood nearly to Willow Hill at Interchange 189, 9 miles east of the halfway point.

By the middle Mississippian, fewer sediments were being carried from the worn-down Acadian Mountains, allowing an eastern regression of the inland sea to cover western Pennsylvania. The resulting Loyalhanna limestone was nearly 50 percent calcium and 50 percent silica, meaning it could almost pass as sandstone. The high silica content actually comes from the underlying Burgoon sandstone, which eroded into the sea from the north due to the rising of the Canadian Shield. Unlike the valley-bottom limestones east of the Allegheny Front, the Loyalhanna outcrops along the crests of Laurel and Chestnut Ridges. Its high silica content retards the growth of speleothems but aids in the creation of extensive mazelike caverns. Laurel Caverns, honeycombing the western slope of Chestnut Ridge in Fayette County, are in fact the longest commercial cave system in the state.

As the Loyalhanna sea regressed westward, another delta covered the future state from the southeast. The resulting Mauch Chunk red beds signify an arid climate and a gradual rise in the continent to the east. In western Pennsylvania, the Mauch Chunk red beds lie on the Loyalhanna limestone and are interbedded with thinner limestone layers. In the east, they sit above the resistant Pocono sandstone. The uplift continued, spreading a sandy alluvial plain across the state that was to become lower Pennsylvanian Pottsville sandstone.

The anthracite and semibituminous bearing synclinal basins of Pennsylvania's Appalachians are bounded by a double ridge rim of Pocono and Pottsville sandstone, separated by an intervening valley of softer Mauch Chunk shales. The sequence is apparent when traveling north on Route 61 across the Lower and Western Middle Anthracite Fields. Immediately south of Pottsville, Route 61 extends through a double water gap carved by the Schuylkill River through Second (Pocono sandstone) and Sharp (Pottsville sandstone) Mountains. The ridges are separated by the narrow Tumbling Run Valley (Mauch Chunk red beds). For the next 30 miles, strip mines and gob piles—mine tailing dumps—abound, evidence of the basins' long history of coal mining. These scenes of extraction are interrupted only by the forest-cloaked flanks of Broad Mountain, an anticlinal ridge of Pottsville sandstone marking the boundary between the two hard coal basins. Beyond Shamokin, PA Route 61 leaves the Western Middle Anthracite Field by way of another double water gap carved by Shamokin Creek through the same Pottsville–Mauch Chunk–Pocono beds outcropping in Big Mountain, Little Mountain, and the intervening valley.

At the beginning of the Pennsylvanian Period, the climate was changing in response to North America's tectonic drifting away from the arid subtropical latitudes of the Southern Hemisphere and toward the humid equatorial region. Extensive coastal swamps formed in two great periods that were responsible for creating Pennsylvania's future coal seams. In the soft coal bituminous fields of western Pennsylvania, the most profitable seams are associated with the lower Pennsylvanian Allegheny

Group, which includes the Lower Kittanning and Upper Freeport seams; and the upper Pennsylvanian Monongahela Group, with its massive Pittsburgh seam, the richest mineral deposit in the world as measured by the total value of mined rock. The equivalent hard coals in the eastern anthracite fields belong to the Llewellyn Formation.

The coal seams were laid down in repeating cycles of changing coastal environments at the fickle margin of a vast inland sea. The gradient of the adjacent land was so low that small fluctuations in sea level could flood or drain huge areas. A rising sea level buried coastal swamps with mud, allowing the partial decayed vegetation and peat to turn into coal beneath a layer of shale. As the rising sea deepened, coral reefs, shells, and crustaceans provided the raw materials for limestone, which itself was buried under stream-deposited sandstone when sea level receded again in the face of an advancing delta. Over time, another coal-creating tropical coastal swamp formed on the delta, and the cycle began anew. These coal-shale-limestone-sandstone-coal cyclothems continued into the Permian Period, when the last great mountain-building period peaked with the collision of Africa and North America.

This collision, known as the Alleghenian Orogeny, and 200 million years' worth of erosion are responsible for the quintessential landscapes of present-day Pennsylvania—its broad valleys, long parallel ridges, and uplifted dissected plateaus. By the end of the Pennsylvanian Period, most of the world's landmasses were either on the Laurentian continent, with North America and Europe, or part of the larger Gondwanaland, with Africa, South America, Antarctica, and much of Asia. The two land giants were separated by the Iapetus Ocean, a proto-Atlantic, which narrowed and then ultimately closed as the continents were drawn into collision to form the supercontinent Pangaea. The rocks that had been stacking up in the Appalachian geosyncline for the last 300 million years were shoved northwestward along sole thrust faults, from which other faults splayed and ramped upward through the rock package. The rock layers above the upward ends of these faults were bent upward into anticlines separated by downward-folded synclines. The heat and pressure generated by more intense folding of the Appalachian Ridge and Valley rocks is what converted the coal of northeastern Pennsylvania into anthracite.

On our turnpike timeline, the Alleghenian Orogeny took place just beyond the halfway point between Ohio and New Jersey, at Exit 180, Fort Littleton. At their peak, the Permian-age mountains of Pennsylvania looked more like the Rockies, with an average relief between 11,500 and 15,000 feet. The land was high and dry, and the forces of erosion dominated, eroding the softer shales and limestones into valleys while the more slowly eroded sandstones, quartzites, and conglomerates were left standing as ridges.

With the exception of the Triassic red beds and basalts found in a band stretching from Bucks County to Gettysburg, Pennsylvania is devoid of rocks from the Mesozoic Era. This is a 165-million-year chunk of time that encompasses the entire rise and fall of the dinosaurs throughout the Triassic, Jurassic, and Cretaceous Periods. The equivalent distance on the Pennsylvania Turnpike would stretch for 132 miles, from Exit 180 to Exit 312 at Downingtown—more than one-third of the turnpike's entire length. Rock layers were not being deposited during this vast sweep of time; they were being eroded away and carried off as the sand and silt of long-gone river systems. At least six—and maybe as much as ten—miles of rock were eroded away.

The Triassic rocks deposited in Pennsylvania resulted from the breakup of Pangaea, the supercontinent assembled in the Alleghenian Orogeny. The massive landmass lasted only about 60 million years before being wracked and split asunder by the parallel faults of an active spreading center. Huge, linear blocks of the continent subsided along these breaks, forming down-dropped fault valleys known as grabens. The graben subsiding along the most active fault system flooded with seawater, giving birth to what would become the Atlantic Ocean. The cleaving of North America from Africa and Europe created a series of failed rift valleys, grabens running parallel to the spreading center, but not destined to be widened as the Atlantic basin. One such rift was the Newark-Gettysburg Basin, actually a half-graben extending across the southeastern Pennsylvania Piedmont from northern New Jersey to central Maryland. The lower Connecticut Valley, Nova Scotia's Annapolis Valley, the Culpeper Basin in Virginia, and the Deep River Basin in North Carolina are other Triassic lowlands that formed in the same way.

As a half-graben, the Newark-Gettysburg Basin was faulted on only its north-northwest side, along which the floor of the rift valley hinged downward. As the half-graben subsided, it filled with sediments washed into the depression from the adjacent uplands. The sediments were compressed into red shales and sandstones. Faulting occurring so close to an active spreading center also allowed molten rock to be injected into the rock package. The magma cooled to become either basalt sills stretching as sheets of igneous rock parallel to the sedimentary bedding, or volcanic dikes cutting across the bedding. Subsequent erosion has exposed these ribbonlike volcanic intrusions, the most famous outcropping of which is the Devil's Den at Gettysburg.

The red coloring of these Triassic rocks is evidence of their formation as terrestrial deposits in an arid climate. At the genesis of the Atlantic Ocean when these grabens were forming, eastern North America was in the center of Pangaea, far from any coastal moisture. The region also lay astride the subtropical latitudes, where high-pressure systems dominate the weather, such as in the Sahara, providing one dry, sunny day after another for millions of years. In short, today's verdant farmland of Bucks and Montgomery Counties was once a desert.

The Newark-Gettysburg Basin is commonly referred to as a Triassic lowland, since the red beds are weaker and more easily eroded than the surrounding Piedmont metamorphics. The section between Reading and Harrisburg is actually a series of red rock hills, however, as the sandstone that outcrops there is more resistant than the adjacent limestones found in the Lebanon Valley to the north and Lancaster's Conestoga Valley to the south.

Ninety percent of a road trip from Ohio to New Jersey would be over by the time a turnpike traveler reached Valley Forge outside Philadelphia. Ninety percent of all time since the Precambrian would just approach the rise of the mammals, which occurred after the great Cretaceous extinction of the dinosaurs. Pennsylvania's cave-bearing limestones were already hundreds of millions of years old by this time, but the holes that constitute today's caves were still millions of years away from being formed. Even the early evolutionary stages of *Homo sapiens,* beginning some 2 million years ago, predate the solution of most Pennsylvania cave holes. The actual cave holes are chemically weathered by water charged with carbon dioxide seeping into the rock from above. Compared to the age of the limestone, this solution process is a relatively recent activity. Laurel Caverns may be an exception.

Cavities within the Loyalhanna limestone at the location of Laurel Caverns may have begun to form 2 to 6 million years ago. But it is hard to date a hole. If the limestone outcropping recedes, wearing away the rock around the hole while allowing the solution to penetrate deeper into the rock layer—as in the case of Laurel—does the date of the original hole still apply? Even more confounding, the sand that remains after Loyalhanna limestone is chemically weathered is nearly the same volume as the original rock, meaning the solution cavity stays filled with sand until some subterranean stream forms to flush it out. Millions of years may pass between the dissolution of the rock and the stream removal of the sand residue, so how old is the cave?

Despite these complications in dating, it is safe to say that the limestone is very old, in some cases having been laid down way back at Exit

48 (Allegheny Valley, north of Pittsburgh) on our turnpike timeline, while the holes are fairly recent. Even a 3-million-year-old Laurel Caverns would equate to Interchange 351, Philadelphia, with 98 percent of the turnpike to its west. Most of Pennsylvania's commercial caves are a lot younger than this.

Caves are limestone solution cavities that form at the water table. So one way to estimate the age of a hole is to determine when the regional drainage network was at the elevation of the cave, assuming that the streams have since eroded their beds lower, dropping the water table and draining the cave. Using this method, Indian Echo Caverns and the long-closed Baker Caverns are estimated to be 600,000 to 750,000 years old. Crystal Cave and nearby Onyx Cave are assumed to be about 300,000 years old. Lost River Caverns may be as young as 100,000 to 250,000 years old. With an age of 750,000 years, Indian Echo and Baker Caverns would show up within a half mile of the New Jersey border on the turnpike timeline. Crystal and Onyx would be halfway up the approach span on the Delaware River Bridge. A 100,000-year-old cave would be located about 300 feet away from the far end of a 360-mile Pennsylvania Turnpike representing 600 million years of geologic time since the Precambrian. The entire commercial history of Pennsylvania's caves, starting with the 1871 opening of Crystal Cave, would be contained within the last 5 inches of the timeline. The current cave proprietors are the momentary stewards of rock-encrusted time.

3

Rock Plus Hole
Equals Cave

A great gulf of time separates the creation of the average cave-forming limestone from the actual formation of the caves it currently contains. Indian Echo Caverns was hollowed out of the Beekmantown Epler Formation, which was laid down in an early Ordovician sea some 500 million years ago. But the hollowing did not start until about 600,000 years ago. For nearly 99 percent of that rock's entire buried existence, it just sat around doing nothing. Then all of a sudden—geologically speaking—a cave formed; became decorated with spectacular flowstone, stalactites, and other colorful calcite gewgaws; and was opened to the public. What took so long? The answer: water. And not just any water, but water mixed with enough carbon dioxide to make the weak carbonic acid necessary for both eating away the limestone like a rotting tooth and filling the void with fanciful speleothems.

The water comes from the sky in the form of precipitation—rain or snow, it doesn't matter. After seeping into the ground, the water picks up carbon dioxide released from plant matter rotting into the soil as humus. The combination of water with carbon dioxide makes carbonic acid, which penetrates the underlying limestone through a myriad of hairline cracks, making its way to the water table, where the real action begins.

While the carbonic acid is passing down through the aerated zone above the water table, it does not stay in contact with the limestone long enough to do much dissolving. Well below the water table, the water is in constant contact with the limestone and becomes supersaturated with dissolved calcite to the point that it cannot dissolve any more. Immediately above and below the water table, conditions are just right. Here the carbonic acid from above stays in contact with the limestone long enough to dissolve cavities into which carbon dioxide is released, providing a ready supply to prevent the water near the surface from being supersaturated with calcite. The uppermost part of the water table is also moving ever so slowly toward some distant spring, carrying the dissolved calcite away with it. Dissolution at the water table explains why most caves form along a horizontal plane regardless of the tilt of the rock beds.

A solid block of limestone is impervious to water. The water actually moves through natural cracks created by clay partings in the bedding plane, by faulting during periods of tectonic activity, or by jointing. Joints can form due to the gradual bending or stretching of the rock or, more often, as a result of earth tides, the constant flexing of the rock caused by the gravitational pull of the moon and sun.

It is common to have two sets of joints running perpendicular to each other and the bedding plane, providing a myriad of tight fractures through which water can move. Dissolution within these fractures is very slow and somewhat uniform, but as soon as one of these tiny channels reaches a diameter of 5 millimeters, enough turbulence is introduced into the water stream to accelerate the chemical weathering. This draws a disproportionate amount of water into the channel, increasing the rate of dissolution at the expense of the other fractures. The result is a joint controlled passageway that is significantly larger than all others, a common occurrence in many caves.

The necessary requirements for the birth of a cave explain why there is such a lag time between rock and cave formation. The cave does not start to form until it is attacked by carbonic acid descending from the surface. This also defines caves as fairly shallow features. Most Pennsylvania caves are no more than 200 feet underground. Even Laurel Caverns, with a 464-foot descent from the cave entrance, achieves its depth by following the downward dip of a limestone bed that runs parallel to the overlying slope of the mountain the cave sits within. When compared with the maximum depth of the rock package, caves are mere pockmarks near the surface outcropping of limestone beds that can slope to a depth of 15,000 feet.

Cave passages will continue to increase in size until the water table drops or an opening to the outside world ventilates the cave, dissipating the carbon dioxide. The water table is linked to the regional drainage network and will be lowered as streams incise deeper courses and erode away the land surface. As the water table drops, however, additional passages may form beneath an abandoned cavity, creating a multilevel cave. After being abandoned by a dropping water table, some cave passages are further eroded by surface streams that find their way into sinkholes and flow underground to some distant spring. These subterranean streams leave their own mark in the form of scalloped walls. They can also deposit sediment or carry it away.

Not only are caves recent, shallow features, but they are also relatively short-lived. Maybe a paltry 1 million years separates the opening of a cave passage from the inevitable collapse of its cavernous roof. The death of a cave may occur as the outside forces of erosion gradually strip away the roof or, more spectacularly, when a widening cave passage can no longer support the heavy expanse of its ceiling. Ceiling collapse accounts for the breakdown boulders that commonly accumulate on the floors of caves and may ultimately be expressed as sinkholes on the surface above.

The forces of erosion respect no splendor. The colossal columns of Carlsbad, Mammoth's massive interior, Merremac's stunning Stage Curtain, the dramatic dripstone of Luray, and all the caves of Pennsylvania are equally doomed to end up as piles of dust and rubble ignominiously carted off by some ordinary stream. See them now while you still can.

Some old cave holes don't die by being opened up, but by being filled up with speleothems. Colorfully named features like the Garden of the Gods, Rainbow Room, Crystal Ballroom, and Palace of Splendor belie the fact that cave formation and the growth of calcite speleothems take place in complete and utter darkness. The color is an incidental by-product of the rock's chemical composition and is not intentionally meant to entertain. Cavernous voids exist in tomblike blackness underground, and under the right conditions, they can be gradually choked closed by calcite crystals growing in the dark. The time it takes to do this, however, may be greater than the time it takes the forces of erosion—or man—to break into the shallow-seated caverns and alter the process.

The chemical reaction between water and carbon dioxide that hollows caves out of limestone also runs in reverse to fill those voids back up again. Carbon dioxide picked up from the soil is released into the subterranean atmosphere as soon as the water reaches the cave, like the fizz from a soda bottle. Since carbon dioxide is the critical ingredient that allows the water to dissolve the limestone, its loss to the dark, damp air of the cave causes the calcite in solution to be deposited as a limey residue. One drop after another issuing from a hairline crack in the ceiling leaves a calcite ring in the place where the drops drip. After centuries of relentless dripping, a hollow, soda straw–shaped stalactite is created. Two millimeters a year would be a fast-growing stalactite. Eventually calcite deposits clog the end of the soda straw, but water continues to flow down the outside of the stalactite, precipitating calcite that increases its girth. More calcite is deposited at the top than is carried down to the bottom, giving stalactites their characteristic icicle shape. As long as the water continues to flow, size is just a matter of time.

Each of the operating Great Valley caves—Lost River, Crystal, and Indian Echo—has a beefy stalactite in the 3- to 5-foot range that formed in the described manner. Interestingly, all three carry the same name, Ear of Corn, a testimony to the influence of agriculture in the valley and the preference for corn as the major field crop on the region's dairy farms. Central Pennsylvania's Indian Caverns also has an Ear of Corn stalactite. Another food-item speleothem, cave bacon, is a common stalactite variant. Bacon, or drapery, forms when water runs across a slanted ceiling, leaving a line of calcite deposits that descend over time in a wavy, translucent sheet frequently striped with orangy stains of iron oxide.

When a drop of water falls from the tip of a stalactite, it still carries some calcite in solution. The drop's splash on the floor deposits the calcite, which, drop by drop, gradually rises to become a stalagmite. Drops dripped from the ceiling versus splashed on the floor is what causes stalactites to be pointy and stalagmites to have rounded tips. With all this dripping going on, it is no surprise that the resulting speleothems are also known as dripstone. Travertine is another word for it, and in the old days, these calcite formations were referred to as cave onyx.

It is not uncommon for a stalagmite to rise up from the splash points of several variable drip streams, allowing the formation to grow into a

Alexander Caverns's Garden of the Gods contains a dazzling array of speleothems, including stalactites, stalagmites, columns, and flowstone.
DEAN SNYDER

bulbous, towering mass of sizable dimensions. Woodward Cave's Tower of Babel was formed this way, standing 14 feet high, 8 feet wide, and estimated to weigh 50 tons. Nearly all of Pennsylvania's caves seem to have a signature stalagmite. Upon entering Crystal Cave, visitors are grouped around the Inverted Ice Cream Cone, a conical white and brown stalagmite with green algae highlights. In similar fashion, Coral Cavern cavers are greeted with Pikes Peak. The Cave Guardian, a.k.a. the Fur Trapper, Santa Claus, or Jabba the Hut, is the bulbous stalagmite personality that presides over Indian Echo's Indian Ball Room. Lincoln Caverns has the Pagoda, which was also temporarily renamed Jabba the Hut during the *Star Wars* craze of the 1980s. A fourteen-foot Statue of Liberty stands in Penn's Cave.

Even the closed caves are not without their signature stalagmites. Onyx Cave was famous for its Giant Fallen Stalactite, a large, tilted stalagmite that was originally thought to have been a huge stalactite that had broken free from the ceiling and speared itself deep into the cave's clay floor. Centre County's Veiled Lady Cave was named for a white stalagmite near its entrance that had the appearance of a seated lady shrouded in a veil. In Bedford County, the white calcite Pillar of Salt, or Lot's Wife, still stands in the long-darkened passageway of Hipple Cave.

Given enough time, a stalactite-stalagmite pair will grow together to form a column. Lincoln Caverns's Whisper Rocks section is graced with two long, slender columns that were formed in this way. Hipple contains a column around which a grouping of stalactites hang like fronds to this aptly named Palm Tree.

Probably the most common speleothem is flowstone, a smooth but rippled calcite formation caused by water flowing down the cave walls. Although quite ordinary, some flowstone formations can reach wall-size proportions, may be very colorful, and can contain an infinite array of forms and shapes—subtle and spectacular, gaudy and grotesque. Recognizable shapes seen in Indian Echo Caverns's Wall of Imagination include everything from a Snowy Owl and Monkey to a Sixteen-Legged Elephant. Indian Caverns's Formation Wall has a Goose hanging by its feet. A large flowstone formation in Woodward Cave is called the Bible Wall for its mineral renditions of Moses, the Nativity, and Jesus Ascending to Heaven. The most common perception is to see the entire flowstone formation as a frozen waterfall. Both Lost River Caverns and Crystal Cave have specific formations named Frozen Waterfall. Indian Echo Caverns, Penn's Cave, Indian Caverns, and Lincoln Caverns all have Frozen Niagaras. Other stony cataracts include the Purity and Diamond Cascades in Lincoln and Indian Echo's Honeymoon Falls.

Flowstone will appear as a suspended shelf wherever it formed over a mound of clay that was subsequently washed away by a stream flowing through the cave. The Umbrella, in the now closed Baker Caverns, formed this way, as did Onyx Cave's Natural Bridge. A long shelf of suspended flowstone clinging to the wall of Penn's Cave contains a tableau of formations, including Niagara Falls, the Chinese Dragon, and a Big Turtle.

Flowstone, columns, stalagmites, and stalactites are the most common speleothems that most limestone caves contain in one form or another. Many more truly exotic and unique formations are also found in caves. Not all caves are equally festooned, however. Oddly enough, the most famous solution hole in the country, Kentucky's Mammoth Cave, has relatively few speleothems due to its sandstone overburden. Laurel Caverns in Pennsylvania is equally devoid. Speleothems exist, to be sure, but they are relatively small and few in number due to the high silica content of the Loyalhanna limestone. Interestingly, what Mammoth and Laurel lack in speleothems, they make up for in sheer size and number of mazelike passages.

The commercial cave enthusiast has nine holes to choose from in Pennsylvania. In times past, there were seven others. This refers only to the limestone caves that were developed as tourist attractions through a capital investment in electric lighting, walkways, steps, buildings, and other infrastructure to support a for-profit business. It does not count the dozens of little holes around the state that functioned as subterranean curiosities and picnic places for local residents, or even larger caves that were shown to tourists in the wild by hired guides armed with torches but never developed.

Sixteen commercial show caves are a small sample of the state's many caves, but they are a good sample. After all, if someone is going to pay money to see the inside of a hole, there had better be something down there to see. And most tourists are not going to want to work too hard to see it. It is safe to say that the inexorable forces of capitalism sorted through Pennsylvania's underground offerings and selected the largest, most sumptuously decorated, and easily accessed caves for exploitation.

Limestone is readily found throughout the state, but large solution caves are not just found in any old limestone. Of the 6,000 feet of carbonate rocks exposed by the Nittany anticlinorium near State College, only 600 feet exhibit good cavern development. Some limestone is too shaley, other limestone too dolomitic, meaning there is more magnesium than calcium and thus the rock is less likely to form extensive cave systems. Pennsylvania caves are quite cozy when compared with caves found in the South and farther west. The difference is largely attributed to climate. Much more carbon dioxide infiltrates the limestone in places with thicker soils that have experienced warmer climates longer. As such, there is more carbonic acid to weather bigger holes and longer passageways, and to fill these voids with more massive speleothems.

Relatively speaking, Pennsylvania has just recently come out of a prolonged deep freeze. A mere ten to fifteen thousand years ago, the northwestern and northeastern corners of the state lay buried beneath the icy grip of the Wisconsin continental glaciers, giving the rest of Pennsylvania the climate of a polar tundra. The time since the retreat of the glaciers amounts to barely the last 10 percent of the life span of the youngest Pennsylvania caves. And there were at least four other glacial advances *before* the Wisconsin advance. This means that Pennsylvania caves have spent much of their time forming in a cold-weather climate where organic material breaks down more slowly, providing less carbon dioxide in the soil for limestone-eating carbonic acid.

Not that Pennsylvania caves are inconsequential. As the second longest mapped cave system in the state, Laurel Caverns has 16,305 feet, or 3.1 miles, of passages. Nearly twice again as large, Harlansburg Cave in Lawrence County is the keystone king of caves, with 21,808 feet, or 4.1 miles, of mapped passageways. Of course, this pales in comparison to Mammoth Cave's 300-mile length.

If a garage had the same dimensions as Indian Echo's commodious Ball Room, 25 feet wide, 88 feet long, and 43 feet high, it could easily hold two tractor-trailer rigs on each of two floors. It would still, however, be nothing more than a closet in Carlsbad Caverns's Big Room, which is a whopping 656 feet wide, 4,270 feet long, and 328 feet high—more than twice the height of Niagara Falls. A garage that size would be sixteen stories tall, with a capacity of more than fifty thousand trucks. To keep this in perspective, it should be made clear that Mammoth Cave is not just a large cave system, it's the *world's* largest. Likewise, as underground chambers go, there are none in the United States bigger than Carlsbad's Big Room.

Pennsylvania's sixteen currently active and former show caves are not scattered about the state in just any old limestone. They are limited to fairly narrow bands of limestone from the Cambrian, Ordovician, Devonian, and Mississippian Periods that have just the right characteristics to be good cave formers. These limestones outcrop in three distinct regions, thus determining the general locations for caves. Five caves are found within the Cambro-Ordovician carbonates of southeastern Pennsylvania's Great Valley, that broad sweep of fertile farmland that extends southwest from the Lehigh Valley through the Lebanon and Cumberland Valleys to the Shenandoah Valley of Virginia. Central Pennsylvania's Appalachian Ridge and Valley section contains seven Ordovi-

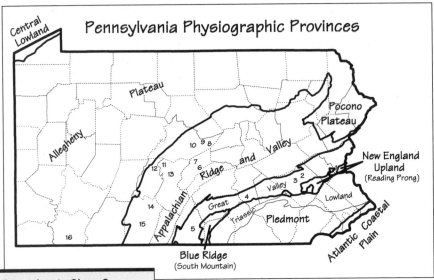

Pennsylvania Physiographic Provinces

Central Lowland

Plateau

Pocono Plateau

Allegheny

10 9 8

7

12 11 13

6 Ridge and Valley

New England Upland (Reading Prong)

2 3

Valley

14

Appalachian

Great

Lowland

15

Triassic

Piedmont

16

5

Atlantic Coastal Plain

Blue Ridge
(South Mountain)

cian and three Devonian show caves. Finally, there is one commercial cave in the Mississippian rocks of western Pennsylvania's Allegheny Plateau. Each of these clusters contains caves with enough similar features to proscribe a pattern, while also being uniquely varied.

Great Valley Caves

Lost River Caverns, on the outskirts of Hellertown, has the distinction of being in the oldest rock layer of any Pennsylvania commercial cave, the Cambrian Leithsville Formation. This rock was deposited near the beginning of a 200-million-year period during which most of what would become Pennsylvania was beneath the waves of a shallow sea most of the time. That's how the limestone got there in the first place. Lost River is the eastern- and northernmost commercial cave in the Great Valley Cave Belt, which includes not only other Pennsylvania caves like Crystal Cave and Indian Echo Caverns, but also Maryland's Crystal Grotto and Virginia's Luray, Skyline, and Endless Caverns in the Shenandoah Valley. Technically, Lost River is in an outlier of the Great Valley, being nearly surrounded by more-resistant hills of Precambrian granitic gneiss belonging to the New England Upland's Reading Prong. The cave sits at the edge of the Saucon Valley, a saucer-shaped depression underlain by limestone that reaches around the east end of South Mountain from the Lehigh Valley.

Lost River Caverns gets its name from a stream that passes through the bowels of the cave. No one is quite sure where this water comes from or where it goes. Ping-Pong balls let loose in the stream were never seen again, although a more sophisticated dye trace did show up in some local wells. The results were inconclusive. The stream is not the carver of the cave, however, but is subsequently using the cave as a conduit. Like most caves, Lost River formed under phreatic conditions, meaning saturated beneath the water table. Most of its calcite speleothems formed in the vadose zone, the air-filled region above the water table. As the surrounding landscape was worn down, surface water found its way into the honeycombed limestone, where it is now being piped to points unknown. Opportunistic vadose streams are not unusual. In times past, they have been used as a ready supply of fresh water, and unfortunately as a cheap and short-sighted way to dispose waste water and sewage.

Lost River is a Y-shaped cave entered through a passage that forms the short right branch of the Y. The cave's namesake, Lost River, is encoun-

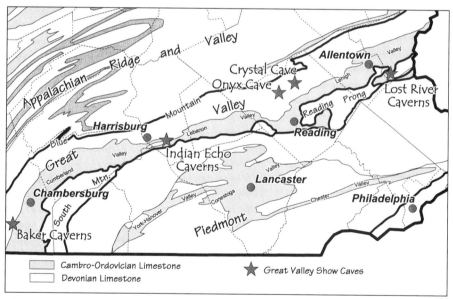

The Great Valley show caves are in Cambrian and Ordovician limestones. Lost River is at the edge of the Saucon Valley section of the Lehigh Valley. Crystal and Onyx caves are in isolated limestone outcroppings of the Hamburg Klippe. Indian Echo is on the banks of Swatara Creek, which drains the western half of the Lebanon Valley. Baker Caverns is in the southern part of the Cumberland Valley.

tered at the junction of the two branches with the main passage. The stream flows out from beneath the wall and down the Y's left branch, passing through the New Room to a sump, a low point in the cave beyond which the passage is completely underwater. The New Room is well decorated with dripstone, including a three-foot-long stalactite called Ear of Corn. This section of the cave also contains a small helictite, a stalactite that grows sideways due to the capillary action of water being drawn through a constricted tube in the formation. A related formation, the delicate cave flower, or anthodite, can be found nearby.

Early cave tourists were ferried across Lost River in a small boat pushed by wader-clad tour guides. The subterranean ferry was retired in 1932, when the concrete Long Bridge was constructed to allow dryfoot inspection of the New Room. Lost River flows through a chamber running parallel to and below the main passage. Rarely is the water low enough to allow people to enter this chamber, but it was during the drought of 1961, and the stunning stalactites, stalagmites, and flowstone discovered within provided the inspiration for its name, the Queen's Room. The main passage opens into the Crystal Chapel, with its wall-size flowstone formation known as the Frozen Waterfall. The Crystal Chapel continues upward and to the left, where there is an elevated landing created by an ancient breakdown of the ceiling. The main passage continues deeper into the cave, terminating at the Blacklight Room, beneath which the Lost River flows through a lower channel.

Lost River Caverns was broken into during quarrying, as were three of the four remaining Great Valley caves. Quarrying plays a curious role

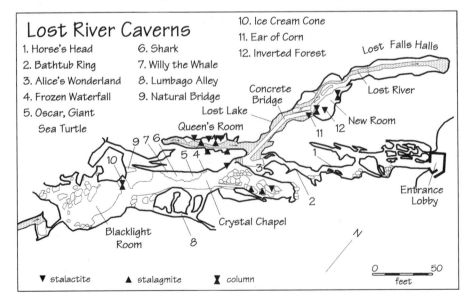

Lost River Caverns

1. Horse's Head
2. Bathtub Ring
3. Alice's Wonderland
4. Frozen Waterfall
5. Oscar, Giant Sea Turtle
6. Shark
7. Willy the Whale
8. Lumbago Alley
9. Natural Bridge
10. Ice Cream Cone
11. Ear of Corn
12. Inverted Forest

Lost Falls Halls

Lost River

Concrete Bridge

Lost Lake

New Room

Queen's Room

Entrance Lobby

Crystal Chapel

Blacklight Room

N

0   50
feet

▼ stalactite   ▲ stalagmite   ✗ column

in the human story of caves, being both the primary activity through which caves are discovered and the main threat to their existence.

Despite the Cambrian age of Lost River's rock, eleven of sixteen current or former show caves are found in Ordovician limestones. Down the valley in Berks County, Crystal Cave and Onyx Cave are in Hamburg Sequence limestones embedded within Ordovician Martinsburg shales. The limestone layers are part of the klippe that originated as a broken chunk of ocean floor thrust westward onto the younger shales of an ancient coastal plain during the Taconic Orogeny. The later Alleghenian Orogeny broke the rock along a fault that would mark the location of Crystal Cave when enough overburden was eroded away to allow the acid-charged water to penetrate the limestone. The dissolution of nearby Onyx Cave and eighteen other known wild caves began at about the same time.

It was a common practice for farmers to neutralize and enrich their soil with crushed limestone dug out of local hillsides and burnt in nearby kilns, and workers quarrying agricultural lime broke into

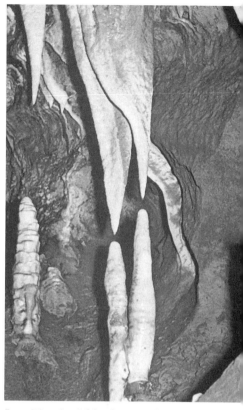

Lost River's richly decorated Queen's Room is protected by the cave's subterranean river and is accessible only during the severest of droughts. AUTHOR'S COLLECTION

both Crystal and Onyx Caves. Two other caves, Eckert and Frazer, punctuate the amphitheaterlike walls of Onyx's old quarry, but neither has proven to extend too far. Frazer Cave is the larger of the two, a spacious, downward-trending conduit floored with breakdown, currently sealed behind a door. Eckert Cave is an opening in the rocks to the right of Frazer.

Geologically speaking, finding these caves was not too surprising, as the nearby Dragon Cave was already well known as an outing destination. Dragon Cave first showed up on a map of the region in 1770 and was described in Charles B. Trego's 1843 *Geography of Pennsylvania*. After 1839, the cave was owned by the Dreibelbis family, who used it as an attraction for their Virginville hotel. The cave's namesake formation is an 8-foot-high stalagmite known as the Dragon, which rises from the floor of the cave's largest room, aptly named the Dragon's Den.

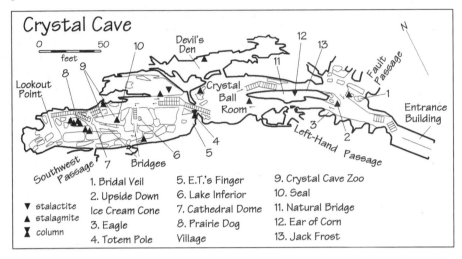

The more famous Crystal Cave is essentially two large, end-to-end rooms. The first, christened the Crystal Ballroom because of its aragonite-adorned flowstone, is entered by walking beneath the Natural Bridge, a huge slab of breakdown that fell from the ceiling eons ago. The return leg of the Crystal Cave tour passes over the top of the Natural Bridge. The rear room is heaped high with breakdown, which impeded the

The Frozen Fountain stalagmite, now the Upside Down Ice Cream Cone, is center right, separating the left passage taken by inbound tourists from the return passage followed on the outbound leg of the tour. AUTHOR'S COLLECTION

progress of initial explorers. The jumbled pile of calcite-covered cave-in has since been neutralized by steps and bridges over which tourists walk. The breakdown itself is ages old, as evidenced by the dripstone that covers its surfaces, implying that the tectonic activity that brought the roof down has long since ceased. Water continues to drip into the cave, keeping the abundant, iron oxide–stained speleothems alive. There are, however, no streams or sumps in Crystal, as the water table was lowered by the incision of regional streams thousands of years ago. The cave entrance is in fact perched eighty feet above the base of the hill. Although Crystal Cave does have a dry wishing well to capture charitable coin tosses, its only standing water collects in a small, dripstone-rimmed puddle ignominiously named Lake Inferior.

Although well decorated with speleothems, Onyx Cave never gained the reknown of its more famous neighbor. It got its name from its calcite formations, which resemble onyx. Onyx Cave reaches into the hillside on at least two levels, the lower of which collects water that can be seen at Swan Lake. After about 100 feet, the main passageway branches into a loop at the Giant Fallen Stalactite. The tighter passage extends under the Natural Onyx Bridge, a 50-foot-long calcite ceiling that presumably formed on top of fill when the passage was choked with clay. Subsequent stream action carried the clay away, leaving the dripstone suspended over the tube. Like the other Great Valley caves, Onyx contains a main chamber graced with a wall-size flowstone formation. The chamber is known as the Cathedral Room, and the flowstone contains the cave's famous Elephant's Head formation. Two joint controlled cross passages connect both sides of the loop. The inaccessible western cross passage is crowded with the Ice Jam, an irregular surface of dripstone over ceiling breakdown. The other passage, which functioned as the return corridor for cave tours, has a ceiling covered with intricate

Huge stalagmite weighing between three to four to In Onyx Cave near Hamburg, Pa.

Onyx Cave's signature stalagmite was once mistakenly interpreted as the Fallen Stalactite. DEAN SNYDER

boxwork, a weblike pattern of calcite deposited by water issuing from minute cracks.

Indian Echo Caverns is the only Great Valley commercial cave with a natural entrance. Its historic maw is in a cliff of Beekmantown limestone of the Epler Formation overlooking Swatara Creek a mile south of Hummelstown. Beekmantown limestones are well-known cave formers, accounting for dozens of solution holes throughout the Lebanon Valley. Swatara Creek is not coincidentally located at the entrance to Indian Echo, but it is part of the regional drainage network that eroded the valley, lowered the water table, drained the cave, and then intersected the cavity. Throughout the cave, there is evidence of two levels that formed as the water table dropped. The massive pile of breakdown between the Wilson Room and the Indian Ball Room was once the floor of the upper level before it collapsed in on the lower level, creating one big room. Like a mountain of partially melted then refrozen ice cream, the flowstone Wall of Imagination hangs on the north side of the Ball Room.

Two high ceiling passages extend from the Ball Room in different directions, forming a large L. The longer passage is known as the North Canyon, and to the right of it is the East Canyon. The Giant Ear of Corn, Indian Echo's largest stalactite, hangs suspended at the entrance to the East Canyon, which is entered by passing beneath a Natural Bridge of travertine. The East Canyon terminates at a massive pile of breakdown and fill in the commodious Dead End Room. The room sits beneath a sinkhole that once had an opening to the outside world. It was filled in when the cave was developed. The more spectacular North Canyon still retains sections of the upper level. In places, the ceiling that once capped the former upper level is visible forty feet above the floor. Speleothems line the passage, especially in the Rainbow Room. An orangy brown sheet

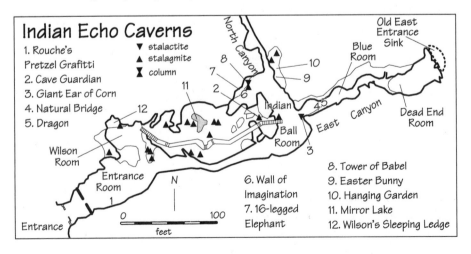

Indian Echo Caverns

1. Rouche's Pretzel Grafitti
2. Cave Guardian
3. Giant Ear of Corn
4. Natural Bridge
5. Dragon

▼ stalactite
▲ stalagmite
Ⅹ column

6. Wall of Imagination
7. 16-legged Elephant
8. Tower of Babel
9. Easter Bunny
10. Hanging Garden
11. Mirror Lake
12. Wilson's Sleeping Ledge

North Canyon
Blue Room
Old East Entrance Sink
Indian Ball Room
East Canyon
Dead End Room
Wilson Room
Entrance Room
Entrance
N
0   100   feet

of flowstone, christened Niagara Falls, formed along the wall of the upper level and can be seen through a hole in the ceiling.

The North Canyon originally terminated at a sparkling, calcite-encrusted pocket cupping a pool of water as clear as air, called Crystal Lake. A crawlway behind Crystal Lake leads to an even larger and more brilliant chamber that could not be accessed by widening the existing passage without destroying the very formations that made it worth seeing. Two years after the cave was commercialized, a 50-foot bypass

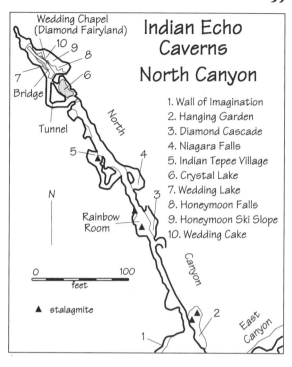

Indian Echo Caverns

North Canyon

1. Wall of Imagination
2. Hanging Garden
3. Diamond Cascade
4. Niagara Falls
5. Indian Tepee Village
6. Crystal Lake
7. Wedding Lake
8. Honeymoon Falls
9. Honeymoon Ski Slope
10. Wedding Cake

tunnel was dug through solid limestone to lift the lid on Indian Echo's most impressive jewel box. Originally christened the Diamond Fairyland, the room is filled with heaping mounds of snow white flowstone and sheets of bronze drapery that glimmer with the specks of a million calcite crystals. A reflecting pool lies at the bottom of the chamber, and a wooden bridge allows visitors to take in the subterranean spectacle from all angles. The chamber has since been rechristened the Wedding Chapel, with the bridge spanning Wedding Lake.

Limestones underlie the south side of the Great Valley between Allentown and Harrisburg. Martinsburg shales outcrop to the north. The difference is readily apparent on the surface, with the limestone part of the valley being more level and intensively farmed compared with the hillier shale side of the valley, which is also farmed but contains more wooded areas. Crystal and Onyx Caves are actually in the hillier shale side of the valley, having formed in isolated chunks of klippe limestone. Indian Echo is on the limestone side of the valley, in an area where once-prosperous farms are giving way to suburbanization between Harrisburg and Hershey.

West of Harrisburg, the Great Valley bends to the southwest and is locally known as the Cumberland Valley. Here the geology is a little different. Limestones that outcrop on the east side of the valley, hard against South Mountain, return to the surface in the middle of the val-

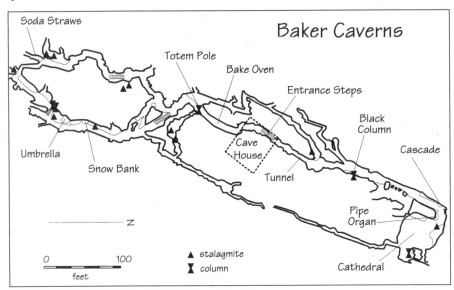

Baker Caverns

Soda Straws

Totem Pole

Bake Oven

Entrance Steps

Black Column

Cascade

Umbrella

Cave House

Snow Bank

Tunnel

Pipe Organ

Cathedral

▲ stalagmite

Ⅺ column

0   100

feet

Manganese has stained Baker Caverns's Black Column.

ley because of a downward fold known as the Massanutten Syncline. A broad swath of Martinsburg shales occupies the middle of the syncline between the outcropping ends of the limestone layers. Baker Caverns sits right on the limestone edge of this boundary in the middle of the Cumberland Valley. The cave formed in Chambersburg limestone but is so close to the Martinsburg contact that the eastern wall of the cave is quite shaley. In fact, the shaley nature of the rock is probably what prevented any more solution passageways from forming to the east, while in the limestone to the west, two and in places three other semiparallel galleries exist.

Baker Caverns is a strike cave, which means its main passage follows the strike of the rock, or the direction in which the rock is outcropping. Just south of Williamson, the Chambersburg limestone outcrops in a narrow band running northeast-to-southwest, the same alignment as Baker's main passageways. This is a very common cave alignment in the Appalachian Ridge and Valley section of Pennsylvania, where the cave-bearing limestones tend to outcrop in narrow bands along the bases of the ridges. The entrance to Baker Caverns sits in a collapsed sink over which a house was built, so that access to the cave is made by descending a flight of concrete steps from the basement of the house. It has been closed since 1954.

The commercial caves of eastern Pennsylvania may have complex geology, but their geography is quite simple. They all line up along the exposed limestone part of the Great Valley.

Appalachian Ridge and Valley Caves

The distribution of caves in the Appalachian Ridge and Valley section of central Pennsylvania is not as clear as in the Great Valley, but a pattern nonetheless exists.

The wooded slopes of Nittany Mountain fall away from Mount Nittany Inn's outdoor deck. Overlooking Centre Hall and Penns Valley, the panoramic view is a picture postcard of Pennsylvania's Appalachian Ridge and Valley section, featuring steep-sided, forested ridges and broad, farmed valleys. It seems improbable that the bucolic mountain scenery was once a flat, sandy coastal plain, but that's what the rocks say. They also say that before the emergence of the coastal plain, the territory around the future Mount Nittany Inn was nothing but open water, a vast inland sea stretching to the horizon.

The ridge-forming Tuscarora quartzite that outcrops along Nittany Mountain was initially a sandy Silurian beach. The limestones beneath Nittany, Penns, and Brush Valleys formed tens of millions of years earlier at the bottom of Ordovician seas. The two strata were folded into broad anticlines and synclines during the Permian Period. In the process, the sandstones were turned to quartzite. Subsequent erosion breached the anticlines, exposing the tilted beds of quartzite and limestone. In such a matchup of erosional resistance, the weaker limestones have weathered faster, forming low-lying valleys, while the more slowly eroding quartzites were left holding up the ridges.

Nearby State College and the Nittany Valley dairy farms to its southwest and northeast sit along the axis of the Nittany Anticline, an upwarp of rock that brings Ordovician and, in places, Cambrian limestones to the surface across the length and breadth of the valley floor. The Nittany Anticline stretches in a great sweeping arc for more than 100 miles, from the Susquehanna River at Muncy southwest to Hollidaysburg. Like a high garden wall, Bald Eagle Mountain borders the valley to north-northwest. It stands as a truncated limb of Tuscarora quartzite

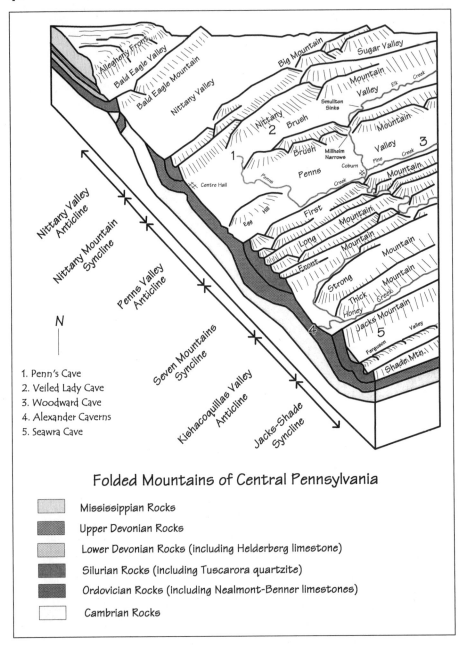

Folded Mountains of Central Pennsylvania

1. Penn's Cave
2. Veiled Lady Cave
3. Woodward Cave
4. Alexander Caverns
5. Seawra Cave

- Mississippian Rocks
- Upper Devonian Rocks
- Lower Devonian Rocks (including Helderberg limestone)
- Silurian Rocks (including Tuscarora quartzite)
- Ordovician Rocks (including Nealmont-Benner limestones)
- Cambrian Rocks

that once vaulted 10,000 feet above the anticlinal valley to connect with the same quartzite strata outcropping in Tussey and Nittany Mountains, the next ridges to the south-southeast. The quartzite and nearly 2 miles of underlying rock have been eroded off the anticline to expose the Ordovician limestones beneath.

East of State College, the Tuscarora quartzite is down-warped into a tight syncline, the upturned edges of which form Nittany Mountain's double crests. The crests merge westward into a great rocky finger that points toward Penn State. Mount Nittany Inn is perched atop the southern crest, the truncated limb to the next series of anticlinal folds that arched over Penns Valley to the south. Farther east, a synclinal crease in the anticline is occupied by another double crested Tuscarora quartzite ridge known as Brush Mountain. Brush Valley occupies the anticline between Nittany and Brush Mountains, while the anticlinal valley south of Brush Mountain is an eastward extension of Penns Valley.

This is the pattern of central Pennsylvania's mountains: broad, anticlinal valleys underlain with limestone separated by synclinal ridges of Tuscarora quartzite. South of Penns Valley, the pattern is repeated in the synclinal folds of the Seven Mountains complex, beyond which lies the anticlinal Kishacoquillas Valley, where the Ordovician limestones outcrop once again. Southeast of Kish Valley, this package of cave-bearing limestones does not outcrop again until the Great Valley near Harrisburg. Southwest from State College, however, the Ordovician anticlinal valleys continue. The Nittany Anticline plunges in Sinking Valley, a tri-

This view north across the anticlinal Penns Valley shows Millheim Narrows in the distance where Elk Creek has cut a water gap through the synclinal Brush Mountain. Beyond the narrows is the anticlinal Brush Valley, bounded to the north by the synclinal Nittany Mountain, glimpsed through the water gap. The valleys are underlain by limestone and the mountains are held up by Tuscarora quartzite.

angular limestone lowland cupped in the double back fold of a different Brush Mountain south of Tyrone. Canoe Valley, a scenic ribbon of limestone-rooted farmland west of Water Street, connects Sinking Valley to Morrison Cove, the next large anticlinal valley to the south. Morrison Cove lies above the resurfacing of the Nittany Anticline, which plunges farther south to rise again in Bedford County's Friendship Cove, where the same Cambro-Ordovician limestones are found.

In the midst of these spacious limestone valleys and sharp-backed ridges, there is a tiny crossroads hamlet named Water Street. It might just as well be named Cave Corner, because it is from this innocuous spot at the junction of U.S. Route 22 and PA Route 453 that the would-be cave tourist has to make a decision as to which cave to see, with no more guidance than that provided by a flurry of brightly painted billboards. In the old days, competition to control this corner with visual proclamations of subterranean superiority was fierce. The junction, a sharp-turned Y, forced traffic to slow down no matter what the approach or desired trajectory, making the billboards visible longer.

Eastbound travelers were implored to turn left 1 mile . . . 1/2 mile . . . then 500 feet ahead to visit historic Indian Caverns, or to "See Penn's Cave by Boat." At the same time, classic billboard yellow and black graphics encouraged the motorist to stay the course on U.S. 22 to see Lincoln Caverns, a mere 8 miles farther down the road. If the U.S. 22 traveler passed the 453 Y without deviation, other signs called attention to the obvious error, giving the hapless wayfarer one last chance to turn back to see Indian Caverns. Likewise, once on the road to Indian Caverns and Penn's Cave, signs were quick to point out that Lincoln Caverns was the other way.

Not mentioned by billboard, at least not in recent years, Woodward Cave is accessed by the same route from Water Street as Indian and Penn's, PA Route 453 to PA Route 45. In the opposite direction, Coral Caverns is west on U.S. Route 22, then south on U.S. Route 220. Thus, all five of central Pennsylvania's active commercial caves can be approached with a turn of the wheel at Water Street. But since the 2002 opening of a new U.S. 22 alignment, there are fewer billboards, and the 453 Y has been eliminated. Traffic now whisks safely through a light-controlled intersection of minimal noteworthiness.

In addition to the five show caves currently open to the public, there are five others in central Pennsylvania that once operated commercially but are now closed. Seawra Cave and Alexander Caverns are in Mifflin County. Veiled Lady Cave is down the road from Penn's Cave in Centre County. Tytoona Cave is in northern Blair County's Sinking Valley, and Hipple Cave is in Bedford County's portion of Morrison Cove. That makes ten show caves scattered over five counties in a region crisscrossed by limestone valleys and the zigzag ridges of the folded Appalachian Mountains. So what's the pattern?

Although limestone is readily found in the valleys of central Pennsylvania, not all of it is good cave-forming limestone. As with Great Valley limestones, which were laid down at the same time, most of the rock is either too dolomitic or too shaley. The rocks with just the right chemistry were laid down in the prehistoric oceans of two different periods: the middle Ordovician, and the upper Silurian/lower Devonian. Caves are found wherever limestones of these ages outcrop. Of the hundreds of holes that exist, ten are extensive and spacious enough, and reasonably well decorated, to have been developed for tours. Half of those have since closed.

Of the region's ten current or former show caves, seven are found within a single 200-foot-thick layer of limestone: the Ordovician Nealmont/Benner Formation. All of these caves are close to or straddle the unconformity that separates Nealmont limestone from Benner limestone. Benner is also known as the Linden Hall Formation and is frequently described as being separated from the Nealmont by the Curtin Formation. The entire package was traditionally referred to as the Trenton group of limestones. The Nealmont/Benner outcrops at the margin of central Pennsylvania's major anticlinal valleys. Penn's Cave and Veiled Lady Cave are both in Brush Valley. Nearby Woodward Cave is in Penns Valley, and Mifflin County's Alexander Caverns is at the southern edge of Kishacoquillas Valley. Hipple Cave sits in the shadow of Tussey Mountain at the eastern edge of Morrison Cove. Indian Caverns is farther north along the same flank of Tussey Mountain, but located in the southwest extension of Nittany Valley. Just to the southwest is Tytoona Cave, at the southern edge of Sinking Valley. Tytoona is actually in the Hatter Formation, about 350 feet below the Benner but similar in geography and geology. In short, the seven Ordovician caves are all located near the base of some major ridge at the margin of an anticlinal valley.

The three remaining show caves share a different set of geographic and geologic similarities. All three are part of the lower Devonian Helderberg Formation, which outcrops at the margins of valleys that are adjacent and parallel to the anticlinal valleys. These are valleys that lie between the axis of an anticline and the axis of a syncline. Geologically speaking, the Helderberg limestone lies beneath the Ridgely (Oriskany) sandstone, which tends to form smaller secondary ridges. The openings to Lincoln and Seawra Caves are actually partially up the slope of these Ridgely ridges. Lincoln Caverns stretches beneath the western flank of Warrior Ridge. To the northwest, Hartslog Valley is underlain by older Silurian Keyser limestone (positioned beneath the Helderberg). Tussey

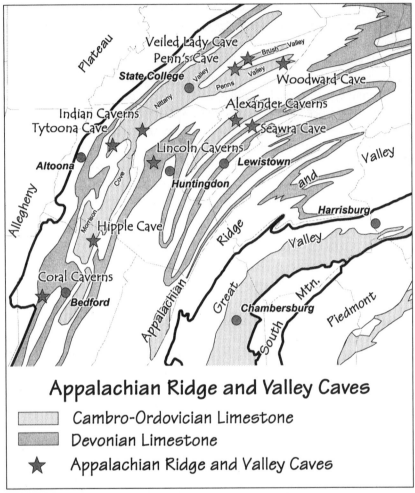

Appalachian Ridge and Valley Caves

	Cambro-Ordovician Limestone
	Devonian Limestone
★	Appalachian Ridge and Valley Caves

The folded bands of Cambro-Ordovician and Devonian limestones in Central Pennsylvania are separated by Siluruan Tuscarora quartzite ridges. The Ordovician caves are in anticlinal valleys. Alexander Caverns is in Kishacoquillas Valley; Woodward, Veiled Lady, Penn's, Indian, Tytoona, and Hipple are in different parts of the Nittany Valley Anticlinorium. The Devonian caves—Seawra, Lincoln, and Coral—are located in a thinner belt of limestone that outcrops along the base of minor ridges.

Mountain stands parallel and northwest of Hartslog Valley and, beyond it, the Nittany anticlinal valleys. Southeast of Lincoln Caverns, the Broad Top Syncline crosses U.S. 22 between Huntingdon and Mount Union.

The pattern of rocks and ridges around Lincoln Caverns is repeated at Seawra Cave. Seawra lies north of Alfarata along the western flank of Chestnut Ridge. A very narrow valley of Keyser limestone is immediately to the northwest, paralleled by Jacks Mountain, beyond which lies the anticlinal Kishacoquillas Valley. To the southeast, the synclinal Pleasant Valley is on the other side of Chestnut Ridge.

The relative location of Coral Caverns in Bedford County is a mirror image of the other two caves. In this case, the anticline is to the east and the syncline to the west. Coral Caverns is just inside the west flank of Buffalo Mountain. The canoe-shaped Milligan Cove anticlinal valley is just over the mountain to the east. To the west, a synclinal axis runs parallel to Buffalo Mountain between the cave and the Allegheny Front. The inverted ordering of the rocks means that the older Keyser limestone outcrops between the cave and the Silurian Tuscarora quartzite at the top of Buffalo Mountain. There's not much space on the slope, meaning the Helderberg and Keyser outcroppings are narrow and steeply pitched. The void that is Coral Caverns may in fact extend into the Keyser. This inverted arrangement of rocks also means that the Ridgley sandstone is to the west, curiously located at a lower elevation than the weaker Helderberg limestone that holds the cave.

The geography of caves in central Pennsylvania reveals a predictable pattern that explains not only their location within the Appalachian Ridge and Valley region, but also their form and appearance at a more localized scale. Why can you see Penn's Cave by boat, while the only water in Lincoln Caverns is a shallow pool at the very lowest level? Likewise, there are no significant pools in Seawra Cave, but just over Jacks Mountain, the stream running through Alexander Caverns is large enough to have supported boat tours when the cave was open to the public. Streams either flow into or out of all the Ordovician caves with the exception of Indian. None of the Devonian caves contain streams, although evidence suggests that they once did. All of the Ordovician caves have natural entrances. All of the Devonian caves were broken into. These differences deserve a closer examination.

Ordovician Caves

Caves are just one of the many peculiar features common to karst landscapes, regions underlain by soluble limestone. Sinkholes, blind valleys, dry valleys, natural bridges, fensters, swallow holes, and stream rises, or springs, are also karst features typically found in the vicinity of caves. Pennsylvania's anticlinal valleys are collectively one of the most renowned karst landscapes in the country. Water is the critical land-shaping agent, having the ability to erode limestone physically or chemically. It can flow aboveground, in a subterranean conduit, or both. Six of central Pennsylvania's seven Ordovician show caves have natural entrances that are in some way the result of stream action.

The Benner's cave-pocked Valentine Member outcrops in two narrow bands along the northern and southern margins of Brush Valley, a curious realm where mountain runs disappear upon reaching the valley floor. The streams draining the clastic flanks of Nittany and Brush Mountains drop into swallow holes eaten into the carbonate rocks of the valley and continue their journey through underground conduits. The swallow holes are, in a sense, the opposite of springs, where water flows *into* the ground instead of out of it. Each of a dozen different runs flowing down the south flank of Nittany Mountain east from Centre Hall terminates in a blind valley at the base of the ridge. A blind valley is a steep-sided depression where the stream runs into a hole at the base of the high wall on the downstream side. Ceiling rockfall at the mouth of the hole has opened a few of these up into caves, meaning they're large enough for someone to crawl into them.

In the 1930s, the Grenoble Run swallow hole was commercially developed as Veiled Lady Cave. The opening is 15 by 15 feet, and when the cave was mapped in 1949, it extended back 1,050 feet. Just inside the cave, up and to the left, sat the cave's namesake—a white stalagmite thought to resemble a woman wrapped in a veil. Fifty feet into the cave, Grenoble Run drops over a 10-foot waterfall, and then gurgles away into the darkness beneath a ceiling that, according to the map, descended from 15 feet to 9 feet to 4 to 2 before pinching out.

The danger of putting improvements into a swallow hole cave is that the watery god who provided the opportunity is fickle and may just take it away. The Great Depression closed Veiled Lady Cave just a few years after it opened, and in 1936, a flood bore down the mountain and wreaked havoc with the cave's electrical system, paths, and planks. The cave never reopened. It did, however, receive an occasional visitor, including members of the Nittany Grotto, a local caving association that recorded its field trips in its newsletter. The March 1962 *Nittany Grotto News* reported that the 2½-foot-high crawlway mapped in 1949 had diminished by a foot. The March–April 1969 issue noted that half the cave was no more than 20 inches high, with 1 to 4 inches of water flowing across the floor. The incredible shrinking cave was actually filling up with dirt and debris carried into it by Grenoble Run. The muddy flood waters of Hurricane Agnes virtually sealed much of the cave in 1972. Meanwhile, the Veiled Lady formation suffered its own dark fate over the years, gradually being battered to a nub by vandals and the freeze-thaw ravages of weather. The cave entrance is on private property and no longer opened to the public.

Veiled Lady is a lesson in the ephemeral nature of caves. A cave spends most of its existence as an unrecognized void in the rock, sealed up like a tomb, the tomb of the unknown void. In a cave like Veiled Lady, surface drainage exploits a fracture and breaks the seal on the void, opening the netherworld to the stream. The dynamic nature of the stream ensures that the cave opening is, geologically speaking, short-lived, susceptible to the collapse or deposition that will eventually reseal the hole. In the end, it all has to go. The whole rock house is ultimately brought down and carried away by the forces of erosion acting through the drainage network.

Although the water of Grenoble Run, and all the other Nittany Mountain runs, may be flowing underground at times, it is still part of a regional surface network that ultimately ends up in the Susquehanna River. The typical Pennsylvania anticlinal valley is drained by creeks flowing along the edges of the valley that collect the water of the mountain runs. The creeks drain into larger streams that cut across the valleys and through narrow mountain water gaps to the Susquehanna River. The southern margin of Brush Valley is drained by Elk Creek, which collects the water shed from the north slope of Brush Mountain. Downstream from Smullton, Elk Creek meanders around the south end of a limestone hill *and* through it. Water disappears beneath a rocky ledge on the upstream side of the hill and reappears as a spring on the downstream side. In between, two sinkholes provide glimpses of the underground stream rising on the

Just before turning south through Millheim Narrows, part of Elk Creek is diverted into a subterranean channel that can be seen flowing across the bottom of two fensters known as the Smullton Sinks. It this view, the water is rising from the upstream wall.

upstream side of each sink and disappearing again beneath the cliff on the downstream end. Like portals through the roof of a watery tunnel, the sinkholes are known as fensters, German for windows. The two fensters are separated by a farm lane that has been built over the top of the natural tunnel that connects the sinks. Elk Creek leaves Brush Valley through Millheim Narrows, a twisting gorge cleaving Brush Mountain. It then flows across Penns Valley and into Penns Creek, which has cut its own gorge through the Seven Mountains complex en route to the Susquehanna.

The northern side of Brush Valley has no equivalent to Elk Creek. It can be assumed that an underground stream connects the mountain runs after they sink. Penn's Cave sits on the other side of the valley, but outside the Elk Creek basin. It has a drainage mystery opposite to that of Veiled Lady. At Penn's Cave, no one is sure where the water comes *from*. The logical connection between the dots is that the water swallowed up in Veiled Lady Cave and the other sinkholes along the base of Nittany Mountain is somehow crossing beneath Brush Valley to rise at Penn's Cave. This is no mean feat, since the water would have to pass through the axis of the anticline and against the bedding plane of the limestone.

Tourists have enjoyed the novelty of taking a boat through Penn's Cave since 1885. Only Crystal Cave has been open longer. I remember my own childhood trip to Penn's Cave. My mother got the idea that the kids could see the inside of a cave *and* get a boat ride. It was like a two-for-one deal. Penn's Cave is the headwater source of Penns Creek, which flows southeast across Penns Valley to a confluence with Elk Creek at the longtime fishing resort of Coburn.

The spectacular maw of Penn's Cave arches over a pool of crystal-clear water 13 feet deep. A long flight of stairs descends to the boat

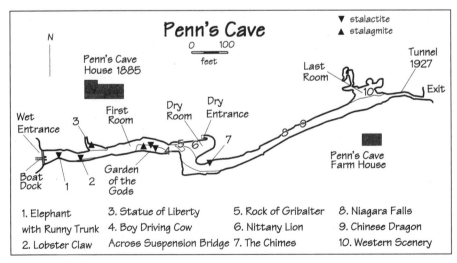

Penn's Cave

▼ stalactite
▲ stalagmite

N

0   100
feet

Penn's Cave House 1885

Tunnel 1927

Last Room

Exit

Wet Entrance

3

First Room

Dry Room

Dry Entrance

10

Boat Dock

1   2

Garden of the Gods

Penn's Cave Farm House

7

8   9

1. Elephant with Runny Trunk
2. Lobster Claw
3. Statue of Liberty
4. Boy Driving Cow Across Suspension Bridge
5. Rock of Gribalter
6. Nittany Lion
7. The Chimes
8. Niagara Falls
9. Chinese Dragon
10. Western Scenery

Boats await the next trip at the Wet Entrance to Penn's Cave.

dock at the water's edge, where the rocky cliffs of the sinkhole rise up on all sides, partially obscured by trees and vines. The cave entrance has a classic triangle shape provided by the tilted bedding of the limestone and the perpendicularly eroded joint that acts as the lifeline to the cave. The boat basin is a spring that discharges 4,000 gallons a minute. The water issues from the sinkhole breakdown beneath the dock, then drifts silently into the cave following the main strike passageway for nearly 1,000 feet. Penn's Cave originally terminated at a sump, where the ceiling dips below the water level barring farther passage. The water then resurfaced at the source spring to Penns Creek outside the cave. In 1929, however, a 75-foot-long tunnel was blasted through the back of the cave to allow the boat tours to continue out onto Lake Nittanee, a small impoundment built just downstream from the spring.

Before the cave was commercialized, visitors favored the Dry Entrance. The Wet Entrance was at the bottom of a 75-foot-deep sinkhole surrounded by cliffs and steep slopes choked with vegetation. This is a condition that can hardly be appreciated by today's visitors, who comfortably stroll down a winding asphalt path to a staircase that descends to the boat dock. Precommercial visitors also had to bring their own boats. Not surprisingly, they opted for the Dry Entrance, located in a shallow sink 500 feet to the east. That entrance is still there along an outcropping of limestone in front of the Penn's Cave Hotel.

The Dry Entrance connects with a higher, and presumably older, cave passage that is now expressed as upper rooms and ledges along the

The narrow straight between the Rock of Gibralter, a huge block of break-down, and the south wall dictates the width of Penn's Cave's boats.

first half of the water passage. As seen from the boat, the majestic Statue of Liberty stalagmite stands on this ledge, as does a mineral forest of calcite formations presented as the Garden of the Gods in the First Room. The Dry (or Second) Room, located some 500 feet back into the cave, is where the Dry Entrance passage descends to the water level. Ceiling heights, which range from 15 to 25 feet in the rest of the cave, soar to 40 feet in this sizable breakdown room. The room is decorated with an array of dripstone formations, including the Petrified Nittany Lion and the Chinese Buddha. A large slab of breakdown sits in the water as the Rock of Gibraltar, which constricts the stream to a size slightly larger than the width of the boat.

At the Dry Room, the cave jogs across the bedding to the south, then eastward again along the strike. This long passage has a lower ceiling, averaging 10 to 15 feet, but dropping as low as 5. In the low Archway, a row of broken stalactites possibly illustrates the handiwork of ancient floodwaters but more than likely is the work of early souvenir vandals. An orangy flowstone shelf along the north wall has the appearance of Niagara Falls and continues as the bulbous Chinese Dragon chasing a Big Turtle. The entire calcite ensemble formed on a bank of cave clay that was subsequently eroded away. Another remnant piece of the upper passage appears in the Last Room, which also includes the cave's largest stalagmite, a 14-footer known as the Giant Pillar.

Penn's was not the only see-it-by-boat cave in Pennsylvania. Before 1954, Alexander Caverns also had a boat tour component. The small number of cavers who have seen it, and the even fewer tourists who remember it, claim that Alexander Caverns was one of the most awe-inspiring show caves in the state. It is located near the small town of Naginey in the Kishacoquillas Valley where the Nealmont/Benner limestone resurfaces south of the Seven Mountains. The limestone is a valuable commodity that is mined and crushed for gravel at a number of large quarries upstream from Alexander.

Like central Pennsylvania's other Ordovician caves, Alexander Caverns is integrally linked to the surface streams that drain the surrounding ridges and sink upon hitting the limestone floor of the valley. The eastern end of Kish Valley is drained by Laurel Creek, Havice Creek, Treaster Run, and Honey Creek. After tumbling out of a reservoir in a high hollow tucked against Front Mountain, Laurel Creek flows south through the town of Milroy, then disappears into a series of swallow holes located in its streambed, which terminates in a blind valley at Goss Cave.

The other streams drain three parallel valleys separated from each other by Tuscarora quartzite ridges. All three are swallowed up in similar fashion soon after flowing out onto the karst surface of Kish Valley. Exactly where these streams sink depends on how much water is flowing in them at any given time. Their beds are riddled with small swallow holes, which are only bypassed by overflow. During low flow at the end of summer or under drought conditions, the water does not make it past the first swallow hole. At flood stage, however, the stream can fill all the swallow holes to overflowing and still have enough water to run down the streambed. These are textbook examples of dry valley streams, typically characterized by channels of rounded cobbles and washed gravel devoid of the water that has been siphoned off into an underground conduit somewhere upstream.

Alexander Caverns is on the downstream receiving end of the underground flow in the eastern end of Kish Valley. The water resurfaces in the cave, flows through an L-shaped tunnel, then exits as the lower reaches of Honey Creek. The rise is known as Mammoth Spring, and at 14,000 gallons per minute (three and a half times the flow of Penn's Cave Spring), it is the second largest spring in the state.

Alexander Cavern's Wet Entrance is actually located just up the bank and immediately west of the spring. Like the top bar of a capital T, the Dry Cave and the upper part of the Wet Cave cross the head of the lower Wet Cave as part of the same strike passage. A tributary stream probably once occupied the Dry Cave portion, which was subsequently abandoned, allowing Honey Creek to incise the Wet Cave 30 feet deeper. The Wet Cave continues upstream for another 500 feet to the terminal sump.

Today the cave is privately owned, on property that is now a dairy farm, and it is not open to the public. However, the owner has entered into an agreement with the Bald Eagle Grotto, which holds the keys to the cave and runs a limited number of trips for National Speleological Society members.

A third spring cave was commercially developed in yet another anticlinal valley to the west. The little known and short-lived Hipple Cave was opened to the public in 1928 and closed in the 1940s. The cave is located near Waterside, Bedford County, at the eastern edge of Morrsion Cove, and although the location is different, the geology and geography are very similar. As with Penn's and Alexander, a stream flows through the length of Hipple Cave, surfacing to form a spring on its downstream end. Much smaller than Penns or Honey Creek, Hipple Cave Run has its headwaters up on the west slope of nearby Tussey Mountain and sinks into the limestone at the base of the ridge.

The main entrance to Hipple is through a 50-foot-deep hole on the upstream end of the strike cave passage. Known as the Bake Oven, the hole sits within an outcropping of limestone along a low ridge. The run issues out from beneath a ledge at the base of the stairs and parallels the path through most of the cave. After an uncomfortable 5-foot stoop for a short distance, the ceiling lifts to a height of 6 to 10 feet until the very rear of the cave, with chimneys extending up as high as 40 feet. Halfway along its 1,000-foot length, the cave jogs to the left and opens into

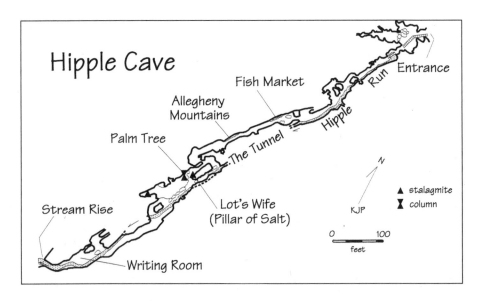

a large room surrounding a huge block of breakdown. A large, 8-foot stalagmite known as Lot's Wife, the Pillar of Salt, or simply The Statue stands at the head of the block. Opposite it is the Palm Tree, a column that flares at the top and is surrounded by an array of small stalactites that have the appearance of palm fronds. The cave formed along the bedding of the limestone, and toward the rear of the cave, the ceiling descends to within a few feet of the floor. At this point, a luminous haze of natural light emanates from the downstream spring and pierces the total darkness of the cave.

Whereas Penn's, Alexander, and Hipple Caves are associated with springs, the entrances to Veiled Lady, Woodward, and Tytoona are in sinks. Although dry now, the entrance to Woodward Cave was once a huge sink for floodwaters on Pine Creek. The headwaters of this stream drain the hollow between Brush Mountain and Buffalo Mountain before dropping into the eastern end of Penns Valley near the village of Woodward. Like so many other streams in the region, Pine Creek's persistent downward erosion intersected a phreatic cave formed in Nealmont/Benner limestone.

The dual lines cutting across the Palm Tree column were part of Hipple Cave's self-generated electric lighting system. DEAN SNYDER

Rockfall at the mouth of Woodward has created a large, arched entranceway. The interior blueprint of a cave is in part determined by the dip of the soluble limestone. Steeply dipping beds, like those found in the folded Appalachians, are likely to form long, linear strike passages. Hipple and Penn's Caves dip at 28 and 30 degrees, respectively, and both are linear strike passages. Woodward dips at a shallower 20 degrees because it is located closer to the axis of the southernmost of two anticlines that run through the eastern part of Penns Valley. When the cave formed at the water table, sealed off from the outside world, water infiltrated the intersecting joints that run perpendicular to the bedding and dissolved them into mazelike passages. Pine Creek carved the two largest passageways, which run parallel to each other and at 90

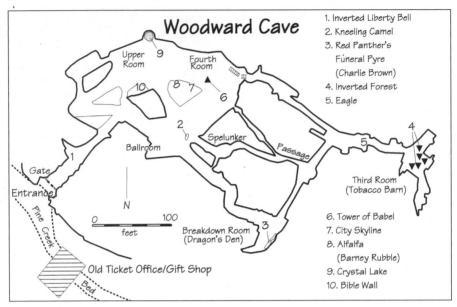

Woodward Cave

1. Inverted Liberty Bell
2. Kneeling Camel
3. Red Panther's
   Funeral Pyre
   (Charlie Brown)
4. Inverted Forest
5. Eagle

6. Tower of Babel
7. City Skyline
8. Alfalfa
   (Barney Rubble)
9. Crystal Lake
10. Bible Wall

Upper Room · 9 · Fourth Room · 10 · 8 · 7 · 6 · 2 · Spelunker · Passage · 5 · 4

Ballroom · 1 · Gate · Entrance · N · Third Room (Tobacco Barn)

Pine Creek · 0 · 100 · feet · Breakdown Room (Dragon's Den) · 3

Old Ticket Office/Gift Shop · Bed

degrees to the entrance passage. The back passage is 15 feet higher and marks the original course of the stream. The lower, front passage was formed later. Woodward's scalloped walls and elliptical tubes are evidence of stream erosion. The parallel passages are supplemented by intervening passages and connected by cross passages, allowing most of the cave to be toured as a circuit. Sediment deposited by Pine Creek

Pine Creek once flowed from right to left in front of the entrance to Woodward Cave.

completely choked some passageways, burying and breaking speleothems that remained undiscovered until the cave was dug out.

Woodward Cave has a muddy complexion. Part cave clay and part iron oxide, the color of the rock formations runs from orange to brown. The stream-cut passages are spacious. Stalactites cover the ceiling of one room, known as the Inverted Forest or the Lancaster Tobacco Barn, depending on whether you see the stalactites as upside-down trees or hanging tobacco. This room and the Square Room, or the Dragon's Den, end in terminal breakdown beyond which is the outside hill slope. The largest room, known unceremoniously as the Fourth Room, contains the Tower of Babel. This massive, 50-ton stalagmite is reputed to be the largest in Pennsylvania. The large flowstone Bible Wall decorates the side of the Upper, or Fifth, Room.

Woodward Cave's Tower of Babel is a 50-ton stalagmite, claimed to be the largest in the state. AUTHOR'S COLLECTION

Tytoona is the only other sink cave that was commercialized, barely. Historically known as Sinking Valley Cave and Arch Spring Cave, it was renamed Tytoona after the nearby towns of Tyrone and Altoona in 1947 during its brief life as a show cave. The cave is not in the valley shared by these two cities, but over Brush Mountain in the anticlinal Sinking Valley to the south and east. Sinking Valley is one of the Cambro-Ordovician limestone valleys that sit atop the Nittany Anticline. It extends along the north side of Brush Mountain from the point at which that mountain doubles back on itself down to the Little Juniata River north of Water Street. The valley is drained by Sinking Run, which, like other streams of its ilk, drains the clastic rocks of the ridge before sinking into the limestone of the valley. The surface channel continues down the valley as an intermittent stream to Arch Spring, where the state's eighth-largest spring adds a continuous flow of water to Sinking Run. This spring drains Tytoona Cave.

The Arch Spring resurgence is in a steep-sided sinkhole 30 feet deep, which drains through a natural stone bridge—the arch at Arch Spring.

This view across the sink from Tytoona Cave shows the stream rising from the upstream wall of the fenster before disappearing underground again.

Holed through a 20-foot-thick ridge of limestone, the natural bridge is a 12-by-15-foot opening that was originally the downstream end of Tytoona Cave. The sinkhole behind the arch is a collapsed portion of the cave.

At flood stage, water bound for Arch Spring can be seen flowing across the bottom of a fenster nearly a mile up the valley to the west. Tytoona Cave is the opening that swallows the water on the downstream side of the fenster. The subterranean stream rises into the fenster through a number of holes at the bottom of the sinkhole wall on the upstream side. The location of the rise depends on the water level. At flood stage, water gushes out of every upstream hole and mixes with the surface drainage that spills into the sink from a southward-flowing intermittent stream. Tytoona Cave gulps down all of this water and transfers it underground to Arch Spring. As the water level drops, the intermittent stream and the upper rises dry up. The lowest rise is actually within the maw of the cave, so the floor of the fenster is completely dry under drought conditions, with only wave-washed sand and gravel bars showing the location of the streambed. Two more sinkholes upstream from Tytoona are tied to this same system of underground drainage.

A massive, tilted lintel of Hatters limestone tops Tytoona's low-angled, triangular entranceway. Forty feet wide and having a 12-foot clearance on its high side, the cave can easily be entered without stooping. A clay pathway follows the left bank of the stream, which gurgles noisily along the pinched right side of the cave. A Log Jam bars the way some 400 feet back, but the cave continues for another 500 feet, terminating at a sump. Tytoona is only moderately decorated with small, soda straw stalactites, columns, and flowstone. Its ho-hum formations, remote location, and penchant for flooding limit its potential as a show cave. These shortcomings, however, were not enough to deter two separate commercialization attempts by two generations of the same family.

Although unprofitable as a commercial venture, Tytoona has always been popular with amateur cavers. Scuba divers plumbed its depths beyond the sump in the 1960s and 1980s, attempting to reach Arch Spring. Although a number of air-filled rooms and additional sumps were discovered, the passage to Arch Spring has proven to be too far, too deep, and too dark to traverse. The first sump, 8 feet deep and 40 feet long, leads to a room reported to contain speleothems. Subsequent sumps, however, are hundreds of feet long, with depths greater than 100 feet. Diving under these conditions is extremely hazardous and therefore currently prohibited. The Western Pennsylvania Conservancy bought Tytoona Cave in 1985, and in 1997, it became the tenth cave to be purchased by the National Speleological Society.

The remaining Ordovician show cave in central Pennsylvania is unique due to the absence of a watercourse that either sinks or rises at

Tytoona's stream rises again at Arch Spring, an ancient cave entrance isolated into a natural bridge when the ceiling collapsed on the upstream side of the arch.

the cave. Like the other caves, Indian Caverns has a natural entrance that opens at the edge of an anticlinal limestone valley. It is located within the Nealmont/Benner Formation at the base of Tussey Mountain, and along the southern flank of the Nittany Anticline at the village of Franklinville. Spruce Creek drains this side of the valley toward the Little Juniata River, but Indian Caverns sits high on a hillside well above the stream.

Indian Caverns is a bit of a mystery, because it has never been adequately mapped beyond the scaled sketch map made by Ralph Stone and published in *Pennsylvania Caves* in 1930. Stone described the tour, essentially the same route used today, as being 1,700 feet long with 500 feet of retraced passage. Additional passageways exist above, below, and beyond the current show cave, but their combined length is anyone's guess. The cave length has been reported to be anywhere from a reasonable mile to an unlikely 10 miles.

Indian Caverns formed at the water table and was drained when the water table dropped with the incision of Spruce Creek into its valley. This was some time ago, judging from the vertical distance between the cave entrance and the creekbed. Inside the cave, Frozen Niagara is one of two formations that have claimed the title of Pennsylvania's largest piece of flowstone. Five feet thick at its base and as high as a two-story house, Frozen Niagara is estimated to be a million years old. Since the speleothem could not have formed until the water drained, the passage

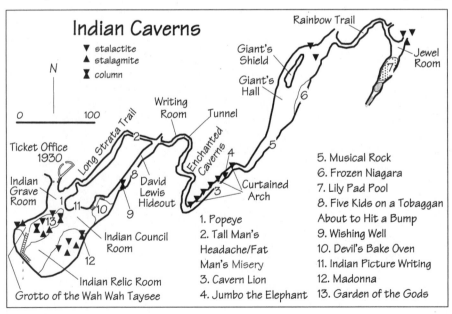

Indian Caverns

▼ stalactite
▲ stalagmite
✕ column

N

0 ——— 100

Rainbow Trail

Giant's Shield

Giant's Hall

Jewel Room

Writing Room   Tunnel

Ticket Office 1930

Long Strata Trail

Enchanted Caverns

Indian Grave Room

David Lewis Hideout

Curtained Arch

Indian Council Room

Indian Relic Room

Grotto of the Wah Wah Taysee

1. Popeye
2. Tall Man's Headache/Fat Man's Misery
3. Cavern Lion
4. Jumbo the Elephant

5. Musical Rock
6. Frozen Niagara
7. Lily Pad Pool
8. Five Kids on a Tobaggan About to Hit a Bump
9. Wishing Well
10. Devil's Bake Oven
11. Indian Picture Writing
12. Madonna
13. Garden of the Gods

it sits in must be older still. The water table now rests at the level of the Jewel Room, but during high water can rise to flood the cave's lower passage. The passages are assumed to be even older toward the entrance, closer to the axis of the anticline. The cave once extended beyond the entrance until it was eroded away with the rock. The overlying hard rocks of the ridge protect the present cave from erosion—for now.

The upper part of Indian Caverns is a rectangular circuit formed along intersecting joints and oriented to the northeast strike of the rock. It includes the Indian Council Room, the Indian Relic Room, the Indian Grave Room, and the Grotto of the Wah Wah Taysee. The Indian Council Room, where Iroquois rituals are assumed to have taken place, is the largest breakdown room in the cave. It, like most of Indian Caverns, is covered with dripstone formations. The nearby Grotto of the Wah Wah Taysee (Iroquois for fireflies) gets its name from the tiny, green specks of luminescent radium on the walls and ceiling that glow in total darkness, a rare phenomenon not found anywhere else in Pennsylvania. The absence of soot on the walls and ceiling led to the assumption that Indians

Harold "Hubby" Wertz orchestrated Indian Caverns's tourist circuit to penetrate as far as the Jewel Room, a dripstone-encrusted lower chamber where water collected in reflecting pools. AUTHOR'S COLLECTION

had avoided this room, fearing that it was haunted by evil spirits, a supposition that was later used to give shivers to tourists.

An angular passage, christened the Enchanted Caverns, links the Writing Room tunnel with a northeast-oriented strike passage that ends at Giant's Hall. In Giant's Hall are the Giant's Shield, a 6-ton wedge of limestone that longitudinally bisects the room.

Beyond Giant's Hall, the passage meanders down a dip as Rainbow Trail to the Jewel Room, 140 feet below the level of the entrance. Here stalactites drip into colorless reflecting pools, and the cave passage narrows and pinches out toward the water table.

Devonian Caves

Lincoln Caverns sits just over Tussey Mountain from Indian Caverns, Seawra Cave sits just over Jacks Mountain from Alexander Caverns, and Coral Caverns is over Evitts Mountain from Hipple Cave. Despite their geographic proximity to the Ordovician caves, Lincoln, Seawra, and Coral are of a different geologic breed, belonging to a family of caves formed in Devonian Helderberg limestone.

Several subtle points separate Pennsylvania's Devonian show caves from the Ordovician caves that occupy the same region. For one, all of the Ordovician caves have natural entrances, whereas all three of the Devonian caves were broken into. Surface drainage is an important aspect to the current natural qualities of all the Ordovician caves except Indian. No surface stream enters or leaves any of the Devonian caves. The Ordovician caves are located at the edge of anticlinal valleys. The Devonian caves are located in valleys occupying the truncated limbs between the axes of adjacent anticlines and synclines. Rock strata in Ordovician caves tend to have a lower-angle dip, below 40 degrees in most cases. The rocks roofing Seawra Cave dip 55 degrees to the southeast, Lincoln Caverns's rocks dip 70 degrees to the north, and Coral Caverns sits within strata that approach 90 degrees, nearly vertical.

These geologic differences influence the overall character of the caves. For instance, rampant flooding and recent debris accumulation are not relevant to the nature of the Devonian caves, but high, narrow passageways are common features due to the steeply pitched beds. Both cave types accumulate calcite deposits in a similar fashion, but well-ventilated cave passages piping formation-wrecking vadose streams are not likely to have as many speleothems as chambers sealed from rampaging waters since the drop of the water table. The biggest difference between Ordovician and Devonian caves, however, is the impact of a natural entrance on their human histories. The Ordovician caves are much more steeped in legend and lore than the Devonian caves, which were discovered in the 1920s and 1930s, then quickly commercialized.

Seawra Cave, along the side of a ravine between Jacks Mountain and the northeastern extension of Chestnut Ridge, is essentially a northeast strike passage running parallel to the hillside for 424 feet, terminating at a flowstone-covered mass of breakdown and cave clay. Averaging 9 feet high and 15 feet wide, the main passage connects with a broader, lower room toward its far end. The vaultlike entrance intersects the cave near its southwest terminus. Seawra formed along the bedding plane, which is tilted at a steep 55-degree angle. This gives the cave a peaked cathedral ceiling where the sloped hanging wall intersects the master joint at right angles. Following the bedding plane, the sloped foot wall is parallel to the hanging wall. Caves like this can be difficult to traverse because of their funhouse tilt. Seawra's main path, however, was laid out along a ledge adjacent to the foot wall. One step off the ledge, and the cave's steep, down-dip slope continues, pinching out toward the bottom. The main passage is crowded with columns, stalactites, and stalagmites, giving a strong vertical component to the cave's cockeyed cross section. Toward the rear of the cave, steps descend the bedding slope to access a lower room, christened the Bridal Chamber due its wealth of calcite filigree.

Today Seawra Cave is on private property owned by Carl Hopper. It is gated, with the keys in the hands of various Pennsylvania grottos (caving clubs).

Coral Caverns is another cave that was blasted into while quarrying for agricultural lime. In the Helderberg Formation, it lies 80 miles away from Seawra, on the flank of Buffalo Mountain above Manns Choice in Bedford County.

Although embellished with the usual array of speleothems, the cave's signature feature is a wall of fossils representing a Devonian coral reef that contains brachiopods, stromatoporoids, and horn corals. These creatures lived and died in a prehistoric, subtropical coastal ocean. Their calcium-rich bodies fell to the bottom of the sea and were buried and fossilized in the muddy ooze that would become Helderberg limestone. One hundred fifty million years later, Coral Cavern's portion of Helderberg was tilted 90 degrees in the Alleghenian Orogeny. Two hundred fifty million years after that, carbonic acid seeping down from the surface eroded the cave along the upturned bedding plane, exposing a slice of seafloor containing the fossils.

Like Seawra, Coral Caverns is a strike cave oriented in the same direction as the limestone outcrop, and located just inside and parallel to the slope of the ridge. Unlike Seawra, its vertical pitch provides more headroom, from 8 to 30 feet, and much of the cave is a broader gallery rather than a narrow passage. The Cathedral Room is the cave's central cavity. In addition to stalactites, large pendants of more resistant limestone hang down from the ceiling.

The lower levels of the cave contain the gravel and clay footprint of a former streambed, while the walls of the upper chambers are studded with calcite crystals, most covered with a layer of brownish flowstone. This evidence suggests that a vadose stream once flowed through the cave. At some point its exit was constricted, damming the water and flooding the cave. Calcite crystals can only grow underwater, so their location on the cave wall is a clue to the water level. The water was eventually released and the cave drained. The crystals, some an inch long, were then covered by flowstone subsequently deposited on the cave walls.

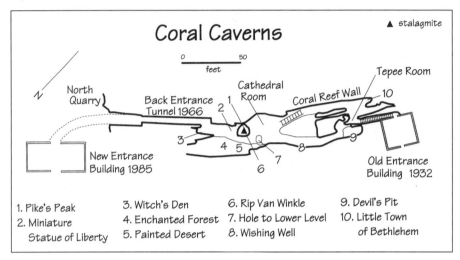

Coral Caverns

▲ stalagmite

0 ——— 50
feet

↖ N

North
Quarry

Back Entrance
Tunnel 1966

Cathedral
Room

Coral Reef Wall

Tepee Room

10

New Entrance
Building 1985

Old Entrance
Building 1932

1. Pike's Peak
2. Miniature
   Statue of Liberty

3. Witch's Den
4. Enchanted Forest
5. Painted Desert

6. Rip Van Winkle
7. Hole to Lower Level
8. Wishing Well

9. Devil's Pit
10. Little Town
    of Bethlehem

Current visitors to Coral Caverns actually enter the rear of the cave by way of a 50-foot tunnel. Frear and McDevitt dug the tunnel in 1966 to create a through-trip tour that exited into the old northern quarry. Later owner Steve Hall closed the original entrance in 1985 to avoid the liability of having visitors descend the high, narrow steps into the cave, thus completely reversing the cave tour from its original path. This tour has been retained by Bill VanDeventer, who has owned Coral since 1992.

Wherever Helderberg limestone outcrops, so outcrops the possibility for caves. Lincoln Caverns is located in a spur of Helderberg along

Pike's Peak is Coral Caverns's signature stalagmite. The cave opened as Wonderland Coral Caverns in 1932. DEAN SNYDER

U.S. Route 22 in Huntingdon County. Nearby is a completely separate section of the cave, with its own entrance, named Whisper Rocks after the sound the air made rushing through the sinkhole at the time of its discovery. Although it is assumed that the two cave networks link up, a connecting passage has yet to be found.

The interior layouts of Lincoln Caverns and Whisper Rocks are much more complex than Seawra or Coral. Whisper Rocks sits above and to the east of Lincoln Caverns. Both sections contain an irregular branchwork of passageways, with high-ceilinged canyons following the east-west strike of the rock. The limestone beds dip at 70 degrees against the north flank of Warrior Ridge. This high-angle dip and strike orientation influenced the formation of the cave's main passage, which begins in the 40-foot-high Lobby Room and extends eastward through the tight Wall Street Canyon. The Lobby Room was truncated to the west by the road cut and resealed with a masonry wall containing the original entrance doorway. At the far end of Wall Street Canyon, the passage splits. To the left, the passage enters the Palace of Splendor, within which a large stalactite extends down from a flowstone wall and barely touches the still water of the coin-filled Wishing Well. The passage jogs right and drops into a deep crevice, the entire wall of which is covered with a massive sheet of flowstone. Forty feet high, this Frozen Niagara rivals the one in Indian Caverns for the title of state's largest. An opening ducks beneath Frozen Niagara and into the Purity Room, where a flowstone formation of stark white calcite decorates the wall as the Purity Cascade. A low strike pas-

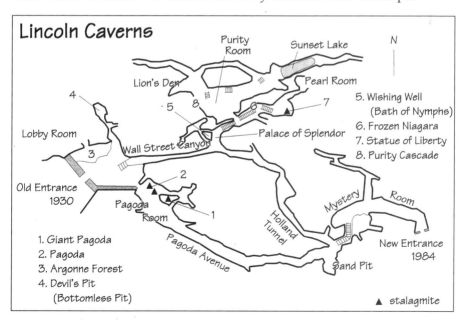

Lincoln Caverns

N

5. Wishing Well (Bath of Nymphs)
6. Frozen Niagara
7. Statue of Liberty
8. Purity Cascade

Purity Room
Sunset Lake
Lion's Den
Pearl Room
4
5   8
7
Lobby Room
Palace of Splendor
3
Wall Street Canyon
2
Old Entrance 1930
Pagoda Room
1
Holland Tunnel
Mystery Room
Pagoda Avenue
New Entrance 1984
Sand Pit

1. Giant Pagoda
2. Pagoda
3. Argonne Forest
4. Devil's Pit (Bottomless Pit)

▲ stalagmite

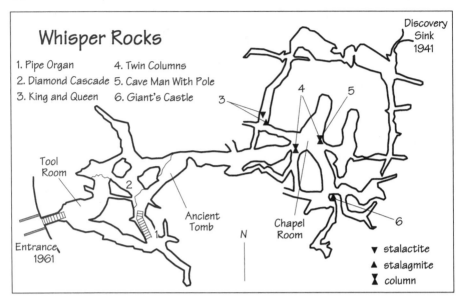

Whisper Rocks

1. Pipe Organ
2. Diamond Cascade
3. King and Queen
4. Twin Columns
5. Cave Man With Pole
6. Giant's Castle

Discovery Sink 1941

Tool Room

Entrance 1961

Ancient Tomb

N

Chapel Room

▼ stalactite
▲ stalagmite
✕ column

Frozen Niagara is Lincoln Caverns's largest flowstone formation, and one of four rocky renditions of the famous waterfall that can be found in Pennsylvania show caves.

sage leads down to Sunset Lake, a pool of water lying at the deepest part of the cave, 130 feet below the surface.

A narrow, 8-foot-high passage charts a crooked path southeastward from the east end of Wall Street Canyon. Originally this passage narrowed into an impenetrable crevice that was blasted open to create a circuit. The break is the opening to a tube known as the Holland Tunnel, which leads to the Sand Pit at the southeastward end of another passageway. Christened Pagoda Avenue after a grouping of pagoda-shaped stalagmites, this corridor leads back to the Lobby Room to complete the circuit.

Beyond the Sand Pit is a chamber called the Mystery Room. A large stalagmite stands in the middle of the room beneath a suspended stalactite. Closer inspection reveals the pair to be a broken column, although the missing pieces have never been found.

Whisper Rocks is entered through a tunnel driven into a small chamber in its western end that still carries the name Tool Room from the days of excavation and development. A short walk down a flight of steps leads to the Diamond Cascade, a vertical mass of orange and white flowstone shimmering with calcite crystals. The main passage extends eastward as a 20-foot-high canyon roofed with a ceiling channel. Ceiling channels appear as upside-down streambeds and are assumed to be solution features formed when the water table was up against the ceiling of the cave. They are frequently discontinuous, which is why they are unlikely to have been formed by flowing water. A similar channel exists above Wall Street Canyon. The cave popcorn on the walls of Wall Street Canyon and the calcite crystals in Whisper Rocks suggest that these passageways were once submerged. The Whisper Rocks passage ends in the Chapel Room. The room is bounded by Twin Columns, two very slender pillars that are Lincoln's longest.

An early Lincoln Caverns claim to fame was the discovery of cave pearls in a small pool of water at the end of the Frozen Niagara passage. The small chamber where the rare spheres were found is still referred to as the Pearl Room. Cave pearls are small concretions of calcite that form as loose beads or irregular nodules in pools constantly disturbed by light currents, such as that generated by dripping water. The calcite precipitates out of the water as carbon dioxide is released to the atmosphere, and adheres itself to a small nucleus of sand or fragment of speleotheom. As successive layers of calcite are built up, in a fashion not unlike the formation of an actual pearl, the light but persistent circulating current rolls the nodule into a ball while preventing it from adhering to the bottom of the pool. Unfortunately, the fate of most cave pearls upon discovery is to be carted off by the discoverer. Lincoln Caverns's cave pearls were no exception. They were reportedly sent to Harrisburg for analysis and were never seen again.

Allegheny Plateau Caves

Allegheny Mountains were the western limit to Pennsylvania's show cave country until 1964. It's not that western Pennsylvania lacks limestone or caves; there are plenty of both. It is that the location and characteristics of these caves, with one exception, have made them less suited for development. Five of the state's ten longest cave systems, and four of the five deepest, are in Allegheny Plateau limestone. This includes the absolute longest, Harlansburg Cave, at 21,808 feet. More than 4 miles long, Harlansburg is a mazelike cave discovered in the Vanport Formation during a road-widening project. Reasonably well located along PA Route 108 east of New Castle, Harlansburg has

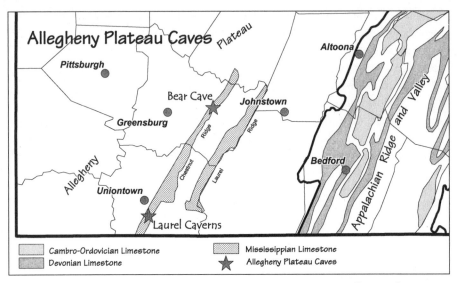

Laurel Caverns and Bear Cave are in Mississippian Loyalhanna lime-stone, which outcrops from beneath the surrounding Pennsylvanian age rocks along the crests of Chestnut and Laurel ridges. Although both caves were popular 19th century tourist destinations, only Laurel Caverns was commercialized.

nonetheless proven to be too wet and muddy with too few speleothems to be commercialized.

The cave-bearing limestone in western Pennsylvania is much younger than that in eastern parts of the state. Vanport is Pennsylvanian age, slightly older but of the same period as most of the state's exploitable bituminous coals. Loyalhanna limestone, the Allegheny Plateau's other big cave former, is Mississippian age. Vanport limestone is found throughout Lawrence, Butler, and Armstrong Counties. Typical of the rocks underlying the Allegheny Plateau, Vanport is slightly undulating. The nearly horizontal pitch of the beds encourages maze caves, in which slow-moving water has more uniformly infiltrated and eroded the intersecting joints into a gridlike network of passageways. Unlike the folded and steeply dipped valley limestones farther east, plateau limestones are generally buried beneath other rock strata and outcrop only in hillsides where streams (or humans) have dissected into the plateau.

Laurel and Chestnut Ridges present an exception to this pattern. These are two anticlinal ridges that run parallel to each other and the Allegheny Front, from central Cambria and Indiana Counties, respectively, southwestward to the state border and beyond. As anticlines, the upward crest of the rock is the same as in the breached anticlinal valleys farther east, but the surface expression is reversed due to the resistant Pottsville sandstone that still shields much of the mountain from erosion. Normally buried beneath these Pennsylvanian-age rocks, Loyalhanna limestone outcrops along the crests of these ridges where the overlying sandstones and shales were fractured in the up-warp and eroded away. The Loyalhanna is a prodigious cave former, with 134 mapped caves in Westmoreland County alone. Because the limestone outcrops on the mountaintop, that's where most of the caves are, with the sharper, more highly fractured Chestnut Ridge containing many more caves than Laurel Ridge.

Unlike the eastern limestone valleys, Chestnut Ridge is still densely forested. It has few roads, no towns, and is rarely entered by anyone other than recreational sportsmen, loggers, and quarry workers. In short, it's not the best place for a roadside tourist attraction. Despite this fact, Bear Cave, on the mountaintop above the small hamlet of Hillside, did enjoy a brief period of tourism during the railroad era.

With 8,500 feet of passageways, Bear Cave is the fourth-longest mapped cave in the state. Its 12-foot-high entrance is in a jumble of boulders and rocky ledges on the north side of a ravine. A small mountain stream trickles into the dark, subterranean warren of cave passages and rooms. This is a maze cave that extends northward beneath a spur of Chestnut Ridge. At first following an 8- to 12-foot-high corridor

Gated in 2003, the south entrance to Harlansburg Cave is discernable above the car hood within the Route 108 road cut that exposed the cave.

The Chestnut Ridge top entrance to Bear Cave is in an outcropping of Loyalhanna limestone.

known as Appian Way, the cave stream is eventually lost to a narrow crevice, only to reappear at Shirey Run in the next hollow north.

Streams such as the one found in Bear Cave are nature's way of excavating passages through Loyalhanna caverns. The calcium carbonate acts as a cement binder in a limestone that is nearly 50 percent sand. When the calcium is dissolved away, loose sand is left behind clogging the passageways. Surface streams that subsequently find their way into the cave system carry the sand away and open the passages. The only other way to clear the sand is for humans to dig it out. Calcite formations that have survived the vandal's hammer include occasional patches of flowstone, small stalactites, stumpy stalagmites, and stout columns.

Bear Cave is still popular among cavers, but it was never commercialized and has fallen off the average tourist's map. It is currently owned by Tom and Kim Metzgar and is open only to those who obtain a permit first. Farther south along Chestnut Ridge, however, an even larger Loyalhanna cave carried its fame into the era of auto tourism and earned its title as the last commercial cave developed in Pennsylvania.

With 16,305 feet of passageways, Laurel Caverns is not only the state's longest show cave, it is also the deepest. From the highest point in the cave to the lowest, the vertical distance is 446 feet, nearly the height of a forty-five-story building. There is only one wild cave deeper than 400 feet, and no other show cave comes close. Laurel's stupendous dimensions are the product of Chestnut Ridge's geology, hydrology, and physical geography. Like Bear Cave, Laurel Caverns is a solution cave in highly siliceous limestone. Cave corridors erode along the joints, freeing the sand to clog the passages as the calcium carbonate is dissolved away. Unlike Bear, Laurel is not isolated within a mountain spur, but extends down the dip a much greater distance from the mountaintop outcrop. This accounts for the cave's great vertical drop. The Loyalhanna beds dip at 15 degrees, on average the same as the overlying west slope of Chestnut Ridge.

The old Main Entrance is in a collapsed sink near a prominent ledge of limestone. Two other lesser entries were discovered among the craggy cliffs and boulders of the outcropping, but these were historically less significant. Locals were familiar with the old Main Entrance in the early days of exploration and settlement.

Three great passageways extend down the dip on the inside of the mountain, each of them stripped of sand by vadose streams that have since dropped to lower reaches, and deepened by the shoveling of more recent cave developers. The Main Entrance leads to the Hall of the Mountain King, with its row of brightly lit chandeliers giving the tunnel the appearance of a grand concourse slanting down to some rock-hewn subway system. The markings of long-gone transients still mar the walls of the hall, the earliest dating to 1834. Grand Canyon, an even broader passageway, follows a parallel joint to the south, and Devil's Staircase Passage follows a joint beyond it. The Devil's Staircase is a 35-foot drop marking the onetime location of a subterranean waterfall.

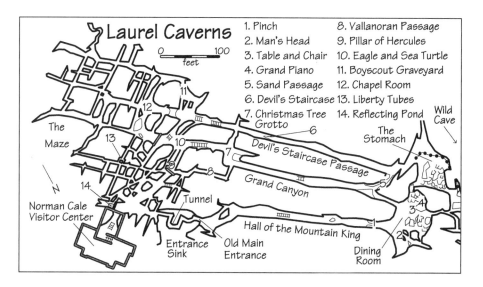

Laurel Caverns

0 ———— 100
feet

1. Pinch
2. Man's Head
3. Table and Chair
4. Grand Piano
5. Sand Passage
6. Devil's Staircase
7. Christmas Tree Grotto

8. Vallanoran Passage
9. Pillar of Hercules
10. Eagle and Sea Turtle
11. Boyscout Graveyard
12. Chapel Room
13. Liberty Tubes
14. Reflecting Pond

The Maze

Norman Cale Visitor Center

Entrance Sink

Old Main Entrance

Tunnel

Devil's Staircase Passage

Grand Canyon

Hall of the Mountain King

The Stomach

Wild Cave

Dining Room

The three passageways connect on the down-dip end at the Dining Room, a huge breakdown chamber housing a haphazard heap of boulders. Conspicuously poised on the heap is a set of rocks shaped like a dining table and chair, for which the room is named. The Ballroom yawns beyond the breakdown where the streams of three different branching passages join and flow into a long, irregular tunnel of twists, turns, and boulder breakdowns. The passage narrows and becomes more angular before intersecting the Millstream Passage. The cave continues a little farther, then pinches out at a sand-choked terminal sump.

Despite its proximity to the surface, an intricate maze network at the top of the caverns and closest to the outcrop may have been one of the last sections discovered by early cave explorers. Although the two smaller entries open into the maze, torch-toting cavers in the days of yore probably accessed this section from the inside by descending to the Dining Room, then turning back up the dip through Grand Canyon, or by a strenuous ascent of the Devil's Staircase. Known as the Catacombs, the maze was a confusing warren of tortuous, sand-filled crawlways about 3 feet high. These characteristics did not encourage frequent visitation.

The cave's lack of tourist-pleasing speleothems has been offset by a layout design that uses indirect colored and natural lighting to highlight naturally sculptured rock formations like the Pillar of Hercules. Over

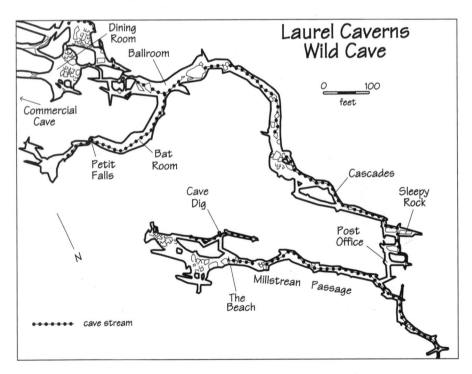

Buried within the west flank of Chestnut Ridges, Grand Canyon Passage is one of three joint corridors that link Laurel Caverns's upper Maze with the lower reaches of the cave.

time, more cave passages have been added to the tour, so that it extends down the Hall of the Mountain King to the Dining Room, then back up the Grand Canyon by way of a side trip to the base of Devil's Staircase.

Imagination Formations

In the earlier days of show caves, part of the appeal of caving was trying to recognize the visual reference of named rock formations, or in fact naming them. Even today the most scientific of show cave operators realize, sometimes begrudgingly, that tourists expect to see what the trade refers to as "imagination formations." Should the tour guide sidestep this traditional element, someone in the group is inevitably going to point to a prominent something-or-other and ask, "What's that one called?" In the time-honored tradition of the past, visitors are more than welcome to come up with their own names. This is, after all, how many of the features were labeled in the first place. But the original names, where preserved, maintain a link to the cultural context that existed when the cave was first brought to light.

Animals, food items, and human faces and figures were common associations applied to smaller formations, but larger or grander features required more significant touchstones. For these, Euro-American cave name

The flowstone formation once known as the Cascade stands at the entrance to Baker Caverns's Cathedral Hall, where 24 weddings took place before the cave closed in 1954. DEAN SNYDER

creators turned to the sources they were most familiar with: Old World history, mythology, and Christianity. Dripstone-rich subterranean halls were likened to the Moorish palace at Alhambra in Granada, Spain, with its exotic architecture and impressive gardens. European cathedrals were almost invariably referenced in the naming of sizable rooms with vaulted ceilings. Equally common were Pulpit rocks, prominences that commanded reverence and respect, and an analogy known to all churchgoing Christians.

Religious references were natural, due to the era's cultural obsession with seeing sublimity, the widespread awareness of symbology, and the Victorian's penchant for surrounding themselves with reminders of their own mortality and the final judgment that awaits. Early cave visitors had the sense that they were walking through an environment fresh from the hands of the Creator, a wilderness cathedral hewn from solid stone. Artificially lit speleothems shone with heavenly splendor, while dark, mysterious underground passages could easily be imagined as housing the damned. Not surprisingly, cave perceptions swung both ways, presenting as many positive images of angels and paradise as negative ones of demons and hell.

Pennsylvania cave formations standing up for the forces of good include Jesus Christ, the Madonna, Moses, two pairs of Angel's Wings, and a couple of Buddhas. Like the people who named them, the references are overwhelmingly Christian. Penn's Cave's Hindu Idol, which Robert Campbell probably named more as an exotic reference than a religious one, is rarely pointed out anymore.

Based on religious references, Woodward is the holiest cave in the state. In addition to the Tower of Babel stalagmite, with its Stairway to Heaven, the cave has an entire flowstone Bible Wall depicting Christ Ascending to Heaven, Moses, and the Nativity. Like cathedral stained-glass windows, the Bible Wall stands as an excellent example of the type of speleo visual aids early ministers would use to teach scripture to followers while on outings to area caves.

Hipple Cave's largest stalagmite has been alternately known as the Statue or Pillar of Salt, but its original name, as stated on the few rare postcards that still exist, was Lot's Wife.

On the side of evil, the state's show caves contain six devil references. Invoking the devil above- or belowground is typically reserved for patches of earth deemed worthless by agrarian place namers: deep holes and gullies, rocky outcroppings, and bizarre rock formations seemingly assembled by some demented design. Following suit, the cave references are various Devil's Pits and Dens, as well as Laurel Caverns's Devil's Staircase, a rock-strewn cliff 35 feet high formed eons ago by an underground waterfall. The Prince of Darkness himself makes only a partial appearance in the form of his tail in Coral Caverns.

Of all the categories, animals are imagined most, accounting for more than fifty references. Possibly the abundance of rounded flowstone attached to singular wall column "trunks" explain why elephants show up in five of nine caves. An equal number of lions—Nittany and otherwise—top the list, followed by four monkeys, including one on the back of an elephant, three sharks, and three dinosaurs, two of them brontosauruses, as fictitious as their speleo namesakes. In the aviary department are two ducks, two eagles, two owls, two bird's wings, a pair of parakeets, and an ostrich. A couple of camels, a moose with one horn, a pile of prairie dogs, two snakes, and a dozen other animals from lizards and lobsters to seals and salamanders round out the menagerie.

With forty references, food follows next. Bacon strips are identified in every cave except Laurel. Like bacon, cave popcorn is practically a scientific term. Formed underwater, the kernel-size wall formations are found in abundance in Lincoln, Coral, and Indian Echo caverns. All three of the Great Valley caves have

The facial features of Woodward Cave's Figure of Christ were somewhat enhanced in this vintage postcard. DEAN SNYDER

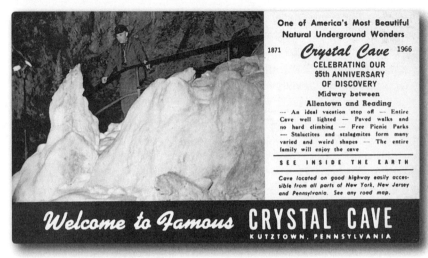

One of America's Most Beautiful
Natural Underground Wonders

1871 *Crystal Cave* 1966

CELEBRATING OUR
95th ANNIVERSARY
OF DISCOVERY
Midway between
Allentown and Reading
— An ideal vacation stop off — Entire
Cave well lighted — Paved walks and
no hard climbing — Free Picnic Parks
— Stalactites and stalagmites form many
varied and weird shapes — The entire
family will enjoy the cave

SEE INSIDE THE EARTH

Cave located on good highway easily accessible from all parts of New York, New Jersey
and Pennsylvania. See any road map.

Welcome to Famous CRYSTAL CAVE
KUTZTOWN, PENNSYLVANIA

Crystal Cave's Seal Rock in 1966. AUTHOR'S COLLECTION

prominent Ear of Corn stalactites, with three other lesser cobs located elsewhere. There are smaller, more scraggly carrot stalactites, bulbous turnips, and Penn's Cave has a parsnip. Three caves have ice cream. Indian Caverns has both a dressed chicken and a hanging goose in its larder. Cave versions of regional specialties include funnel cake (Coral), Hershey kiss (Indian Echo), and Lebanon bologna (Penn's). Tobacco hangs in Crystal, Woodward, and Penn's Caves, all in places where the Amish actually grow it. And fried eggs are served up in Crystal Cave and Indian Caverns.

Fictional characters outnumber real ones two to one. The generalized forms found in caves particularly lend themselves to cartoon characters, especially classic ones like Woodward's Barney Rubble (pun intended), Charlie Brown, and Droopy Dog; Indian's Mutt and Jeff; and Coral's Porky Pig. Popeye's head is the first thing pointed out upon entering Indian Caverns, only now it is more likely to be called Jay Leno. From the screen, big and little, old and new(ish), there are Shirley Temple's Curls (Indian), the Little Rascals's Alfalfa (Woodward), E.T.'s Finger (Crystal), and Sesame Street's Snuffleupagus (Indian Echo). *Star Wars's* popularity was responsible for renaming two signature formations, albeit temporarily, when Jabba the Hut unseated Indian Echo's Cave Guardian (a.k.a. the Fur Trapper, a.k.a. Santa Claus) and Lincoln's Giant Pagoda.

The few real-person references include two American presidents, the only two anyone would recognize as cartoony cave creations: George Washington (Indian) and Abraham Lincoln (Crystal), although Abe's pro-file also moonlights as the Old Man of the Cave, an indirect reference to

New Hampshire's late great Old Man of the Mountain. Although no longer shown, somewhere in the depths of Penn's Cave lies Lindbergh's Plane and King Tut's Stenographer Carrying a Jug of Water. I kid you not.

From the world of fantasy, Pennsylvania show caves hold three dragon references, Dracula's castle, witches and wizards, an Abominable Snowman, an Enchanted Forest, the Easter Bunny, gnomes, and giants, giants, giants, with a Giant's Castle, Giant's Hall, Giant's Shield, at least four Giant's Footprints (one doubling as Big Foot's Footprint), Giant's Tooth, Giant's Salad Bowl, the Giant's Hand, and finally, the Giant's Other Hand. Curiously, in a constricted place filled with tiny nooks and crannies, there are a lot more references to giants than elves or gnomes.

Naturally, Indians are well represented, being referenced in the names of two Pennsylvania show caves, five different rooms, and a dozen other imagination formations, including two Indian Chiefs, two Totem Poles, an Indian Head, an Indian Tepee Village, an Indian Woman Carrying a Papoose, and an Indian Riding Pony on the wall at Penn's Cave.

Sumptuous connotations of royalty are conjured up in the ballrooms that exist in six of the state's show caves. In addition, there are five castles (besides Dracula's), two palaces, and a Queen's Room.

Twenty-five different well-known international landmarks are evoked on Pennsylvania's underground tours, the criteria being sites readily recognized when rendered in random rock. Niagara Falls heads the list, due

Corn and tobacco are two Pennsylvania Dutch Country crops commonly represented in show cave stalactites. Woodward Cave's Hanging Forest is suspended in the Third Room, formerly known as the Lancaster Tobacco Barn. AUTHOR'S COLLECTION

Indian Caverns tourists returning from the Jewel Room are invited to reinterpret Frozen Niagara as the Abominable Snowman. Although this postcard view is marked for Frozen Niagara, the beast within can be seen staring down at passing visitors. AUTHOR'S COLLECTION

to the proliferation of flowstone formations that look like static waterfalls. Lincoln, Indian, Penn's, and Indian Echo all have Frozen Niagaras. As prevalent as Niagaras are Statue of Liberty stalagmites. They're easy enough for Mother Nature to make: heap up some calcite, and off-center the top like an upraised arm. Any cave tourist in America would identify this as the Statue of Liberty. They stand in Penn's, Lincoln, Coral, and Indian (in this case, a column). Lincoln Caverns is a regular underground tour of New York City in itself, with Lady Liberty, the Holland Tunnel, and Wall Street Canyon. An Upside Down New York City clings to a ceiling in Indian Echo Caverns. European landmarks include Coral Caverns's Leaning Tower of Pisa and Roman Coliseum, and the Straits of Gibraltar, which set the width limits on the boats run through Penn's Cave. Lincoln Caverns's rubble wall of cemented formations broken during the opening once went by the name of Argonne Forest, a famous World War I French battlefield with shell-blasted tree trunks.

Backlit groupings of stalagmites and stalactites create scenic panoramas that are variously interpreted as cityscapes, seascapes, deserts, and forests. Six such forests occupy Pennsylvania caves, four of them Hanging or Inverted Forests made of stalactites. Similarly lit Gardens of the Gods exist in Indian Caverns and Penn's Cave. Penn's Cave also has one of the more elaborate Western Scenery displays, where sunrise, full daylight, and sunset are simulated by illuminating different sets of colored lights.

Scale is sometimes confusingly elastic. Visitors can be shown in quick succession an 8-foot Ear of Corn followed by an 8-inch Statue of Liberty. An entire western landscape with cacti and buttes can reside within the oversize grin of a giant clown face. That's the reason for the guide's flashlight pointer and the astounded-looking cave models providing a sense of scale in postcards and brochure pictures.

Four show caves, Crystal, Woodward, Lincoln, and Laurel, have wishing wells. Many visitors seem to be afflicted with an irresistible urge to throw coins into holes. It seems that the attraction is not the wishing, but the throwing.

Named formations often helped provide a narrative that could be presented in travelog format made more interesting by legends and lore.

Cave legends were a natural part of the earliest tours, which were much longer and sometimes involved an overnight stay. Romantic tales of Indians, robbers, gothic tragedy, and lost treasure were standard fare for the day, and they were exploited to give added meaning to the landscape. The tales have not gone away, but they are no longer emphasized on today's shorter cave tours highlighting science education and karst geology. The science lesson has become much more fulfilling to the modern cave tourist, especially for parents desiring an educational activity for their children.

The imagination formation is an expected part of the show cave experience, as is "total darkness." There isn't a show cave in the country in which the guide doesn't at one point turn off all the lights so everyone can get creeped out by the eerie sensation of being completely without light. Likewise, many show caves have strung certain sets of imagination formations together in short, tongue-in-cheek "formation fairy tales," which have come to replace the pseudohistory of legends.

Formation fairy tales are minifables in which the static features of a cave are used as characters in a story frozen in midaction like a diorama. Sometimes they have a moral, often they don't, with the desired response being a chuckle. Although not the terror-stricken response of the awesome sublime, an emotion is nonetheless evoked from the lesson learned. In a way, they are similar to the Bible lessons taught through the religious labeling of cave features in times past.

Some long-name formations labeled before World War II were precursors to the formation fairy tale, like Penn's Cave's Boy Driving Cow Across Suspension Bridge, and Indian's Five Kids on a Toboggan About to Hit a Bump (a.k.a. Toboggan Slide). Both of these formations are action-frozen mininarratives. Tour guides at Indian Echo attribute its 16-Legged Elephant to the cave's proximity to Three Mile Island nuclear generating station. By coupling independent formations, fairy tale tellers can weave a story where there was none. A show cave favorite coupling is the cave bacon that shows up along the tour to go with the fried egg previously seen. In Indian Caverns, cartoon crazies Mutt and Jeff are not simply *there,* but are actively sticking their heads out of the ceiling to get a good look at Niagara Falls. And you just know that once Popeye the Sailor is introduced, his Can of Spinach cannot be too far away. It isn't.

Some of the formation fairy tales have gotten quite elaborate. Lost River patrons are introduced to lovable cave mascot Oscar the Giant Turtle, only to find that he is actively being attacked by a Giant Shark. Fear not, however, because Oscar is being protected by Willy the Whale. Jack Frost (a.k.a. Old Man Winter) resides in Crystal Cave in the summer, keeping it cool. Upon entering Coral Caverns, visitors are shown Young Rip Van Winkle. The same formation seen on the way out, however, is *Old* Rip Van Winkle, a measure of the long period of time tourists have spent in the cave. Nearby, a diminutive Statue of Liberty holds up the entire cave ceiling with an upraised arm, as long as she doesn't reach for the nearby Ice Cream Cone.

Just about every formation in Indian Echo's Blue Room is strung together in a story about a Mummy who falls out of a wall pocket sarcophagus, scaring awake a Giant who had been turned to stone by an evil Wizard. The Giant runs for the exit and bangs his head against the Natural Bridge, denting it in the process. He then falls back, kicking his Footprint into the ceiling and awakening the vicious Dragon on the bridge. Fear not, however, for the (iron oxide) Dragon is on a (white calcite) leash.

The moral of some fairy tales is intended to keep unruly kids in line, like the Boy Scout Graveyard in Laurel Caverns, or the guides' interpretation of "I. E. C." inscribed above the door at Indian Echo as "I Eat Children"—but only bad ones!

Although executed in whimsical humor, formation fairy tales nonetheless reflect the human need to make sense—even foolish sense—of chaotic patterns in nature. In the storytelling, recognizable shapes appear where previously there was only rock, allowing us to build an acuteness to the environment that aids in sorting everything out so that we can make more astute observations.

In recent years, some caves are emphasizing the scientific over the fanciful. The guide escorting my group through Lost River Caverns pointed up a dark crevice and he called it what I thought was a "free attic chimney." I had never heard of that term before and thought it was an architectural reference, maybe part of some vernacular Pennsylvania Dutch house. Later I realized he had said "phreatic chimney," *phreatic* being a cave science term meaning it had formed underwater. I had been conditioned to think of cave formations as metaphors for something else, and it was disconcerting to have a cave feature named for its intrinsic qualities rather than its coincidental appearance. That implied a naming system tied to a process specific to caves that had nothing to do with mythology, food items, or pop culture.

Sometime afterward, I went to Lincoln Caverns. This cave was like an old friend. It was the first cave I had ever been in, and I had been there several times since. I walked down the passageway with the group, anticipating the Giant Pagoda, and there it was, the pointy-topped, bulbous stalagmite standing there just as I remembered it. But the tour guide just passed it by. We saw the Purity Cascade, Frozen Niagara, the Lion's Head, plenty of soda straws, cave bacon, and popcorn, but dropped from the list were the Statue of Liberty, Ice Cream Soda Complete with Straw, Cave Man with Pole, the Giant's Castle, and the King and Queen. The knowledgeable cave guide gave an excellent tour and could point these things out when I inquired about them, but they were peripheral to the information he gave about cave formation and Lincoln Caverns history. He would humor me and say such things as "Some people think it looks like an ice cream soda." "*Some* people?" I thought. "That's what it's *called.*" Nobody except me seemed to miss it. Even the cave guide was unclear about the Palace of Splendor, Bath of Nymphs, and Argonne Forest. And forget Jabba the Hut. The 1980s are over. Of course, the cave guide was right, *some* people did call it that, and when it ceased to have meaning, they didn't call it that anymore.

The little girl next to the Wishing Well (also called the Bath of Nymphs) is Patricia Ann Dunlavy, daughter of cave owners Myron and Marion, and the future proprietor of Lincoln Caverns. AUTHOR'S COLLECTION

4

Pennsylvania's Early Cave Discoveries

Hundreds of millions of years after the rock was formed, and hundreds of thousands of years after the holes were made, humans began to crawl into Pennsylvania's caves. Indians actually had little use for caves, as they were dark and damp. Cave entrances were used as temporary shelters, but the utility of such natural rock houses was limited by the impenetrable darkness that enveloped the passages a few score feet into the cave. Certain commodious rockshelters were the exception. Rockshelters form in cliff faces when less-resistant shales are eroded out from beneath an overhanging ledge former like sandstone. Unlike caves, their shallow depths are bathed in light, yet the overhanging rock can roof a sizable area, affording protection from the weather while allowing campfire smoke to rise and dissipate.

The cliff faces of western Pennsylvania's dissected plateaus are replete with rockshelters, the most famous of which is the Meadowcroft Rockshelter. This overarching sandstone ledge crops out along Cross Creek, a tributary of the Ohio River, just east of the West Virginia border near Avella. Archeologists have radiocarbon-dated Paleo-Indian artifacts found at this site to between 16,000 and 17,000 years ago. This immediately sent up a storm of controversy, since the oldest human settlement in North America prior to the Meadowcroft site was at Clovis, New Mexico, which dates to 11,200 years ago. If accurate, the Meadowcroft evidence suggests that humans crossed the Bering Land Bridge from Asia thousands of years before what was previously assumed.

More recent Indian artifacts have been found just inside and around many of Pennsylvania's caves, proving a human history that goes back centuries. For most of that time, however, caves were little more than idle holes in the ground. The next big step in their human development had to await a perceptual change that brought caves from the realm of wilderness into the world of tourism. Caves may have been peripheral to the lives of Indians, but Indians were central to the tourist interpretations of caves. Following a European tradition, Americans found meaning in their natural environments by linking them to folklore and legend. Indians were mythologized as noble savages and commonly woven into tales about caves whether they ever set foot in them or not. By the mid-twentieth century, show caves and Indians were inseparably joined and referenced at five Pennsylvania operations.

To colonists in the frontier environment, caves had limited utility and were often considered in a negative context—as dark dens that sheltered dangerous wild animals or nefarious humans, or unwanted holes that could swallow up livestock or unwary children. Many small openings were blasted shut or filled in upon discovery. In some cases, they were a source of freshwater springs or repositories for saltpeter, a critical ingredient for gunpowder. The earliest profitable use for many Kentucky caves, Mammoth chief among them, was as saltpeter mines during the War of 1812.

But tourism put caves in a whole new light and provided the ultimate profitable end use that justified their exploration and preservation. For the traveling public, they were curiosities—weird, fantastical, and sometimes horrific places that aroused a range of emotions, from a solemnity akin to viewing the grand Niagara Falls to giddy fears like those experienced in an amusement park funhouse.

One of America's early scientific cave explorers was Thomas Jefferson, who drew a map of Virginia's Madison's Cave in 1782 and published it in his *Notes on the State of Virginia* two years later. Already attracted to the Shenandoah Valley by Natural Bridge, curious tourists soon arrived to see the cave Jefferson had described. Down the valley, at what is now Grand Cavern, Bernard Weyer tapped into this growing crowd of Virginia landscape tourists in 1806 by opening America's first commercial show cave. By then, the Devil's hole along the Delaware River in Durham, Pennsylvania, was already attracting the curious. After 1849 however, the first two of its three chambers was quarried away. Now known as Durham Cave, the current entrance penetrates what was actually the third chamber.

The commercial history of Pennsylvania show caves began on November 12, 1871, when William Merkel and John Gehret discovered a cave a few miles from Virginville. They had blasted into it while quarrying for fertilizer lime on William's father's farm. After the dust settled from one of their explosions, they discovered a fissure that led into the mysterious underground darkness. Without torches, William and John penetrated the darkness only as far as natural daylight filtering into the newfound hole would allow.

Within a few days, an ad hoc discovery party was formed and outfitted with candles, coal oil lanterns, rope, and other necessary gear needed for underground exploration. The cave must have revealed itself as a fairyland, thoroughly decorated with white and rust-colored stalactites, stalagmites, and flowstone with crystal-studded walls that shimmered when illuminated. These crystals were initially thought to be diamonds. Samples were taken to a mineral assessor, who judged them to be nearly worthless aragonite crystals, tiny calcite gems that form below the water table.

Although Lookout Point at the back of the cave is barely 500 feet from the entrance, it took explorers several days of scrambling over breakdown in torch-lit semidarkness to get there. Impeding their progress was an uneven floor with openings that led into side passages and lower levels, all meticulously explored. The astounding discovery was soon christened Crystal Cave.

A bust as a diamond mine, it was assumed the cave could be used as a convenient cold cellar. Unfortunately, the humid environment of a cave only caused food to rot all the faster. It took Samuel D. F. Kohler, a farmer from nearby Greenwich Township with an avid interest in geology and Indian relics, to recognize the cave's potential as a tourist

CRYSTAL CAVE.   MAIN ENTRANCE.

Opened in 1871 as the state's first show cave, Crystal Cave was attracting 50,000 visitors a year by the time this postcard was printed in the early 1920s. AUTHOR'S COLLECTION

attraction. He bought the hole and 47 acres for $5,000 in March 1872. His first order of business was to build a wooden door over the cave and prohibit entry. In the few months since its discovery, souvenir hunters had already carted off an untold number of calcite formations. To this day, one of the first formations seen upon entering Crystal Cave is a row of broken stalactites from this period.

In preparation for visitors, who had already started to arrive, Kohler graded a path to the entrance, which was 80 feet up the side of a steep hill, and constructed wooden walkways, handrails, and steps throughout the cave. He added a gate, a ballroom where dances would occasionally be held, and concessions with food, drink, and souvenirs. By spring, he was ready. Kohler advertised his "Grand Illumination of the Crystal Cave" for Saturday May 25, 1872. The Greenwich Cornet Band would be on hand to provide music. This was to be the birthday of the show cave in Pennsylvania—admission, 25 cents.

In developing Crystal Cave, Kohler converted a dark, wild cavern filled with irregular breakdown, calcite deposits, and mud into a picturesque fantasyland. Nature had designed these features at random and in the dark through chemical and mechanical processes. Kohler isolated and highlighted each feature, gave them new meaning relative to a human world, and arranged them in a linear collection connected by a path of his making. Visitors entered the cave through a special door as if walking into a museum or looking into a curio cabinet of Victorian collectibles. Once inside, tourists were guided along a predetermined path laid out through a hall of wonders, passing dripstone oddities, vignettes, rock-framed vistas, and panoramas, all bearing evocative names and tied to a general narrative. Early Crystal Cavers marveled at the Angel's Wings, Preachers, Pharaohs, Woman in White, Pulpit Rock, Frozen Fountain, Seal Rock, and Prairie Dogs. This would be the dominant formula followed for the interpretation and presentation of show caves for the next century. Kohler did not invent the format, but adapted it from the prevailing landscape aesthetic then being used in the design of urban parks, cemeteries, and mountain resorts.

It took only 195 days from discovery through exploration, purchase, and development to the grand opening of Crystal Cave. Within four years, enough tourists were paying to see the cave that Sam Kohler quit farming to become the state's first full-time commercial cave owner-operator, a profession he maintained until his death and then passed on to a second generation. Although an unprecedented business venture in Pennsylvania, Crystal Cave achieved quick success.

There is no accepted discovery story for Indian Echo Caverns. John Peter Miller was on the edge of the settlement frontier when he entered the cave in 1753, and it was already known at that time, making it one of America's earliest limestone show caves to have been discovered by Europeans. Jefferson did not render his map of Madison's Cave for another twenty-eight years, and Weyer's discovery of Grand Caverns was half a century into the future. The original warrant for the tract containing what was then known as the Swatara Grotto was patented by William Penn Proprietors to Hugh Hays in 1754, a year after Miller's cave trip.

Indian Echo's early discovery was a function of America's geographically induced migration patterns. Philadelphia was the primary port of immigration during the eighteenth century, and the Great Valley was the settlement funnel that directed the migration stream to the southwest. This easily traversed valley with its productive limestone soils provided an attractive alternative to the difficult terrain of the Appalachian Mountains farther west. From Philadelphia, the doorway to the Great Valley was through the low range of hills between the southern tip of the Reading Prong and the northern end of the Blue Ridge. That put the Swatara Grotto squarely in the path of the migration stream.

Indian Echo's clerical connections run deep. Scholar John Peter Miller was a Reformed Church pastor who eventually joined the celibate cloister at Ephrata. Across Swatara Creek, three generations of Engles ministered for the Brethren in Christ Church from 1810 to 1953. In 1872, the Stoverdale Campmeeting was established on the Engle farm. A wire suspension bridge spanned Engle Ford, where full-immersion baptisms were conducted. The closing Sunday of the 1888 meeting season drew ten thousand people. Many crossed the creek to tour what was then known as Echo Cave, which had been gated the year before by its owner, Rev. Samuel E. Brehm. Although Reverend Brehm charged a 25-cent admission, the fee was rarely collected. Brehm was more interested in keeping vandals out than running a show cave, and the commercial development of the cavern was left for future owners.

From the Great Valley, the cavernous source of Penns Creek is 100 miles away and thirteen mountains back. Not exactly convenient to the beaten path of migration, Penn's Cave lies in a fertile limestone valley that was nonetheless settled as soon as a retreating hostile frontier would allow. Like Indian Echo, Penn's Cave has no specific discovery story. It was recognized by early settlers, especially as a reliable spring, but with little more attention than a curious outcropping or mountain stream. Its early history is therefore defined by frontier land transactions. The tract was warranted to James Poh, a distant relative of Edgar Allan Poe, in 1773 and patented in 1789. Poh lived on the tract long enough to build a sturdy log cabin adjacent to the spring, but he soon returned to his main seat of residence some miles south in what would one day become Poe Valley State Park. After his death, the spelling of the family name was changed and the land was bequeathed to his daughter, Susanna M. Poe. Susanna married Samuel Vantries and lived in Linden Hall while renting the Penn's Cave farm to Jacob Harshbarger after 1855. Edgar Allan Poe himself actually toured Naginey Cave in Mifflin County while visiting central Pennsylvania in 1838. Naginey was locally famous at the time, but that did not save it from being subsequently quarried almost completely away.

By this time, Penns Valley had been thoroughly settled, and the cave was becoming popular among the local residents as a place for picnics or Sunday outings. Visitors entered through what was subsequently known as the Dry Entrance, an opening in a shallow sinkhole planted as an orchard. The spring marking the source of Penns Creek was over the hill from the cave, and a large, cliff-rimmed sinkhole containing water was not far away in the opposite direction, but it was not clear how these features related to one another. Most visitors were content just to scramble into the dry part of the cave, torch in hand, and descend no farther than its watery terminus.

The historian and folklorist Henry Shoemaker gives Jacob Harshbarger, the tenant farmer present to witness this early surge of inquisitive guests, as the source that claimed Rev. James Martin to be the first white person to have entered the cave, toward the end of the eighteenth century. An Irish émigré and graduate of Dublin's Trinity College, Reverend Martin was the pastor of the earliest Presbyterian congregation in Penns Valley. He died in 1795.

Shoemaker also tracked down Penn's Cave's first exploration story, attributed to Isaac Paxton and Albert Woods. Paxton was a schoolteacher from Spring Mills, and Wood was a friend and neighbor. While exploring the dry part of Penn's Cave one June around 1860, Paxton and Wood noticed light in the upstream direction of the sinkhole. They exited the cave, acquired some lumber at a local sawmill, carried it back into the dry cave, built a raft, and set sail. They became the first to float a boat through the wet entrance, but from the inside. They poled the raft all the way to the rear sump and back again, reportedly discovering the skeletons of two large mountain lions.

Word of their discovery spread, and a few days later, another Presbyterian pastor, Rev. J. E. Long of Hublersburg, came over to Spring Mills to request a guided boat trip. That Independence Day, a gang of picnickers were treated to boat tours of Penn's Cave, which became the favorite way of viewing the water cavern until 1868. In that year, Samuel Vantries sold the cave farm to George Long, who realized that the water being boated on in the cave was returning to the surface as his spring. To protect his drinking water, Long put an end to the casual tours. Years later, when the cave was commercialized, cut timber that had accumulated at the back of the cave was pointed out to tourists as the remains of the original raft.

The Chestnut Ridge entrance of Delaney's Cave, now known as Laurel Caverns, was only a few miles south of where Braddock's Road was cut across the mountains during the British general's 1754 march against French Fort Duquesne. The existence of this rough road from Virginia encouraged early settlement, with the valley bottom along the Monongahela River filling first. A small limestone quarry operated in the outcropping along the ridge in the 1780s, ensuring that the cave must have been known by then, but its first printed reference is not until 1798, when it was mentioned in a local newspaper. By then the cave tract had been owned by Richard Freeman for four years.

Like the other substantial caves on the frontier, this one was a local curiosity and the destination of occasional outings. But the innate fear of caves as dangerous returned after 1801, when two men lost their light and were trapped in the darkness. They reportedly were found locked in each other's arms, awaiting death from lack of water and food. Locals responded to the tragedy by sealing the cave. Nevertheless, cave visits were resumed some years later.

It was not called Delaney's Cave until after John Delaney purchased the cave tract in 1814 to expand his adjacent farm. Although John Delaney died in 1823 and his heirs sold the abandoned cave farm in 1836, his name remained affixed to it for the next 128 years. The cave's first official name was actually Laurel Hill Cave, given to it by John Paxton in an 1816 article he wrote for Brownsville's newspaper, the *American Telegraph,* which was reprinted in 1832 in *A Gazetteer of the State of Pennsylvania.* Paxton had made an extensive exploration of the cave with a party of local dignitaries. They took measurements, marked their way with chalk arrows to avoid getting lost, and claimed to have found the name of one of the men lost in 1801 written in the sand toward the bottom end of the cave. Despite the notoriety Paxton's study generated, locals still insisted on calling it Delaney's Cave.

After 1818, traffic started coming over the mountain on the National Road, and visits to Delaney's Cave increased. In the 1850s, it was a well-advertised attraction for guests staying at the Fayette Springs Hotel, a summer resort several miles to the southeast, and the Summit House, located on the National Road at the crest of Chestnut Ridge. Cave touring guests were outfitted with horses and guides from both establishments.

For seventy-five years after 1851, the Delaney Cave Farm was operated by the Humbert family. They tilled the land and were apparently tolerant of the numerous caving parties, but never developed the cave as a tourist attraction. Although it was well known and within a few miles of the resort hotels, the cave was remotely located at the top of the ridge and could not be easily reached without horses. In order to become a commercial attraction, caves at this time had to be directly linked to the railroad. Easy access to Delaney's Cave would not exist until well into the age of the automobile.

Studying Caves

Scientific notoriety came early to the caves of Pennsylvania because of their proximity to Philadelphia, the eighteenth-century Renaissance capital of North America. The American Philosophical Society, organized by Benjamin Franklin as the premier scholarly forum of its day, was but a stone's throw from the State House. On March 3, 1783, John Peter Miller presented the society's first cave-related paper, which was published in their *Transactions* three years later. In describing the "Grotto on the Swatara," Miller provided an early treatise on what would become Indian Echo Caverns. Although in Pennsylvania, the Swatara Grotto is physiographically linked to the East's other famous early caves, Weyer's and Luray, in that they are all located in similar-age limestone within the Great Valley, through which settlers migrated west.

One of the more blatant examples of cave vandalism, this advertisement for Roush's Pretzels was painted just inside Indian Echo Caverns before commercialization restricted access.

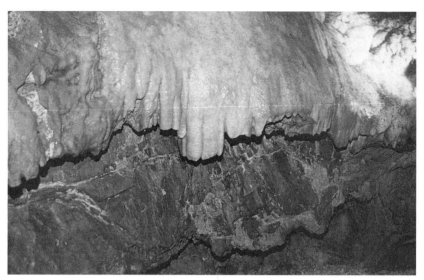

Before commercialization provided registry books and gift shops, few open-access caves escaped the effects of visitors' obsessions with leaving names and taking souvenirs. This row of stumps is all that is left of stalactites snapped off by early visitors to Crystal Cave.

As cited by Richard H. Hartwell in *Indian Echo Caverns,* Miller was familiar with the latest cave science, explaining that "water drops incessantly from roof upon the floor, by which, and the water petrifying as it falls, pillars are gradually formed to support the roof." He found the water "wholesome and pleasant to drink when it has discharged its petrifying material." He noted the possibility that the cave might be connected to the abyssal sea, the subterranean repository of Noah's floodwaters assumed to have been drained off the surface through caves: "We found several holes at the bottom of the cave, going down perpendicularly, perhaps to the abyss, which renders it dangerous to be without a light." Miller also noticed, even as early as 1753, when he made his trip, the innate human obsession with souvenir taking and name leaving: "Some of the stalactites are of a color like sugar candy, and others resemble loaf sugar; but it is a pity that this beauty is now destroyed by the country people."

Other early Swatara Grotto chroniclers also reported the ill effects of human visitation. Alexander Hayden, in a 1789 letter to geographer Jediah Morse, identified another source of interior marring: the smoke from the torches used when tourists were led through the cave. A considerable amount of the cave marring was deliberate. An article in the August 1, 1905, *Hummelstown Sun* surmised that the cavern, known by then as Echo Cave, was losing its attraction because "most if not all the beautiful formations have been defaced by the hammer of the relic hunter. The stalactites so beautiful under the light of the torch no longer are to be seen, while stalagmites are battered completely out of shape." Smoke damage and historic graffiti tempered by time into quaintness mar the walls to this day yet much beauty remains.

The Westmoreland Lyceum undertook a scientific expedition to Westmoreland County's Bear Cave in 1839. Lyceums were popular liberal studies associations that sponsored educational outings and lectures. They were fostered by Enlightenment principles of rational thought and empirical study. The Westmoreland Lyceum camped at Bear Cave for three days, exploring its passageways, taking measurements, and speculating on its genesis, entertaining such theories as earthquakes and volcanic gases in addition to erosion by water. Their exploits were reported in the Greensburg paper.

Cave creatures were also the object of scientific scrutiny, especially after Charles Darwin's *Origin of Species* was published in 1859. Samuel Kohler encouraged the scientific community to direct their attention to Crystal Cave, and then printed whatever they wrote as promotional material for the cave. Professor Burrows, correspondent for the Philadelphia *Public Ledger,* arrived at Crystal in 1873. Inspired by Mammoth Cave, he named one room the Star Chamber and proclaimed to have found blind fish, quite a feat, since it would have been a challenge even to find enough water for the fish to live in. Regardless, Kohler turned Burrows inventive description into a promotional pamphlet the next year.

Other caves achieved temporary fame through the discovery of prehistoric mammal bones. Depending on their configuration, caves could function as Pleistocene animal traps, preserving the bones of long extinct creatures. Not too spacious and virtually devoid of decorative speleothems, Durham Cave in upper Bucks County grabbed attention in 1865 through state geologist H. D. Rogers's collection of bones removed from the cave. An even more intensive investigation was made by Dr. Henry Mercer of the University of Pennsylvania in 1893. This bone bed, however, paled in comparison to what was found in Port Kennedy Cave, along the banks of the Schuylkill River just below Valley Forge. Through the efforts of three different studies spanning nearly twenty-five years, from 1871 to 1895, the bones of fifty-four mammals were identified, forty-one of which were from animals now extinct. The bones were saved, but the cave was not. Despite its scientific significance, most of Port Kennedy was quarried away by the early twentieth century, and the remains buried in lime sludge.

Cave rat and bat studies kept scholars crawling into caves throughout the twentieth century. One evening in 1922, Earl L. Poole climbed Berks County's Pinnacle, a rocky promontory on Blue Mountain, to dispel the myth that it was haunted. In addition to mountaintop spooks, the location was also associated with a persistent dragon legend. Pinnacle Cave, a small tectonic passage through Shawangunk quartzite, was thought to be the dragon's lair. With baited traps, Poole captured what he thought to be responsible for the Pinnacle's late-night shrieks—an Allegheny woodrat.

Cave Dwellers

In Philadelphia's early days as the new colonial capital, many settlers lived in man-made hollows dug into the banks of the Delaware River until more substantial housing could be constructed. John Key, Philadelphia's first baby of European parents, was born in one of these caves in 1682.

In addition to Indian legends, tales of hermits were used by Victorian romantics to make natural landscapes seem more picturesque. In Philadelphia, the story of the Kelpius monks of the Tabernacle of the Mystic Brotherhood was resurrected when tourists began to reinterpret their former wilderness abode as urban park space. The followers of Johannes Kelpius arrived from Germany in 1695 and hollowed out homes for themselves among the stony grottos of the Wissahickon Valley. The forty or so Kelpius monks, also known as Rosicrucians, came to the New World frontier to await the coming of the Lord, but they gradually disbanded and moved away after the 1708 death of Kelpius. Two hundred years later, Kelpius Cave in Hermit's Glen was one of the must-see sites for Fairmount Park tourists.

William (Amos) Wilson, the "Pennsylvania Hermit," came to be the state's most renowned recluse through the recitation and publication of his life story, a tale so romantically tragic that it is difficult to accept as true, but court documents and contemporary accounts verify its authenticity.

Philadelphia's Indian Statue, popularly recognized as Teddyuscung: Leni-Lanape Indians were romanticized in the late nineteenth century when the Wissahickon Valley was reinterpreted as part of Fairmount Park. AUTHOR'S COLLECTION

In this vintage woodcut, Harriot Wilson is sent to her death moments before her brother, Amos, arrives with her pardon, driving him to seek solace in the Swatara Grotto as the Pennsylvania Hermit. INDIAN ECHO CAVERNS

Wilson was born in Lebanon in 1774, and then moved to Chester County with his parents and his younger sister, Elizabeth (some accounts refer to her as Harriot). He apprenticed as a stone cutter, and his sister went off to work in a Philadelphia hotel, where she was seduced by a man who promised to marry her. She got pregnant with twins (some accounts say a son), and he reneged on his proposal. Sometime after Elizabeth returned to Chester County, the murdered infants were discovered by hunters tramping through the nearby woods. A sensational trial condemned Elizabeth to hang for the murder. While awaiting her sentence, Wilson pleaded her case to the governor in Philadelphia, who was so moved that he granted a stay of execution. Wilson raced back to Chester with the pardon but was delayed by rain-swollen streams. He arrived twenty minutes after she had been hanged. Later interpretations of the evidence suggested that Elizabeth was innocent and the father was the culprit, but he was never brought to justice.

Thoroughly discouraged with humanity and the injustices of life, Wilson wandered back toward the valley of his birth to live the life of a recluse. He took up residence in Swatara Cave in 1802 and lived there until his death nineteen years later. He sought a simple life, supporting himself by making millstones, living in solitude to find communion with

God, and writing his precepts for a happy life. Adhering to his wishes, Wilson's writings, "The Sweets of Solitude; or, Instructions to Mankind: How They May Be Happy in a Miserable World," were published in numerous periodicals after his death. Wilson's search for solitude became a legend that only enhanced the popularity of the cave in ensuing years. Today visitors to Indian Echo Caverns are grouped before a simulated campfire in the Wilson Room, shown the travertine ledge on which the hermit slept, and told his tragic tale and of his ultimate salvation through solitude. Between Dingmans Ferry and Bushkill in the Poconos was the ridgetop lair of hermit Austin Sheldon. He reportedly inhabited a cave near Brisco Mountain Road and made his living by weaving baskets and forging kitchen knives until his death in 1886.

A January 2, 1895, newspaper article from Greensburg's *Pennsylvania Argus* tells of two separate hermits who had inhabited a cave on Chestnut Ridge: "Samuel Freeman, a colored man who came from the south, and secured work last spring at the Morewood coke ovens, was discharged two weeks ago on account of his strange actions. Since then he has been living in a cave on Bald Knob, one of the wildest points on Chestnut Ridge, in Westmoreland County, and manages to get a living by digging herbs and roots and stealing from farmers in that neighborhood. Freeman's cave is the same one that the crazy Abe Holland, who is now in Dixmont [western Pennsylvania's state insane asylum], made his abode for five years. Holland imagined he was General Grant and would stand on the cliffs in the mountain for hours at a time, making speeches to his imaginary legions." Harking back to the old perception of caves as dangerous dens of the sly, shiftless, and insane, the article ends somewhat ominously: "Some time this week a posse of officers will go up in the mountain to capture Freeman. He is a giant in stature, and they expect a lively time before he is taken."

Whether true, exaggerated, or completely fictional, tales of cave-dwelling hermits never ceased to delight the Victorian nature tourist.

5

Railroad-Era Caves

Pennsylvania is honeycombed with hundreds of caves, but relatively few of them were ever successfully commercialized. Those that were commercialized possessed a combination of attributes related to the size and length of their passages, the quality of their formations, and their market accessibility. The criteria are mutually supporting, so that a long, well-decorated cave easily accessed by a large urban market would be a tourist-attracting gold mine. Small, tight caves without speleothems and off the beaten path would likely be ignored by the general public. Caves lacking in one set of attributes could still attract paying patrons if it had an overabundance of another. For example, with an entrance-to-rear length of barely 500 feet, Crystal Cave is a lot shorter than many caves that were never commercialized, but none had a greater concentration of dripstone.

Commercial cave criteria were not nearly as rigid during the early days of cave touring, when participants were willing to put up with a more arduous experience for the sake of the adventure. Over time, though, as show cave competition increased, the commercial cave criteria sorted out the good from the bad from the ugly. Up until the 1960s, tourists dressed up for their cave adventures in clothes that favored level paths and stairways over muddy crawls and climbs. Having to crawl or even stoop was undesirable. The passages had to be large enough for people to walk upright, and cave operators invested great effort in digging, chiseling, and blasting to make them so. The tourist would tolerate, and even enjoy, a limited amount of fat-man squeezes and rocks that had to be ducked, especially if they were presented in a novel way.

During the railroad era, cave tours had to be long enough to justify an overnight stay. Tourists arrived by rail and coach and lodged nearby.

In some places, the cave could be entered as often as one wished for the price of room and board at the on-site hotel. The guides could perform any number of cave theatrics to extend the trip, such as torch tossings, lighting effects, or storytelling, but in the end there had to be enough cave there to satiate the curious—and then some. Rare was the cave that was not described as having unexplored sections that continued on indefinitely. Visitors could leave satisfied that there was a lot more cave that could have been explored, while few actually left the beaten path.

Before the automobile, drawing tourists meant access to rail-based transportation, even if it required cave operators to run stagecoaches to nearby depots. The importance of the railroad was evident in the early development of Pennsylvania's first-generation show caves, Crystal Cave and Penn's Cave, both of which were developed and opened with gate fees in the nineteenth century.

Other caves were nonetheless being shown in less formal ways. Mounted guides had been leading tourists up Chestnut Ridge to Bear Cave and Delaney's Cave since the mid-nineteenth century. Delaney's was least dependent on the railroad, located miles from the nearest depot, but many tourists got to the cave by trekking up Cave Hollow from the valley below where the Pennsylvania Railroad had constructed a line along the base of the ridge from Connellsville through Uniontown in the 1870s, a route later paralleled by the Baltimore and Ohio.

A streetcar line helped popularize Rentzheimer's Cave decades before it became Lost River Caverns. Laborers in Charles Rentzheimer's quarry had blasted into the cave in 1883. They were quarrying limestone to be used as flux at the Saucon Iron Works, whose failure a year later may have saved the cave from being dug completely away. Within two years, Charles Weidner had crawled throughout the cave, discovering its spacious, flowstone-draped central room and its "lost river." Recognizing an opportunity, the local street railway company leased the cave, built a horsecar line to it from the center of Hellertown, and erected a wooden dance floor in what is now the Crystal Chapel. A second entrance was opened that allowed visitors for a fee to descend a stairway directly into the Ball Room. The transit company benefited by maintaining both the attraction and the means to get to it. During the day, people also patronized a picnic ground along Silver Creek across the street. In 1898, the Allentown and Lehigh Valley Traction Company took over the Hellertown horsecar line and operated electric trolleys to the cave for a short time. It is unknown how long the cavern Ball Room with its naturally air-conditioned dance floor lasted, but the post holes drilled to support the dance floor are still visible today.

After 1887, Rev. Samuel Brehm occasionally charged people a quarter to enter Hummelstown's Echo Cave. Echo Cave was only a mile south of the Reading Railroad depot in Hummelstown. Summer visitors bound for the Stoverdale Campmeeting had to troop right past the cave property. The Reading's Middletown and Hummelstown line came closer still, opening along the edge of the Echo Cave farm in 1890. The railroad even rebuilt the footbridge over the Swatara at Engle's Ford to discourage the meeting crowd from using its railroad bridge. The spirited soul saving that enveloped the Engle farm each summer ended a century back, but the M & H has recently been revived as a tourist railroad, allowing visitors to once again arrive at what is now Indian Echo Caverns by train.

Soon after through trains started crossing the state on Pennsylvania's Main Line in the 1850s, the "Great Bear Cave" on Chestnut Ridge in Westmoreland County started showing up in railroad guides. This sandy cave was extensive and locally well known, but early visitors stripped out what few speleothems once existed. The convenience of being along the state's most heavily traveled railroad, however, was more than enough to make up for the lack of decorations. The tracks ran along the base of Chestnut Ridge, where travelers were encouraged

Although the Virginville Depot that served tourists bound for Crystal Cave is gone, the East Penn Depot in Kutztown still stands.

After being picked up at the depot by Sam Kohler's omnibus, railroad-era tourists to Crystal Cave typically stayed overnight at Crystal Cave House, opened in 1876 and now used as the cave's gift shop and office.

to disembark at Hillside and secure mounts and a guide to journey up the mountain. After visiting the cave, the traveler could continue to their final destination on a later train.

From Pittsburgh, Chestnut Ridge was the first part of the Allegheny Mountains reached by train, and much of the forested acreage on the west slope above the tracks was purchased by wealthy city dwellers for summer homes. A camp meeting was established along the railroad near Hillside, and from there people made frequent trips to Bear Cave, giving the rock formations and passages biblical names.

Bear Cave became so well known that it was depicted as a point of interest on some early road maps, even though it was never commercialized. Like Delaney's Cave, it was too far up the mountain to warrant development during the railroad era, and even for auto tourists, the cave remained a forty-five-minute uphill hike from the nearest road.

Sam Kohler's Crystal Cave was the epitome of a railroad cave, developed and opened to the paying public who arrived by train. The cave was only a few miles northwest of Kutztown's East Penn depot and 2 miles east of the Virginville depot, which opened in 1876 as the primary gateway to Crystal. Kohler opened a hotel, the Cave House, the same year. Looking like an overgrown farmhouse, the Cave House was connected to the outside world by the omnibus service Kohler ran to both depots. The hotel opened just in time to receive spillover patronage from the Centennial Exposition in Philadelphia. At the time, there was not another show cave operating in the state, and all but the last 2 miles of the 75-mile trip could be covered comfortably by train. Three Paris educators who were in America to visit the Centennial toured the cave, and they left a signed testimonial stating that Niagara Falls and Crystal Cave were the greatest natural wonders they had seen in America.

While Crystal's early fame spread, Pennsylvania's other great railroad cave, Penn's Cave, lay dormant as the water well for the Long farm. After George Long died in 1884, his sons began commercial development. By the summer of 1885, they had built the three-story Penn's Cave Hotel and were open for business.

When George Long had purchased the cave farm twenty years before, Penns and Brush Valleys were peaceful, prosperous, and somewhat isolated. The nearest railroad was at Bellefonte, 14 miles over Nittany Mountain to the west. By the time his sons had taken over, the tracks had crept within 3 miles, and Long's Cave was already showing up in

Penn's Cave's remote location necessitated the building of a hotel for guests arriving by train. The hotel closed in 1919 when guests began arriving by automobile. The hotel also functioned as restaurant, gift shop, and the Campbell family residence. DEAN SNYDER

ENTRANCE TO PENNS CAVE,
NEAR BELLEFONTE, PA.

Penn's Cave's Wet Entrance was virtually impenetrable until 1885, when Jesse and Samuel Long built a staircase into the sink and a wooden dock from which to launch boats. DEAN SNYDER

railroad guides. The Lewisburg and Tyrone Railroad pushed up Penns Creek through the narrow Seven Mountains gorge from the Susquehanna Valley in 1877, terminating at Spring Mills. The line was connected through Centre Hall to Bellefonte the same year the cave opened, an event certainly not lost on the Long brothers.

The Pennsylvania Railroad's 1883 travel guide, *Summer Excursion Routes,* described Spring Mills as "an unobtrusive place" with "good air, taking scenery, and a picturesque nature," as well as "a series of singular and interesting caves. The height of the [cave] roof varies from ten to sixty feet [a 20-foot exaggeration] and is, of course, covered with stalactites. Within the cavern is a large lake upon which the visitor can go boating among queer arches and domes, the grottoes, and winding passages." Accommodations could be had at the Spring Mills House.

Aside from providing a boat and names for some of the cave's formations, the Long brothers, who continued to farm, did little else to develop Penn's Cave. Nevertheless, colorful descriptions written by visitors to the cave drew interest.

Associate editor of the Philadelphia *Public Ledger* and fishing fanatic William E. Meehan visited Penn's Cave for his monograph on "The Mountain Lakes of the State," published as part of the 1896 *Report of the State Commissioners of Fisheries.* He described how a path led through heavy brush to the edge of the sinkhole, where two flights of steps descended 60 feet to the wooden dock at the mouth of the cave. There he was met with a "scene grand beyond description. In this vast cavern slumbers a lake of sparkling water, invariably as clear as crystal, and reaching as far into the black depths as the eye can see."

Jesse Long guided Meehan through the cave with the aide of a gasoline lamp attached to the prow of the boat. "If the visitor is impressed with the beauty at the entrance, he cannot help but gaze in awe at the wonders displayed as the boat glides noiselessly along over the placid waters. The light from the gasoline lamp casts a weird, ghostly radiance on all the surroundings, and the whole seems a perfect maze of fantastic shapes and figures."

Besides giving elaborate descriptions of the cave's formations, Meehan devoted considerable attention to the unique experience of being in an underground environment. "The first sensation that greets the visitor in his descent is the marked change in atmosphere. The temperature may be ninety degrees in the shade at the top, as one goes down the air becomes cooler and cooler and the atmosphere bracing until once at the entrance to the cave, it seems so cold as to actually make one shiver." He also describes the rock as being "exceedingly vibratory. A loud call or 'hello' will reverberate from one end of the cave to the other, and so apparently perfect are the acoustic properties that a person at the entrance speaking in a natural tone of voice can be heard the full length of the cave." He also said that even though the rock overhead was 50 to 75 feet thick, wagons could be heard passing on the road overhead with such clarity as to make it possible to determine whether they were being drawn by one horse or two.

The acoustic qualities of caves have never failed to fascinate, sometimes drawing singers or musicians to perform from some rocky prominence or play over the reverberating waters of a cave river. Some caves delight visitors with musical stalactites whose hollow forms ring with various tones when struck. Meehan described Penn's Cave's Chimes, a grouping of stalactites, as producing sounds not unlike a flute. The Chimes still hang from the ceiling of the cave, but like the Liberty Bell, they are no longer rung for fear of doing damage to the formation.

As towns and railroads expanded across the Keystone State throughout the nineteenth century, caves continued to turn up and attract at least local visitation. Carlisle residents frequented Conodoguinet Cave, a natural opening along the banks of the creek of the same name north of town. A series of hillside openings along Little Chickies Creek eventually became the focus of a picnic ground at the edge of Mount Joy.

The students of karst-country colleges often frequented local caves. Kutztown students commandeered Schofer Cave, discovered in a small limestone quarry a few miles north of the college. Before being filled in, a cave opened right on the campus of Bethlehem's Moravian College. Both Moravian and Lehigh University students used Rentzheimer's Cave for academic study and ritual hazing. "LU" graffiti from 1914 attests to their activities, which included abandoning blindfolded fraternity pledges in the cave with only one small box of matches to find their way out. Lafayette students favored Indian Cave, overlooking the Delaware River 4 miles north of Easton. All of these caves, with the eventual exception of Rentzheimer's, were lacking in some necessary aspect—size, length, quality of decoration, or accessibility—to be profitably commercialized. As a result, they remained in their wild state, but with open access, they also suffered the ravages of careless cavers and vandals.

As the automobile gradually came onto the scene, it slowly overtook the railroad as the main mode of travel. Streetcar lines, interurbans, and branch line passenger service were hard hit first, failing by the score during the 1920s and 1930s, followed by the curtailment of main line service after Word War II.

Penn's Cave and Crystal Cave were destined to become more popular than ever in the ensuing auto age, but not before experiencing ownership changes that would mark the passing of the first generation of rail-oriented show cave entrepreneurs. Despite rave reviews from those who entered, the Penn's Cave farm was out of business and up for sheriff sale by 1905. Even with the railroad, it may have proven too remote to be profitably run, or it is quite possible that the Long brothers lacked the business acumen to make it work. Meehan had levied a harsh critique of their abilities nearly a decade before, when he concluded that the cave was little known outside the region because it was "in the possession of one of the slow-going natives of the county, who either has not the means or the desire to beautify the surroundings and make it the place it ought to be." Meehan was convinced that Penn's Cave could be one of the most popular resorts east of the Mississippi and could make a fortune for its owner. Nevertheless, it was up for sheriff sale again in 1908 after it passed unsuccessfully through the hands of John A. Herman of Pleasant Gap.

The cave farm was next purchased by two local brothers, Robert Pearly and Henry Clay Campbell. Robert was a Penn State–trained civil engineer who had grown homesick working for American Bridge in Toledo. He was anxious to return to Centre County and take up farming like two of his other brothers. Clay graduated from Penn State in veterinary medicine and was teaching at the University of Pennsylvania in Philadelphia. He never became anything more than a silent partner, but he did suggest that the farm had potential beyond its ability to grow crops. In a letter written soon after the purchase, he referenced the booming business being done at Luray Caverns and the need to electrify Penn's Cave to attract paying tourists. It would be some years before the cave was electrified, but tours were resumed almost immediately.

Crystal Cave's Samuel D. F. Kohler, Pennsylvania's pioneer cave showman and promoter, died on August 16, 1908. He was buried at Zion Moselem Church Cemetery beneath a stalagmite sacrificed from his beloved cave. It quickly eroded away and was replaced by a replica of one that continues to mark the grave. His son, David, who was six years old when the cave was discovered and had later piloted the omnibus to and from the train stations, assumed the reins.

The Campbells and Kohlers stood on the threshold of a new era. The age of the railroad was waning, but a new mode of transportation was on the horizon. In 1908, Henry Ford's first Model T rolled off the assembly line. Four years later, Kohler retired the omnibus. With the advent of the automobile, the greatest years of show cave development and patronage lay ahead.

6

Show Caves in the
Early Auto Age

Three machine age innovations—the automobile, hard-surfaced roads, and electricity—were responsible for ushering in the golden age of the show cave, a period of unprecedented growth and development that began in the early 1920s and lasted into the mid-1930s. Self-contained electric generating and distribution systems had been lighting coal mines since the 1880s. Ford's Model T had made automobiles affordable to the masses by the 1910s, and the federal government started funding the construction of all-weather highways in 1916. With these innovations in place, Cave Country, USA, awaited only a prosperous economy of readily available investment capital to develop its assets. This arrived with the Roaring Twenties.

If there were a "show cave highway," in Pennsylvania, it would be the William Penn. The original route passed within 10 miles of nine of Pennsylvania's sixteen limestone show caves and was directly responsible for the discovery of one of them. Even its origins are linked to the state's cave history.

The William Penn Highway Association was founded in 1916 to improve and promote an automobile road across the midsection of the state, from New York City to Pittsburgh by way of Harrisburg, the association's headquarters city. The transcontinental Lincoln Highway was laid through the state between Philadelphia and Pittsburgh three years before, but its southern routing avoided Harrisburg and reached New York by a less direct path. The Lincoln Highway had usurped the most well-trodden path across the state, following much of the route of the historic Pennsylvania Road, including the Lancaster Pike and the Forbes

WM. PENN HIGHWAY AND JUNIATA RIVER BETWEEN HUNTINGDON AND LEWISTOWN, PA

Affordable automobiles and hard-surfaced roads sparked a nationwide expansion of show cave operations during the 1920s and early 1930s. The William Penn Highway became the most important trunk road serving Pennsylvania's cave country. AUTHOR'S COLLECTION

Road. Penn Highway advocates championed Pennsylvania's second most well-used trans-Appalachian route, the more circuitous but lower-grade alignment of the Frankstown Path west from Harrisburg along the Juniata River through Lewistown, Huntingdon, and Hollidaysburg. East from Harrisburg, the road followed the Great Valley, originally passing through Lebanon, Reading, Allentown, and Easton. Its low-grade route put the highway in cave-pocked limestone valleys, from the shores of the Delaware River at Easton to the foothills of the Alleghenies west of Water Street. Laid out over existing roads, the William Penn Highway was continually rerouted here and there in search of better pavement and alignment. After 1925, it became part of U.S. Route 22.

Even before the founding of the William Penn Highway Association, Pennsylvania was a progressive good roads state, having founded its Department of Highways in 1903. In 1911, there were 43,181 vehicles registered in the state. By 1917, there would be 349,720, an eightfold increase in just six years.

Much of the state's early road-building efforts focused on long-distance highways like the Lincoln and William Penn. The Federal Highway Act of 1921 supported this program by providing additional funds for an interstate highway system in which the roads connected with similar roads in adjacent states. In 1925, the uniform Federal Highway numbering system was developed to mark this national integrated network of improved roads with standardized route shields.

The improved accessibility of those caves located near this Federal Highway system increased their potential for commercial development far beyond that which was previously offered by the railroads. Even caves located well off this system received a boost after 1931, when Gov. Gifford Pinchot initiated a campaign to "get the farmer out of the mud" by sending the state's paving crews out onto Pennsylvania's secondary roads. As more backcountry roads were paved, every local cave was reexamined and every doggy hole explored as a potential show cave. Potential cave proprietors in Pennsylvania were anxious to discover, develop, promote, and show whatever hole tourists were willing to pay to see. Some holes were bigger than others, requiring Herculean feats of engineering and effort to make ready for the well-dressed tourists of the 1920s. Painted billboards were erected to entice motorists off the highway. In 1922, the year before Onyx opened, only two show caves were operating in Pennsylvania, plus Cold Air Cave at Delaware Water Gap. Ten years later, the tourist had fifteen to choose from.

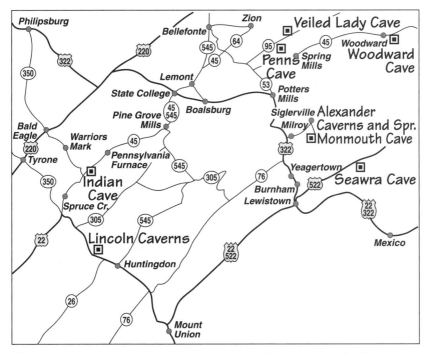

The central section of a 1948 Pennsylvania road map locates half a dozen show caves then in operation, all easily accessible from the William Penn Highway, U.S. Route 22.

Now the lion's share of the show cave business came from day-trippers who returned home after their visit, travelers en route to someplace else, or vacationers already in the area. Forty-five minutes to an hour and a half came to be standard for the length of cave tours. Tours through shorter caves were augmented by orientation presentations. Longer caves were covered by more walking and less talking, or by leaving less interesting parts of the cave undeveloped.

For the most part, Pennsylvania caves were too far-flung to generate competitive animosity. There were occasional billboard battles to redirect tourists approaching a competitor's cave, but as more entrepreneurs entered the field, the spirit was more cooperative than competitive. This was especially true after 1948, when Indian Caverns owner Harold Wertz formed the Pennsylvania Cave Men's Association, an organization of show cave owner-operators that still exists as the Pennsylvania Cave Association.

The State's First Auto-Age Show Cave: Onyx Cave

While Samuel Kohler was preparing for Crystal Cave's Grand Illumination in May 1872, workers blasted into another cave 2 miles west of Virginville. As with Crystal's discovery six months earlier, laborers were after agricultural lime. They were digging the stone from a hillside on Isaac Adams's 1,000-acre farm to be burned in a limekiln that still stands across the road. The chambers within were not as large as Crystal's, but the cave was well decorated with flowstone, stalagmites, and stalactites. Nevertheless, their find went virtually unnoticed by the larger world. It was not unusual to find caves in limestone country; rather, it was unusual to promote them as tourist attractions. For the most part, such discoveries sat idle as local curiosities while cave property owners continued to pursue their main occupation, typically farming.

The new find near Virginville did not even warrant a name until it was purchased by Thomas Luckenbill in the 1880s, then by convention, it carried his name.

Over the years, Luckenbill's Cave changed names as it changed hands. Occasionally visited by adventurous cavers, it sat in the shadow of its more famous neighbor until November 8, 1922, when Irvin E. Dietrich bought the cave. Dietrich promptly set to the task of exploration in preparation for the cave's commercial development. He renamed it Onyx Cave for its abundant brown, red, and white striped calcite deposits, which at the time were commonly referred to as cave onyx.

Like his cave-developing predecessors, Dietrich dug out passageways to create a circuit, laid boardwalks and erected stairs to keep tourists out of the mud, and isolated interesting formations, giving them evocative names like Elephant's Head, Crouching Tiger, Pipe Organ, Ice Jam, Natural Bridge, and Madonna. The Cathedral Room contained the cave's largest flowstone formation. The cave's signature piece was the Fallen Stalactite, a large stalagmite that was interpreted as a stalactite that had been broken from the ceiling during an earthquake.

The "First Annual Opening of the Great Onyx Cave" was set for Sunday, May 20, 1923, and advertised to include a concert by Reading's Farmers's Haymakers Band. Fifteen hundred people showed up for Onyx's grand opening, and the cave maintained its popularity throughout the 1920s. Dance bands, concerts, and the occasional lecture or political rally became staple attractions at Onyx, performed beneath the pavilion Dietrich built on his picnic grounds, along with a restaurant and a refreshment stand. Dietrich lived on the property in a house constructed soon after he purchased the cave.

Onyx was the first cave to open in Pennsylvania since the 1908 reopening of Penn's Cave. During the intervening fif-

Although discovered in 1872, the year after nearby Crystal Cave, Onyx Cave was not commercialized until auto tourists could penetrate the hills and valleys of rural Berks county. DEAN SNYDER

teen years, America had entered the modern machine age. Now cars, roads, and electric lights underpinned the cave's inauguration.

A week before the cave's official opening, it was illuminated. Unlike Crystal's flame-based Grand Illumination fifty years before, Onyx was turned on instantaneously through the magic and power of a 210-volt Delco generator and light system. The typical Delco system consisted of two wires suspended from insulated posts affixed to the cave walls and ceiling, connecting a string of electric lights. By today's standards, the exposed wires were unsightly and the white bulb lighting effect less than spectacular, but it was a vast improvement over carbide lamps and hand-held flashlights.

Onyx was still nonetheless a step behind Crystal Cave. One of David Kohler's first upgrades when he took over from his father fifteen years before was to team up with Kutztown electrician Edward Slonecker and light the cave with a gasoline-powered generator. Penn's Cave's lighting was also updated in 1925, when the Campbells built a hydroelectric dam across Penns Creek, just downstream from its rise beyond the back of Penn's Cave. Prior to that, Penn's Cave was illuminated by a searchlight mounted on the boat. The stream that supported the boat tours was now generating the power to light the cave. Show caving had entered the twentieth century.

Noticeably absent at Onyx Cave was a hotel. Dietrich made no accommodations for railroad visitors requiring an overnight stay. The majority of Onyx tourists were expected to drive to the cave, then leave, as was the case on opening day, when the grounds were crowded with parked automobiles. Dietrich did build a gas station, a new necessity for the cave tourist. Onyx Cave advertisements described its location as 2 miles west of Moselem Station, the next Reading Railroad station south of Virginville, and 5 miles north of Moselem Springs, a crossroads community with no rail service located on the William Penn Highway.

Penn's Cave in the Auto Age

Robert Campbell had made a successful business of Penn's Cave. In 1911, three years after purchasing the cave, he married Edith Picken, whom his sister had roomed with at Williamport's Dickinson Seminary. They set up house on the third floor of the Cave Hotel, where their son William was born two years later as the first of three children. Edith looked after the hotel and restaurant while Robert ran the farm and cave. With babies on the way, however, Edith's job was becoming increasingly more difficult at a time when the automobile was making the hotel a lot less necessary. It was closed in 1919, although the hotel's restaurant continued to serve guests for another ten years. Robert Campbell died in 1932, leaving Penn's Cave in the capable hands of his wife, Edith, and their nineteen-year-old son, Bill. Edith bought out her brother in-law Clay Campbell's share and ran the business with Bill for the next thirty years. By the time of Robert's death, the Great Depression had set in. Penn's Cave attendance records set in 1923 would not be matched again until 1949. Not only was the business pie shrinking, but it had been cut up into many more slices. At the beginning of the 1920s, Penn's Cave was one of just two in the state. By the early 1930s, five other caves were operating within 30 miles, including Veiled Lady, which was right down the road, and Alexander, Pennsylvania's other cave that could be seen by boat.

The hydroelectric dam constructed across Penn's Creek downstream from the cave created a man-made lake that provided a wonderful

Penn's Cave's picturesque back entrance was fabricated rather than found. The artificial tunnel was bored through in 1927 to extend the boat trip onto Lake Nitanee, a manmade pond backed by a hydroelectric dam constructed in 1925 to provide lighting for the cave.

opportunity to add a picturesque extension to the cave boat tour. In 1927, a 75-foot-long tunnel was excavated through the back of Penn's Cave to allow the boats to exit onto the placid waters of Lake Nitanee. Boats carrying tourists drifted from the wilderness cavern through the tunnel, and out onto a bucolic mountain lake surrounded by forested slopes, and then turned to be swallowed up by the underworld again. The effect was astounding, and still is.

Woodward Cave

Legend has it that the Seneca knew of Woodward Cave long before white settlers entered Centre County. It is quite possible, as its mammoth mouth would have been hard to miss, but its plentiful orange and mud-colored speleothems lay somewhat protected behind the watery moat of Pine Creek and a tangled barrier of driftwood, debris, and silt carried into the cave during floods. The creek flowed along the base of the hill into which the cave extended. The water pooled at the cave entrance, then continued down the valley through a hollow between the cave hill and Thick Mountain. During dry spells, Pine Creek would be lost to swallow holes in the streambed, like water down a draining bathtub,

By 1926, Pine Creek had been diverted and Woodward Cave opened to lantern tours. It was electrified a year later. DEAN SNYDER

before ever reaching the cave. At flood stage, however, Pine Creek would fill to overflowing, sending excess muddy water cascading into the yawning hillside hole.

Despite the challenge, an investment group called the Woodward Cave Company was formed in 1924 to convert the natural grotto into a paying proposition. This company actually consisted of the cave farm owners—Luther L. Weaver and his sister, Tammy Meyer—and Oliver M. Hosterman, a bakery chain operator from Buffalo, New York. Hosterman, whose relatives ran the nearby Woodward Inn, chipped in the cash, and the Weavers provided the property.

This was not an unusual arrangement. Farmers across the country were cashing in on the motor trade during the 1920s. They owned most of the land America's new roads passed by, and if their farm happened to abut against a major highway, they could spare a small frontage lot or two for a gas station, café, or string of cabins. This new line of work could be run by the farmers themselves or by outside investors who bought or leased the property. The old adage of farmers being land rich but cash poor certainly favored some sort of partnership with outside investors.

Like farming, cave development required money up front for materials, followed by many hours of labor done primarily by the owner-operators. The first order of business for the Woodward Cave Company was to redirect Pine Creek away from the entrance. Aside from the nuisance of having to bring tours over water, stream sink cave owners always faced the threat of having their internal lighting and walkway improvements destroyed by rampaging flood waters. The fact that much of the initial work at Woodward was removing flood debris gave clear evidence that Pine Creek was prone to bring it all back at some future date.

Much of the sediment and debris excavated from the cave in preparation for its 1926 commercial debut were from the 1889 flood that had devastated Johnstown. To avoid such devastating high water in the future, a ditch was dug along the opposite side of the floodplain and bound by a long earthen dike, topped in places with a concrete wall. The dike redirected the stream into the ditch and left the cave high and dry, even during normal spring freshets and high water. The floodplain was developed into a campground, and a wood-frame dining hall was constructed near the cave entrance. Tickets were sold here until 1987, when the new gift shop was built. The old structure still stands, partially suspended over a swale that once carried Pine Creek.

After the ditching and diking, Weaver and Hosterman began cleaning out the cave, pulling the logs away with a team of horses. After the opening was cleared, they laid a horsecar track into the cavern to cart out tons of silt and debris. Passageways were dug deeper to provide adequate headroom, then graveled. Many of the cave's passages were entirely plugged with clay, offering no hint as to what lay beyond or how much clay had to be excavated to get there.

The original earthen and concrete dike used to divert Pine Creek still protects Woodward Cave and Campground from flooding.

Ongoing "curiosity digs" led to the discovery of the Second Room, christened the Dragon's Den, and the Third Room, named the Hanging Forest or the Lancaster Tobacco Barn, after the mass of pendulous, tobacco-colored stalactites hanging from the ceiling. The Upper (Fifth) Room contained an entire Bible Wall, with flowstone formations suggestive of Moses, the Nativity, and Christ Ascending to Heaven. The Kneeling Camel, a large speleothemic mass moved into the Ball Room to clear a path between the Fourth and Fifth Rooms, gained notoriety by showing up in Ripley's *Believe It or Not*.

Newspaper coverage, including that of the occasional Ball Room dance and church service, made tourists aware of the cave, and billboards directed them to its remote, scenic glen. Woodward Cave opened with lantern tours in 1926. Electric lights powered by a Delco generator were added a year later. Adults gained access for 75 cents, children for 35 cents.

Right from the start, it was recognized that the hundreds of cars carrying excited cave visitors to Woodward could be sent back out again as mobile advertising beetles roaming off in all directions to spread the word. This was done through the precursor of the bumper sticker, a cardboard placard proudly proclaiming the name of the attraction tied onto the bumper while the car's occupants were in the cave. Designed to be seen, the yellow and black placards were 4 inches high and 2½ feet long. If all went well, the car owner left with a free souvenir and proof of his adventure, and the cave owner received far-ranging publicity for the price of the placard.

Tying advertising signs to cars was the job of "bumper kids," who got paid pennies per placard. Many children who grew up in show cave families got their start in the business with this task. Ray W. Stover, who fished Pine Creek with his father from the mouth of the cave before it was developed, started as a bumper kid in 1926. Ray had a lifetime association with Woodward Cave, moving on to become a guide and then general caretaker and handyman.

By the start of its inaugural season, Woodward Cave needed only a good story to complete its romantic place making. Henry W. Shoemaker presented the legend in the August 19, 1926, edition of the *Centre Hall Reporter*. As with all of his legends, Shoemaker claimed to have discovered the tale in his folklore-gathering wanderings around the state. The timing of Shoemaker's *Centre Hall Reporter* story seems uncanny, appearing a matter of months after the opening of Woodward Cave.

"Red Panther's Funeral Pyre" centered on Red Panther, a strong, young Seneca brave and the cherished son of Chief Mountain River, whose tribe lived in the Valley of the Beech Tree. The revered beech tree was a favorite of the Storm God, who promised that it was immune to lightning strikes. During severe storms, the tribe would gather beneath the spreading branches of the beech tree and know that they were safe. Red Panther was a powerful warrior and skilled hunter who became cruel and warlike. He felt nothing but contempt for the sacred beech tree and frequently threatened to cut it down, challenging the wrath of the Storm God. After one particularly successful hunt, an overly confident Red Panther executed his threat and felled the tree. His loyal subordinates cut the mighty tree into lengths, stacked it into a pile, and Red Panther set it aflame. Instantly a great peal of thunder ripped the sky and a lightning bolt struck Red Panther dead.

Upon hearing the calamity, Red Panther's distraught father called the other chiefs together and carried the brave's lifeless body into a cave long used for religious ceremonies. Red Panther lay in state on a stone pyre, while the chiefs petitioned the Storm God with prayer. After engaging in lengthy rituals, the chiefs retired. On their return, they had hoped a forgiving Storm God had restored Red Panther to life. Instead, water dripping from the ceiling had turned the body to stone. Mountain River, his clan, and the Senecas came and went, but the profile of Red Panther upon his stony pyre remained as a warning to the arrogance of youth.

Red Panther's Funeral Pyre is a flowstone-covered block of breakdown in the Dragon's Den. Years later, and after several Woodward Cave ownership changes, the legend of Red Panther is still told, but it ends with his body being buried somewhere in the cave, and Red Panther's Funeral Pyre is now referred to as Charlie Brown lying on his back, to which it does bear a remarkable resemblance.

More legends have been written about Penn's Cave than any other cave in the state, and they are all attributed to Henry W. Shoemaker. A wealthy newspaper man who would become the state's first folklorist, Shoemaker often took great liberties in developing a fictional context for gathered folklore. He insisted that an "aged Seneca Indian" named Isaac Steele told him the Penn's Cave legend in August of 1892, when Henry was twelve years old and spending the summer on a family estate in McElhattan, Pennsylvania.

His "Legend of Penn's Cave" first appeared in the *Centre County Reporter* in 1902. It was republished a year later in his *Wild Life in Western Pennsylvania,* and again in 1907 in *Pennsylvania Mountain Stories.* In 1916, it showed up with a number of other cave-related legends in *Penn's Grandest Cavern,* a booklet sold in Penn's Cave's gift shop that went through eight editions up until 1971. Needless to say, the story became an institutionalized part of the tourist experience at Penn's Cave, where it is still recounted on a sign leading to the boat launch.

According to Shoemaker's Legend of Penn's Cave: "In the days when the West Branch Valley was a trackless wilderness of defiant pines and submissive hemlocks," Malachi Boyer, a young Frenchman from Lancaster County, came to camp along the shores of Spring Creek in the vicinity of Chief O-ko-cho and his tribe. The old chief's pride was his seven sons and "Diana-like" daughter, Nita-nee. Malachi and Nita-nee soon fell in love. Although Malachi was considered a friend of the tribe, a marriage between him and Nita-nee would never be tolerated. Resolved to spend their lives together, they struck out one moonless night for more inhabited parts to the east. By morning, Nita-nee's seven brothers had caught up with them, and in the ensuing battle, one of the brothers was killed. The remaining warriors dragged Malachi back over the mountains to a water-filled cavern and threw him in. They guarded the cave for a week, beating Malachi back every time he tried to escape, until at last, weakened by hunger, Malachi crawled back into a remote part of the labyrinth and died. Two days later, the Indians found Malachi's body, weighted it with stones, and dropped it in the deepest water. After all these years, those who have heard the legend declare that on the still summer nights, an unaccountable echo rings through the cave that sounds like "Nita-nee, Nita-nee."

Hipple, Seawra, Alexander, Indian, Indian Echo, Lost River, Veiled Lady, and Coral Caves

Ten of Pennsylvania's sixteen karst show caves were opened between 1928 and 1932. Three opened for the 1929 season, more than in any other year. This was a national trend. Of the 150 show caves currently operating throughout the country, more opened during these years than in any other five-year span. Like any other popular business opportunity presenting itself during a wave of prosperity, the show cave trend had a life cycle. The diffusion of necessary infrastructure and technical know-how laid the foundation, and a few successful pioneers showed the way. Following their model, other entrepreneurs sought out promising sites, amassed the capital, and invested their time, money, and energy in development, each ignorant of future market demand until after the speculation had already been made.

By the time many show caves were ready to open, it was 1929, with only one prosperous summer season left before the onset of the Great Depression. Lost River Caverns and Veiled Lady Cave were still in development and not opened until 1930. Three other caves were christened over the next two years, as investors held out for a short recovery while searching for Depression-proof businesses. The auto-oriented tourist trade seemed as good a bet as any. The reality of the dismal economic situation was apparent by 1932, after which Pennsylvania witnessed only the closing of show caves. Happy days would come again, but not until after World War II.

The show cave frenzy of the 1920s reached all the way to the venerable halls of the state government in Harrisburg, where the Topographic and Geologic Survey undertook the research and writing of Bulletin G-3, *Pennsylvania Caves*. This branch of the Department of Internal Affairs was in many ways the public sector adjunct to the state's mineral industry. Its bulletins, maps, and reports located and described Pennsylvania's geologic treasure trove so that these resources could be profitably exploited. Published in 1930, *Pennsylvania Caves* differed from the others only in that it did not result in the opening of mines or quarries. It nonetheless was written expressly to encourage the commercial development of this natural resource. The bulletin lamented the loss of nature-loving tourists to other states because Pennsylvania's own attractions had not been properly advertised. It included illustrated descriptions of Pennsylvania's major limestone caves, including eleven commercial ones and twenty more that were undeveloped. A second edition, published two years later, included ninety-two caves. By then fourteen of them were show caves, the most that would ever be operating in Pennsylvania at one time.

No longer open today, Hipple and Seawra Caves joined the ranks of Pennsylvania roadside attractions in 1928. Both have classic cave discovery stories involving hunting and lost treasure. Hipple Cave likely was known to early settlers of Bedford County. This Morrison Cove cavern appears as a substantial opening in a rocky knoll not far from a sizable spring. According to tradition, a pioneer known only by the name of Hipple tracked a bear into the cave. Change the name to Houchins, and this is the Mammoth Cave discovery story. At least seven other show caves around the country are said to have been discovered by hunters, three of them, including Mammoth, by bear hunters.

Hipple was the great-grandfather of H. S. Stonerook, who owned the land and developed the cave in 1928. The cave's main advantage was its location, just a mile west of the state highway through Waterside and 12 miles north of the Lincoln Highway, the nation's primary transcontinental trunk road. Stonerook constructed a dance pavilion, a shelter, and fireplaces for picnickers. A row of peonies graced the path to the

Stair Way Of
Hipples Cave
One Half Mile East Of
Waterside, Pa.

Copyright
MOLL & Co.

Soon after Hipple Cave opened in 1928, the original wooden entrance steps were replaced with concrete. DEAN SNYDER

cave, where a fifty-step staircase led down the hole to a bridge that spanned the cave's interior stream. Boardwalks and sawdust-covered, packed clay paths kept tourists out of the mud—mostly. A Delco generator lit the way to such formations as Lincoln's Head, the Fish Market, Allegheny Mountains, Lot's Wife, and the Palm Tree, and it also ran a pump to carry water to the surface picnic grounds. The tour pushed 1,100 feet into the cave, back to a point where the downward-sloping ceiling made walking difficult. From here, tourists could see daylight filtering into the darkened distance from the stream rise. This gallery had long been used as Hipple's "writing room." Countless signatures carved, smoked, and painted onto the walls and ceiling record the misguided point of pride experienced by generations of subterranean explorers who reveled in having made it to the cave's deepest reaches. The cave's greatest disadvantage was that it contained stretches of low ceiling requiring prolonged claustrophobic stoops. Like most caves, adequate signboards were necessary in order for tourists to find it.

Seawra Cave's traditional discovery story has two boys poking around the wooded slopes near Decatur in 1925, searching for the lifelong savings of a hermit who once lived in the area. The hermit was a Civil War veteran who retired to the mountains of Mifflin County to live as a recluse after being spurned by the girl he was in love with. He continued to draw a veteran's pension but spent very little of it on his meager existence. His death touched off a hunt for this money, which was rumored to be squirreled away in his lair somewhere along the base of Jacks Mountain. As the story goes, two boys, Fern Snook and Ted Snyder, stumbled upon a leaf-covered crevice in the ground. Thinking they had found their mark, they opened it with a pickax. No money was ever found, but the opening led into an extensive cave well decorated with speleothems. An old newspaper clipping from 1927, however, stated that Snook and Snyder were setting traps for skunks, not hunting for lost loot, when they discovered the cave. The boys told Fern's brother Walter and John Wray about their discovery, and they returned a few days later with 50 feet of rope borrowed from Wray's father. It was then that they made the original hole wider so that they could explore the cave.

Like pioneer bear hunters, boys and dogs are attributed to having found more than their share of show caves, including Zane Caverns in Ohio, Virginia's Dixie Caverns, and Crystal Cave in Spring Valley, Wisconsin. Virginia's Endless Caverns and Ohio's Seneca Caverns were both revealed by rabbit-hunting dogs chased by farm boys. Farm boys searching for lost pigs stumbled across Mystery Cave outside Preston, Minnesota, and two schoolchildren, a boy and a girl, discovered Indiana's Marengo Cavern in 1883 when they stopped to explore an opening at the bottom of a sinkhole.

Many of these children remain nameless in the annals of great cave discoveries. Cave developers, on the other hand, are well recorded and, as in the case of Seawra, have lent their names to the caves they operated. C. P. Wray and the Searer brothers teamed up to develop the cave, fabricating a title from the combination of their names. Wray owned the property, and the Searers leased the cave under a company officered by President Homer O. Searer, Vice President I. B. Searer, Secretary and Treasurer W. Perry Searer, and Ground Manager V. Lamont Searer, Perry's son. The Searer brothers went to work in the summer of 1927, enlarging the tight confines of the original entrance by creating a short, lateral cut driven into the hillside to intersect the main strike passage at a point where the cave widened. The artificial opening was reinforced all around with concrete and fitted with a cast-iron gate. Block letters imprinted into the cement above the entrance spelled out "SEAWRA CAVE." A small, concrete-block souvenir stand and ticket office was constructed nearby, and the hilltop above the cave was landscaped into a picnic ground with a shelter.

The cave's remote location at the end of a long, unimproved lane off a dirt road 4 miles north of Alfarata made development that much more difficult. The Searer brothers were banking that the richly decorated cave was worth the effort. Immediately inside the cave, the path to greater visual riches dropped into a rocky, steep-sided pit that required bridging. Following a tilting 55-degree dip, the cave needed a fair amount of railing, steps, and level walkways, which were paved in crushed rock. A Delco generating system converted the cavern from natural darkness to the magically lit fairyland the visitor expected.

By May 1928, Seawra Cave was ready for its first paying customers. In addition to the hermit and lost treasure discovery story, the romance of the cave was enhanced by the Searers's formation naming. Tramping a quarter mile underground, tourists were taken past the Table of the Last Supper, through the Crystal Palace, and into the Garden of the Gods, before descending a flight of stairs into the white, calcite-cloaked Bridal Chamber. Seawra also had a set of stalactite Chimes, a musical must in the early days of the show cave business.

A year after Seawra Cave was discovered, another pair of boys embarked on an underground adventure just over Jacks Mountain to the west. The Pittsburgh youths, John Speilman and Henry Schmidt, built a boat and launched it into the subterranean part of Honey Creek to explore the cave that yawned behind Mammoth Spring. The stream rise was on the farm of Reed McClay "Mac" Alexander and had been known since pioneer days. The boys were not the first to penetrate its interior, a spacious wet cave with minimal dripstone. They went deeper into the cavern than their predecessors, however, leaving their craft to

Gated within, Seawra's original concrete entrance still exists with the name of the cave discernable above the threshold.

SEAWRA CAVE, Lewistown, Pa.

Show cave design depended on a clever orchestration of nature. In order to commercialize Seawra Cave, electric lights were strung and its irregular strike passage was leveled through the use of wooden walkways, bridges, and steps. This allowed the cave and its colorful dripstone formations to be presented as a series of easily accessible vistas, vignettes, and panoramas.

climb a 30-foot clay embankment and crawl through a tight crevice, discovering a dry cavern filled with spectacular dripstone formations.

The discovery astounded Alexander, who realized his property held an overlooked opportunity. Seeking out expert council, he invited Ollie Hosterman and Luther Weaver, who had just opened Woodward Cave in the next valley north, to assess the venture. After exploring the cave, the three men formed a partnership to develop what would be called Alexander Caverns.

At the time, there were only two other show caves in the country that involved a boat trip, one of them Penn's Cave. The idea of bringing guests in through the wet entrance proved problematic, however, as a 600-foot, one-way row was necessary to reach the richly decorated dry cavern. Their solution was to bore a hole through 65 feet of solid limestone from the bottom of a sink on the upland part of Alexander's property to intersect the far end of the dry cavern. They conducted precise surveys to make their mark, then punched into a narrow void off what they christened the Cathedral Room. They widened the void into a human-size passage, poured 115 concrete steps into the doglegged slope, and built a wooden structure over the top of the stairs. A parking lot and other tourist conveniences were laid out nearby. Boat docks

The historic entrance to Alexander Caverns was in the cliff face near the rise of Honey Creek. Cave owner Reed "Mac" Alexander is at center, seated next to his wife.

were erected inside at the junction of the dry and wet caverns and at the entrance to a side passage 300 feet downstream. Farther downstream, a clay dam was thrown across the stream to maintain a reliable boating depth. The touring circuit was wired for light, and Alexander Caverns opened for business on May 30, 1929, under the care of resident manager C. F. Kerstetter. The intensive effort needed to open Alexander illustrates the level of deliberate engineering that went into providing tourists with the sense that they were stepping into a pristine fairyland of natural splendor.

After descending the steps, tourists were led through the Cathedral, a large room with a variety of spectacular formations. Similar wonders were shown in the Garden of the Gods, a standard show cave label for a room filled with stalactites and stalagmites that evoked Colorado's famous red rock garden. After passing through the Chamber of Statues, tourists were loaded into a boat at the wet cavern dock. They were unloaded at the second dock and directed down a short passage to view Crystal Lake, a small pool surrounded by dripstone formations. Each group was then reloaded into the boat for the return trip, retracing the path back to the artificial entrance. The tour took more than an hour, no doubt slowed, as much as it was enhanced, by visitors having to climb into or out of a boat four times.

While Hosterman and Weaver were preparing Alexander, another cave of 1929 was being developed in the obscure village of Franklinville, Huntingdon County. Harold Wertz had a long line of vocations to his credit. The Tyrone resident known as "Hubby" had been a skilled welder for the Pennsylvania Railroad, ran a local taxi service, dabbled in advertising, and owned a restaurant, a laundry, and the High Hat Club, a local bar and pool hall. His real passion however was caving. He and his wife, Lenore, had explored a number of caves, including a legendary hole on a hillside above the banks of Spruce Creek, where the two maintained a summer cottage. The cave had a long history that reached back before the days of early European settlement to a time when Iroquois traveled the valleys of central Pennsylvania hunting game. It was locally believed that the future site of Franklinville was a favored Indian campsite due to the presence of the cave, which could be sought out as temporary shelter during inclement weather.

By 1928, the old Indian trail had become PA Route 45, and Hubby recognized Franklinville Cave's potential as a tourist attraction from the parade of clay-encrusted cavers who came out of the cave. He was also aware of other caves that were being developed in the area. Penn's and Woodward were not that far to the east just off the same highway. Hip-

Despite its billing as the "Carlsbad of Pennsylvania," Alexander Caverns was barely open a year when the Great Depression hit and eventually forced its closure in 1936. Reopened in 1940, the cave experienced minimal visitation during the war years, and closed for good in 1954, just as the postwar boom in mass auto tourism began. DEAN SYNDER

ple and Seawra had just opened that spring, and Alexander was being readied. Hubby and Lenore bought what they planned to call Franklin Cave from the farmer who owned the property, and embraced the life of show cave entrepreneurs.

The Wertz's half-million-dollar investment included a stone cottage house at the base of the hill that also functioned as the first ticket office. A second ticket office and gift shop was built into the side of the cave after the first year of operation. In the past, some visitors had been discouraged from going into the cave because of the need to walk up the steep hill. With the new setup, such visitors had already climbed the hill to reach the ticket office and so were less deterred.

Hubby hired fifty workmen to dig out clay from the passages, level the floor, lay down crushed stone walkways, pour concrete steps, and string wires for electric lights. Like Hipple, the cave terminated in a Writing Room with smooth walls etched with the names of previous visitors, the oldest dating to 1816. Hubby was not convinced that this was the end of the cave, surmising that the water that formed the passage had to have drained somewhere. After digging through the clay floor of the Writing Room, Hubby and Lenore found a hole at the bottom of the wall that led to an entirely new section. Workmen blasted a 14-foot tunnel through the limestone, doubling the length of the cave.

The new section was widely promoted as the Enchanted Caverns and included a number of enticing magical references like the Giant's Hall, which was split by a slab of breakdown aptly named the Giant's Shield, beyond which hid the Jewel Room with its Lily Pad Pool. There was even a Musical Rock, a thin, pointed projection that to this day is still struck with a mallet to produce a vibrating tone. The pride of the new section, however, was the Frozen Niagara, a massive wall of flowstone reputed to be the largest calcite formation in Pennsylvania. To emphasize its bulk, pictures of it were published showing people at slightly less than normal scale. A liquid latex cast of it was made in 1939 for the cave exhibit at Pittsburgh's Carnegie Museum. A black patch of rubber was left behind as evidence for the tourists to see.

As stunning as the new discoveries were, they paled in comparison to another find that would change the course of Wertz's promotion and fix the identity of the cave. In leveling the floor of the Entrance Hall, workers started turning up Indian artifacts and fragments of bone belonging to both animals and humans. Work was halted while archeologists unearthed dozens of relics and skeletal remains. These were examined by Neil M. Judd, curator of American Archeology at the National Museum in Washington, and the museum's paleontologist, Dr. Gerrit S. Miller. Specimens were also sent to Boyd P. Rothrock, director of the State

Built in 1930, Indian Caverns's gift shop was originally designed to have the appearance of a Southwestern Indian cliff dwelling. The building was subsequently refaced with stucco, and in 1954 a second story was added, giving it a streamlined, modern look. With the addition of a concrete replica of a Plains Indian teepee and a totem pole from the Pacific Northwest, three American Indian regions were referenced. AUTHOR'S COLLECTION

Museum in Harrisburg. The total cache of arrowheads, points, pipes, beads, blades, bracelets, and other relics was reported to be more than four hundred items belonging to Iroquois and Algonquin people dating back four centuries.

On June 15, 1929, the cavern opened to a booming first season as Historic Indian Cave. In addition to its newfound Indian heritage, the cave thrilled visitors with another long-standing place-based legend, that of robber David Lewis and his buried treasure. David Lewis was central Pennsylvania's legendary highwayman, who took on the characteristics of Robin Hood with the after-the-fact retelling and embellishing of his tales of derring-do. More than a few places in the Juniata and Cumberland Valleys use David Lewis as their link to a more thrilling past, including Blue Mountain's Sterrett's Gap on the Cumberland-Perry County line, Lewis Rocks on South Mountain east of Shippensburg, and the Seven Mountains area north of Lewistown. From the legends, Lewis must have poked his head into just about every natural cave in central Pennsylvania. He was reputed to have hidden out and/or buried treasure in Doubling Gap Cave on Blue Mountain, Davy Lewis Cave near the Bedford Springs Hotel, Carlisle's Conodoguinet

Cave, where he hid after his escape from imprisonment for desertion, and Historic Indian Cave.

The real Lewis was born on March 4, 1790, and moved to Bellefonte with his family when he was ten years old. He enlisted in the army in 1797, but deserted during the War of 1812. After escaping what was to be a death sentence, Lewis took up a life of crime that favored counterfeiting and robbery. He was said to target only wealthy landowners, merchants, and iron plantation payrolls, laying the foundation for a postmortem history that painted him as a friend to the common laborer. His most famous "Robin Hood" tale tells of his desire to rob a farmhouse by asking for change for a counterfeit bill. In this way, he would see where the household money was hidden. He suffered a change of heart when the elderly widow woman of the house said she was without money and the constable was on his way to claim the property for the unpaid rent. Touched, Lewis gave her the money, and then later robbed the officer to get it back plus an additional $50 for his trouble.

In 1820, Lewis and a confederate were tracked down by a posse and wounded in a gun battle on Seven Mountains Road. He died in the Bellefonte jail, either of pneumonia or gangrene from his wounded arm, which he refused to have amputated. On his deathbed, he claimed to have secreted away $20,000 worth of stolen gold. As the legend goes, Lewis had previously written a letter to a Spruce Creek Valley farmer and friend, telling him the booty was hidden in "a dank hideout room" from which he could see workmen at the old woolen mill going about their tasks. The old woolen mill referred to stood on what is now the parking lot to Indian Caverns.

Ralph Stone picked up on this tale and included it in the Topographic and Geologic Survey Bulletin he wrote on Franklin Township in 1921. Stone claimed that the remains of homemade ladders had been found in a remote section of the cave. One Franklinville resident is said to have spent a lifetime searching the cave with lantern and twine ball for Lewis's lost loot. He died empty-handed not long before the Wertzes bought the cave.

As the consummate showman, Hubby Wertz took full advantage of these stories. Beyond a passage junction called Doubling Gap was a room known as David Lewis's Hideout, which had an ominous-looking pit dubbed the Lost Tunnel, a conduit of unknown length that was said to possibly be the hiding place of Lewis's undiscovered treasure.

The long-standing frontier assumption that caves were the abodes of nefarious brigands was supported by numerous nineteenth-century newspaper accounts of cave-related criminal activity. Historian caver Tom Metzgar has linked three Westmoreland County caves to printed articles of thieves, burgled booty, and counterfeiting. Anderson Cave was named for a local villain, Abraham Anderson, who plagued the Delmont area in the 1830s. He was rounded up and died in Western State Penitentiary in 1834. So many people were attracted to the Anderson's Cave to search for rumored stolen treasure that the farmer who rented the property blasted the nuisance shut in the 1910s. An 1877 *Blairsville Courier* article associated Bear Cave, on Chestnut Ridge above Hillside, with the notorious Ligonier robber Clint Hamilton. A counterfeiting operation was discovered in Cole's Cave near Ligonier, according to an 1893 article in Greensburg's *Pennsylvania Argus*. Highwaymen were reported to have holed up in Woodward Cave as well, and according to Rich Kranzel, several small caves in Bucks County have been associated with the Doan Gang, a band of Tory outlaws preying on patriots during the Revolutionary War.

David Lewis was an interesting side legend, but American Indians clearly took center stage at Historic Indian Cave. Part of the development discoveries included an ancient fire pit found in the large, smoke-stained room beyond the Entrance Hall, along with bear claws, a bone flute, and hundreds of beaver teeth. The chamber was assumed to be the place of sacred rites and rituals, and so was christened the Indian Council Room.

Each summer during the 1930s, Wertz invited Indians to camp at the cave, where they made and sold crafts to the tourists, conducted demonstrations on Indian dance, and exhibited feats of archery and fish spearing in Spruce Creek. A favorite summer resident was a Mohawk named Two Cities, who described the Iroquois ritual of fire and darkness that may have taken place in the Indian Council Room. This all night ritual of the Ho-no-tci-no-ga Society was led by a shaman who would extinguish the fire and facilitate the Chant of Darkness, which would not end until the ambient light of dawn penetrated the cave. As the singing ended, matrons brought in food, the fire was rekindled, and pipes were smoked while the chief held council with his Warriors.

Emphasizing the identity of Historic Indian Cave, Wertz erected a concrete tepee and totem pole at the edge of the parking. Although they had nothing to do with Eastern Woodland Indians, the tepee of the Great Plains groups and the totem pole common to tribes in the Pacific Northwest became twentieth-century roadside icons that told tourists the attraction had something to do with Indians, a perennial favorite. Referencing still another region, Wertz had his cave-side ticket office constructed in the image of a southwestern adobe cliff dwelling. The curve-sided building was covered in white stucco when a second story was added in 1954, sacrificing its adobe appearance for that of streamlined modernity.

The romantic cult of the Indian was alive and well at other show caves as well. In fact, Hubby Wertz was chagrined when his idea of wrapping visitors in Indian blankets to fend off the chill of the cave was mimicked at Woodward, Crystal, and upstart Echo Cave, recently opened and rechristened *Indian* Echo Cave. Although Crystal Cave clearly held no claim to Indian heritage, having been discovered long after the Indians' removal to the West, the operation was not averse to celebrating the aborigines who had once inhabited the area whether they had been in the cave or not, memorializing them with tepees and totem poles.

An even greater stretch was made at nearby Onyx Cave sometime after World War II, when one of the cave's flowstone formations, which bore the resemblance of a human figure lying on its back, showing head, chest, arm, and hand, started to be known as Possible Human Remains. As late as the 1970s, when the formation was also known as Caveman's Bones, postcards claimed that cave owner Lou Rizzo planned "to have the formation examined by experts to determine the possible existence of human remains." The word "possible," which inevitably showed up in any assertion about the formation, provided an ambiguous out for guides confronted by know-it-all tourists who were certain that human remains were unlikely to be preserved in the humid environment of the cave long enough for them to have been encased or petrified by the precipitation of calcite sometime since the cave was first penetrated in 1872.

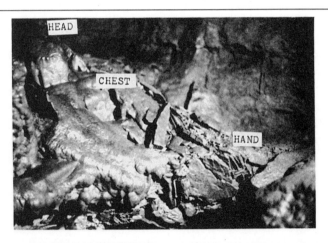

HUMAN-LIKE CHARACTERISTICS are outlined in this flowstone formation at Onyx Cave Near Hamburg, Pa. Owner Lou Rizzo plans to have the formation examined by experts to determine the possible existence of human remains.

This card depicting Possible Human Remains was distributed by Onyx Cave during the tenure of Lou Rizzo, 1978 through 1983. AUTHOR'S COLLECTION

U. S. G. Bieber commercialized Indian Echo Caverns in 1929, transporting the neoclassical pavilion from Kutztown by truck to be used on the picnic grounds. DEAN SNYDER

The mayor of Kutztown, Dr. U. S. G. Bieber, was responsible for commercializing Hummelstown's Echo Cave. Even though it had been known as an open-access cave for years, and suffered for it, Bieber recognized that with some investment, it still had the potential to be a paying operation, especially in the auto-oriented cave-opening frenzy of the 1920s. He purchased the Cave Farm in 1928 from E. M. Hershey, who had acquired the property only two years before, ending Rev. Samuel Brehm's long ownership. The Bieber family and coinvestor D. M. Ryan put up $125,000 to remold the cave into a place worthy of an entrance fee.

Surface improvements included a tree-lined drive leading to a spacious parking lot and the conversion of the farmhouse into the Indian Echo Inn, a restaurant and gift shop. Concrete steps were constructed down the treacherous cliff to the cave's main entrance along the banks of the Swatara. A wood-framed entranceway with sturdy barn doors secured the main cave entrance, while the rear sinkhole entrance at the far end of the East Canyon was sealed with tons of dirt and rock that can still be seen piled to the ceiling in the Dead End Room. This ended the traditional route visitors took through the cave, which was in through the main entrance and out through the sinkhole.

Since 1929, tourists have entered and exited the west end, doubling back through the East Canyon and then the North Canyon before climbing over the dripstone-covered breakdown of the Ball Room to get to the Wilson Room. The arrangement worked well with the presentation given

Indian Echo's original barn door entrance was constructed in 1929 and replaced by the current cut limestone facade in 1956. DEAN SNYDER

by uniformed tour guides. The Entrance Hall and Ball Room provided the setting for the dramatic cave genesis story, with its swirling whirlpool union of subterranean rivers. Leveled walkways paved with crushed limestone led past one scenic vignette after another illuminated by 1,700 electric lights: Ear of Corn, Rainbow Room, Diamond Cascade, Frozen Niagara, Crystal Lake, assorted monkeys, tobacco leaves, and what-not. Returning back through the Ball Room, tourists mounted a flight of concrete steps past the Totem Pole (a large stalagmite now known as the Cave Guardian) and over Potato Hill for a spectacular view of the Hanging Garden, essentially the stalactite-studded ceiling of the Ball Room, whose height protected it from pre-Bieber vandals. In the smoke-marred Wilson Room, the guided narrative concluded with the amazing, tragic tale of the Pennsylvania Hermit.

In addition to the famed William Wilson story, visitors were regaled with tale of the Mystery Box. In 1919, five Hummelstown cavers found a small, copper-bound wooden box decorated with strange markings tucked up on a ledge in the Rainbow Room. The box contained seventeen foreign coins, including one dating from the Roman Empire. The newest was a Turkish coin minted in 1915, suggesting the box had not been secreted away for too long. Two necklace amulets, a multisided hollow block, and a package of tumbled quartz marked "diamonds in the rough" accompanied detailed instructions for making diamonds by harnessing lightning. The find was well reported in area newspapers and has since been told to every cave visitor since 1929. Yet the true owner of the Mystery Box and the reason why it was left in the cave have never been discovered. The box and its contents remain on display in the gift shop.

Nearly forty thousand people from every state in the union except Nevada paid to see Indian Echo Cave in its first six months of operation, from June to December 1929. A gross estimate at 55 cents per person (typical gate fees at the time were 75 cents for adults and 35 cents for children) puts the take at $22,000. Without counting the other half of the year, as show caves were usually closed in the winter, such a revenue stream would have equaled the initial investment by the sixth year of operation. In reality, the cave would be bankrupt by then and facing foreclosure.

In the summer of 1929, however, the future seemed bright for Indian Echo Cave. Even after the September crash, new discoveries were made and the operation expanded. In September 1930, a clay-filled passage behind Crystal Lake at the end of the North Canyon was excavated to reveal a pristine room encased in sparkling flowstone, columns, pendulous stalactites, and corresponding stalagmites reflected in the clear waters of a limpid pool. The Biebers decided to call this Diamond Fairyland. To make it accessible without damaging any formations, a 50-foot tunnel was drilled through the back of the North Canyon and around Crystal Lake to allow visitors to view the chamber from a bridge constructed over what was christened the Wishing Well. The new extension was added to the tour on April 10, 1931, and officially dedicated in an address made by Ralph W. Stone on May 2.

Knowing the auto trade was the business's life blood, Bieber went to great lengths to increase the visibility of his already well-located show cave. Motorists traveling U.S. Route 422 could pinpoint the entrance to Indian Echo by the 10-foot-high, electrically lit sign that read, "CAVE." In 1930, Bieber persuaded the civil leaders of Hummelstown to allow him to erect a classical gateway arch over Main Street in the middle of the town square. Civic gateway arches grew out of the victory arches built in the aftermath of World War I to welcome home the troops. They were popular points of pride constructed over the main streets of small-town America into the 1940s. The Hummelstown Arch was thus in step with a national trend, and it was used as a signboard to announce public events and commonly decorated for patriotic holidays like Flag Day and the Fourth of July. In addition to its civic function, Bieber had the arch crested with a large arrow proclaiming Indian Echo Cave to be only a half mile down the road to the south. The arch stood until 1955, when, like most other over-the-road civic arches, it was deemed a traffic hazard and demolished.

Up the valley from Indian Echo, title changes at Onyx, Crystal, and Hellertown in the 1920s caused the owners of these caves to be interconnected by a web of social relationships. Crystal Cave received twenty-four thousand visitors in 1922, the largest seasonal attendance yet. It may have caused David Kohler to think that it was a good time to get out, or others that it was a good time to get in, because Kohler sold the cave that November to a group of Reading investors including J. Douglas Kaufman, Edwin L. DeLong, and Edgar D. Sibley. They poured new concrete steps and walkways, expanded the parking lot, and in 1928 rewired the cave. They also hired Albert S. Hunsicker in 1924 to be the resident manager of the cave and inn. Hunsicker owned the adjacent farm, which he sold to the Crystal Cave Company in 1929 to get the money to purchase Onyx Cave from Irvin Dietrich.

Hunsicker invested mightily in his new operation, building a dining room onto the main building, relocating the refreshment and souvenir stands, and adding fences, benches, and an acre's worth of new parking. Hunsicker improved the paths underground by removing the old

INTERIOR VIEW—CRYSTAL CAVE, PA.

The concrete dual stairway to Lookout Point was part of the interior improvements made by the Crystal Cave Company during the 1920s. The steps are still there today. AUTHOR'S COLLECTION

boardwalks and steps, digging out up to 2 feet of cave clay. The one remaining set of steps was rebuilt with concrete, and the entire walkway network was paved in crushed stone. He also abandoned the old electric generator, having petitioned Metropolitan Edison to extend their power lines to the cave.

Whereas 1922 may have been a good time to buy a show cave, 1929 was not. Despite all of his efforts, Hunsicker's fate was to be a tragic victim of the Great Depression. Having sold his farm and abandoned his position at Crystal Cave, Hunsicker lost Onyx Cave to hard times and dwindling visitors. The cave was closed by the mid-1930s, and when it reopened some years later, it had new owners.

Although David Kohler gave up ownership of Crystal Cave, he never entirely left the business. He moved onto a nearby farm and continued to lead trips through the cave and sell souvenirs. He ran the Sacony Corner campground and established his own museum in a one-room brick building behind his house. The Kohler Museum was devoted to caves and cave history and contained many specimens, paraphernalia, and old souvenirs from Crystal.

Kohler also assisted an ambitious Philadelphia couple in their search for a suitable cave to develop. Erwin and Marie Gilman met him as a result of a junket to Crystal Cave in the 1920s. The couple had recently moved to Philadelphia from Newark, where Erwin worked in the Radio Department at Bamberger's. After seeing an ad for Crystal Cave in the local paper, Marie persuaded her husband to visit the attraction. They arrived late in the day but were nonetheless given a tour and a meal at the Crystal Cave Inn. The life-changing experience set the Gilmans on the road to becoming show cave entrepreneurs. Each weekend, they followed up leads and explored the quarries of southeastern Pennsylvania for a well-decorated cave located within 50 miles of a major city. Their search ended in an old limestone quarry on the edge of Hellertown, just south of Allentown and Bethlehem, and within 50 miles of Philadelphia.

The neglected Rentzheimer's cave was by then owned by Bethlehem Steel, which quarried local limestone to be used as flux in their blast furnaces. The cavern had a lively history and had recently been leased by bootleggers to store booze. Teenagers under the age of serious prosecution were employed to transport the illegal liquor from the cave to the nearby Sunshine Club. The Gilmans purchased the cave in 1929, too late to get in even one good season before the onset of the Depression.

After a year spent outfitting the cave with the usual crushed stone walkways, concrete steps, and electric lights, the business opened as Lost Cave on May 24, 1930. It was unofficially known by the longer title Lost River Caverns, but it would be years before this name dis-

Erected in the old Rentzheimer quarry, this was the original 1930 entrance building to Lost River Caverns, then known as Lost Cave.

placed Lost Cave on maps, brochures, and promotional materials. The reference was to a subterranean stream that ran through the cave to and from points unknown. Though a good tourist draw, the mysterious stream also presented a challenge, as it separated the front half of the cave from the larger chambers toward the rear. These included the Ball Room, which had been accessed in its dance hall days by a more direct artificial entrance to avoid this problem. Early tourists were ferried across this "Lost Lake" in a boat pushed along by a wader-wearing cave guide. Although novel, this cumbersome transfer was eliminated in 1932 with the construction of the Long Bridge, a concrete span that not only connected the two cave halves, but also branched into a side passage known as the Lake Room and extended the tour past the Inverted Forest and Ear of Corn to the New Room, where the rush of subterranean water could be heard tumbling over the Lost Falls.

The last Pennsylvania show cave to be developed in the optimism of the 1920s was the Grenoble Run sink, located on a Brush Valley farm owned by Franklyn Pierce Duck. Grenoble Run was not unique in that all of the streams draining the south flank of Nittany Mountain east of Centre Hall drained into limestone sinkholes upon reaching the valley floor. Grenoble's easily accessed sink was nonetheless locally famous as Veiled Lady Cavern and was already celebrated with its own legend, immortalizing a white calcite formation that stood just inside the cave entrance and had the appearance of a lady enshrouded in a veil.

Back when Brush Valley was on the settlement frontier, according to the legend, local landowner Michael Q. McCochran proudly boasted that neither side of his family had experienced a "lowly marriage" in twenty generations. This did not prevent his beautiful daughter Patricia from falling in love with a Seneca warrior named Strongheart. Patricia accepted Strongheart's proposal to flee with him to his lodge in Canada. The lovers planned to rendezvous that night at the mouth of the cave, where Strongheart promised to bring ponies for their trip. Patricia stole away to the appointed place, only to find that Strongheart had yet to show. She sat upon a ledge to wait, wrapping herself in a veil against the bitter cold March night.

Unknown to Patricia, Strongheart had already arrived. Walking down the slippery path in the darkness of night, he had stepped on a poisonous barb set there by villainous settlers to kill Indians. Stumbling, he stepped on yet another. Realizing that death was near, he crawled toward the mouth of the cave, hoping to die in the arms of his beloved, but slipped on the ice-covered rocks and tumbled into the rain-swollen Grenoble Run. The rushing waters swept Strongheart into the cavern, hurtling him down the tortuous passage to a hidden lake in the depths of the cave, where his last cry of pain and despair can still be heard. Refusing to believe that she had been abandoned by her one true love, Patricia waited on the ledge, huddled against the biting wind that covered her in snow and numbed her body, then her mind, and then her heart, eventually turning her to stone.

The Veiled Lady legend in many ways parallels the legend of Penn's Cave, which would have taken place just across the valley around the same time. The Veiled lady tale is attributed to John Hall Chatham (1846–1923), who claimed to have heard of it in 1876 from Grandmother Grenoble, who lived on the cave farm. Chatham spent a lifetime collecting Pennsylvania legends and folklore, becoming one of Henry

In 1932, the Long Bridge was built over Lost Lake, extending Lost River Caverns tours into the New Room.
DEAN SNYDER

LEGEND
...of...

The Veiled Lady Cavern

NATURE'S WONDER SPOT
in Central Pennsylvania.....

A Story of love, adventure and pride, as told by the poet-schoolmaster, J. H. Chatham,, to Henry W. Shoemaker

COMP. Of

G. EDWARD HAUPT
BELLEFONTE, PA.

Haupt's Summer Place, Bellefonte, Pa.
and The Veiled Lady Cavern Farms

Veiled Lady was in business for such a short time that few souvenirs, like this rare booklet depicting the cave opening, made it into general circulation. DEAN SNYDER

W. Shoemaker's sources after 1911. Like many frontier legends, Veiled Lady is not an Indian tale passed down from original inhabitants as much as it is a tale about Indians written for European descendants weaned on Victorian romanticism and Shakesperean tragedy.

In 1928, G. Howard Haupt bought the farm to commercialize Veiled Lady Cavern. His labor crew built an upstream dam to divert the water, and then dug out tons of mud, trash, and debris that had been washed into the cave by Grenoble Run. Walkways, steps, railings, and electric lights were installed, and the cave was opened to the public in the summer of 1930. An advertisement in Bellefonte's July 11, 1930, *Democratic Watchman* implored people to spend a pleasant day at Veiled Lady Cave: "See the spectacular ghostly figure of the Veiled Lady, under brilliant electric flood lights in all the colors of the rainbow, many thrills, masses of formations, weird passages and chambers. Free park and picnic ground, open day and night."

Only the exuberance of the Roaring Twenties could have enticed someone to develop Veiled Lady. The relatively small, tight cave sat in the shadow of nearby Penn's Cave, where Robert Campbell was furious that Haupt should open such meager competition in his backyard. Established commercial cave entrepreneurs were sensitive to the opening of shoestring show caves. With only the word "CAVE" painted on a signboard to guide the consumer, such operations were thought to pirate patrons and kill future visitations by reaffirming that caves were dark, muddy holes in the ground not worth the entrance fee to get in them.

Alexander, Indian, Indian Echo, Lost River, and Veiled Lady were all in some stage of development, and Hipple and Seawra were in their second season, when two Bedford County businessmen decided to get into the show cave business. After all, 1929 seemed to be a good year for it. Philip J. Hughes was a local distiller before Prohibition, and a lumberman who specialized in whiskey barrels. Edgar Burkett was the Manns Choice postmaster and a real-estate agent. The two had become interested in a cave that had been discovered in one of the quarries operating on Buffalo Mountain above Manns Choice.

The year before, David Hellegass and Albert Grasser were blasting rock for agricultural lime in the upended Helderberg when one of their charges blasted down into a void. For quarrymen, voids are bad because the value of the mine is based on the amount of rock it contains, not air. The only consolation is if it is a pretty enough void that it might be marketable as a show cave. Caves were nothing new in the Buffalo Mountain quarries. Workmen had lost their tools down deep crevices before, and a cave had recently been blasted into at the adjacent quarry to the north. This one, however, was a bigger hole than usual.

The next day, Hellegass and Grasser conscripted a local boy to explore the cavity. Armed with a flashlight, the Manns Choice boy was dropped into the crevice on Buffalo Mountain. The exploration revealed several large rooms well decorated with speleothems, as well as a wondrous wall of fossils lost to the light of day since its burial as a dying coral reef at the bottom of a Devonian sea.

Inspired, Hughes and Burkett christened their newly purchased underworld Wonderland Coral Caverns, but plenty of work needed to be done before the cave was ready for the public. The entranceway was widened and a steep flight of concrete steps poured to descend 35 feet

Although no longer used, Coral Caverns's first ticket office still stands over the original entrance steps. DEAN SNYDER

into the base of a natural chimney labeled the Tepee Room. A modest cinder-block building was erected over the door with a sealed entrance to act as the ticket office and gift shop. From the Tepee Room, a short tunnel was blasted eastward through a vertical wall of limestone to access the cave's signature Fossil Wall. A flight of steps was also constructed to carry visitors into the Cathedral Room. The cave's irregular, crevice-scarred, and breakdown-littered floor was leveled with clay fill from an abandoned subterranean stream channel, and then paved with crushed rock.

Years had passed before Hughes and Burkett were ready to debut Wonderland Caverns on July 2, 1932. The cave was well located, just 5 miles off the heavily traveled Lincoln Highway down either of two hard-surfaced roads. The timing of the cave's opening, however, could not have been worse. Scant information exists about the cave's fate over the next few decades, except that its name continued to appear on the free gas station road maps of Pennsylvania until the postwar return of prosperity.

Depression-Era Cave Closures and Survivors

Many self-styled show cave kings had literally poured their life savings down a hole in the late 1920s, only to watch the venture fold a few years later. After the money dried up and the banks refused to provide more, the caves just didn't open with the start of the spring tourist season. There were few tourists around to notice, since the lack of visitors was the problem.

By 1933, the chain had been drawn across Veiled Lady Cave, and in the Flood of 1936, the cave folded in on itself. Rampaging waters poured into the sink, obliterating Haupt's improvements. They were never rebuilt. Over the years, the cave silted up while vandals and weather battered the Veiled Lady beyond recognition.

Albert Hunsicker's optimism at Onyx Cave and Dr. Bieber's stunning success at Indian Echo were thwarted by the prolonged Depression. Both families were out of the show cave business by the mid-1930s, and their grottoes quieted. Hummelstown National Bank foreclosed on Indian Echo Cave and put the property up for sale to recuperate its loan losses. The Indian Echo Inn and its parking lot were split off and sold separately. In 1937, a bill was introduced to purchase the cave and turn it into a state park. The bill died in committee. Two years later, the borough of Hummelstown removed the Indian Echo Cave arrow from the top of Bieber's downtown arch.

Seawra Cave was shuttered by 1938. Its protective iron gates were stolen during World War II, and an unknown number of speleothems soon after. By 1946, one of the Searer brothers was working as a desk clerk at the Lewistown Hotel.

Even more remote than the Great Valley caves, four of the seven show caves operating in the central part of the state in 1929 were closed by 1940. Already teetering from weak attendance, Alexander Caverns went down for the count in the 1936 St. Patrick's Day Flood. Despite its spectacular formations and boat ride that rivaled Penn's Cave, there was no money—and little optimism—left to repair the damage. Hipple Cave limped along as an addendum to the farm until about 1940, when it was closed for good.

As the Depression dampened America's growing appetite for auto-oriented family vacations, only the most well-known and easily accessed attractions seemed to have the capacity to survive, and then only through the business acumen and determination of their owners. Those that survived the Depression did so by various economic coping strategies, an important one being farming. This was a viable option only if there was enough land on the property and the knowhow to farm it. Penn's Cave had originally been incidental to the farm, then a supportive sideline. Even when the cave became the primary occupation, the land was still tilled to supplement the seasonal income generated by the tourist business. Bill Campbell raised beef cattle and a variety of grain and forage crops. He married Sara Odenkirk in 1938, and together they raised their only daughter, Jeanne, at the Penn's Cave Hotel. Under Bill's supervision, the cave rarely closed. When visitors arrived, whatever work was being done around the farm was halted to take them through the cave. Even mealtimes could be interrupted by the crunch of tourist tires on the gravel parking lot.

Crystal Cave was surrounded by farmland, but the popularity of the attraction had allowed it to abandon agriculture years before. A large barn that once supported this activity was torn down to make way for parking in 1928, when much of Crystal Cave's former farm fields were being planted with thousands of trees to create a more natural setting. The evergreen-cloaked glen that cups Crystal Cave today like a primordial forest owes its existence to deliberate landscaping decisions made in the 1920s. Complementing the forested slopes, the cave's substantial natural stone-faced entrance was laid in 1935. Crystal's notoriety and market proximity allowed it to weather the Depression better than most other caves.

The Gilman family had just moved into their Spanish Mission–style house and ticket office at Lost Cave when the Depression set in. Committed to their dream of running a show cave, the Gilmans continued to make underground improvements while augmenting their income any

Mirroring national trends in forest conservation, Crystal Cave planted thousands of trees on its property, then constructed a new cave entrance in 1935 in a style similar to Civilian Conservation Corps buildings.

way they could. As a reminder of these tough times, a storage shed still stands that was constructed as a chicken coop where two thousand hens laid eggs during the 1930s. As a trained civil engineer, a handy skill to have for developing a show cave, Erwin Gilman supplemented his income through public school and road-building contracts, while his wife worked at a nearby textile mill. Erwin also made crafts to sell at the cave, including wooden jigsaw puzzles. They even showed outdoor movies on summer evenings, projecting the film on a bedsheet for patrons who paid a nickel each.

Some show cave operators perfected the sideline circus during the Depression. When the crash left Hubby and Lenore Wertz with only $50 to their name, they were forced to rethink the operation. It was immediately apparent that auto-oriented tourism would not keep them through Pennsylvania's long, cold winters, so they closed up the cave for the season, packed their two young children into the car, and drove to Miami, where Hubby opened the Aboriginal Golf miniature golf course. They soon sold it and bought a souvenir-selling Indian trading post in nearby Hallandale. For the next twelve years, the Wertzes wintered in Florida and returned each summer to run the cave.

An early roadside showman, Hubby Wertz now made his living in two different states by selling everything Indian to the tourist. His trading post drew heavily from southern Florida's Seminole culture and craft items readily available at nearby reservations. Each spring, he loaded tourist trade goods into the car to stock the shelves at Indian Cave, adding to them Cherokee and Chickasaw crafts picked up en route. Exotic flora and fauna were packed to Pennsylvania as well, including two hundred baby alligators that made the trip one year to be sold from a pit dug at the cave. Wertz's American-Indian amalgam was augmented by the Algonquin and Iroquois culture presented by Two Cities and crew camped at the cave each summer.

All the while, Hubby and Lenore's son Harold Jr. was learning the business. Destined to be known as "Bear" Wertz, Harold Jr. guided his first cave tour at age ten and became a partner in the business at fourteen. Tragically, Lenore Wertz was killed in a Florida traffic accident in 1941. That summer, Bear returned to Pennsylvania alone to run the cave. He was eighteen. The trading post was shut down for good, and the family reunited in Pennsylvania. Although it had survived the Depression, the Historic Indian Cave was finally forced to close in 1942 due to travel restrictions imposed during World War II.

Woodward Cave provided a different kind of roadside show. During the Depression years, penned animal attractions were becoming popular, and the number-one, crowd-pleasing Pennsylvania roadside circus animal had to be the bear. Penned white-tailed deer were a favorite, but nothing could beat a caged den of bears for traffic-stopping fun. Bear cages sprang up all over the roadside, at gas stations, cafés, resorts, and

Dorothy Burd at the bear den used to house Old Bill and Maggie during the 1930s.

attractions. As a native species, black bears were lumbering clichés of the Pennsylvania mountain country, and their omnivorous habits could be easily exploited for the amusement of tourists.

Ollie Hosterman brought bears to Woodward Cave in 1934. Maggie, Old Bill, and their cubs were set up in concrete dens within a caged area near the entrance to the cave. Although a hit with the tourists, their act did not run long. That September, a flash flood broke through the dike, sending water down Pine Creek's old channel where the bear den now was. The bears were turned loose, and in a state of agitation, Old Bill attacked Earl Vonada, one of the cave guides. While Earl's wife and son beat on the bear with rocks, a flashlight, and an umbrella, Ollie ran for his shotgun. Old Bill took one to the throat, and Maggie took to the hills. She was later tracked down and also shot. The cubs stayed on for a while, enjoying free rein of the place, but were eventually sold to a gas station and fruit stand in Bloomsburg.

New Depression-Era Show Caves: Lincoln and Baker

Road building was the salvation of down-and-out America, keeping millions off the dole by constructing the modern infrastructure needed for economic recovery. The quaint names of the old privately sponsored auto trails were fading in the face of a standardized system of numbered shields that were erected along every new section of hard-surfaced highway as soon as the concrete dried. Public funds were available to straighten treacherous curves and level steep gradients by cutting through rocky spurs and using the shattered earth to fill in the adjacent hollows. The resulting all-weather highways left twisting remnants of older roadway in their wake to ossify off the beaten path.

By the spring of 1930, road-building crews reshaping the old William Penn Highway into a modern U.S. Route 22 had arrived in Huntingdon County to realign the road over Warrior Ridge. While pounding a road cut through a spur of Helderberg limestone, a worker lost a drill bit into a subterranean chamber. As more of the rock was removed, workers realized they had sliced into the front room of an extensive cave that glistened with dripstone. Curious members of the road crew penetrated the cave's dark recesses, snatching a few speleo souvenirs, and drinking from a cool pool of water that would one day capture tourist pennies as Lincoln Caverns's Wishing Well.

For Harry B. Stewart, the farmer who owned the land, it was like someone had found a gold mine on his property: a show cave located directly on the state's second most important trans-Appalachian trunk

The old William Penn Highway (Old U.S. Route 22) bends to the left down the west flank of Warrior Ridge. To the right is the straight stretch of current U.S. Route 22 that was under construction in May 1930, when Lincoln Caverns was discovered.

road. But like a gold mine, it would require a tremendous amount of investment before any payout would ever be realized.

After the road crew finished its task, Stewart boarded up the cave entrance and set to work with his sons Lester, George, and Warren through the winter of 1930–31. They dug out passageways and leveled floors, carrying the fill across the new road to build up a parking area. Since the cave's front room had been cleaved in half by the highway, they were forced to close the gaping hole with a 35-foot-high masonry wall. The roof was reinforced with steel I-beams that supported a wooden ceiling installed to collect small bits of dirt and rock that occasionally rained down. This was to be the Lobby Room, where tickets and souvenirs were purchased. The wall safe can still be seen from these early days.

As they worked building walkways and pouring concrete steps, the Stewarts conjured up names for the cave's noteworthy features, mixing Old World romantic classics with modern New World references. A deep hole off the Lobby Room was christened the Devil's Pit, and for years tourists were told that it was bottomless. The highway workers' drinking fountain was rechristened the Bath of the Nymphs. The watery sump at the cave's lowest point was reinterpreted as Sunset Lake and a flowstone wall became the Great Falls before taking a more recognizable form as Frozen Niagara.

As soon as the passageways were cleared of clay, the Stewarts had the cave surveyed. They discovered that a short tunnel opening a crawlway beyond the Palace of Splendor would connect with Pagoda Avenue, making a desirable tour loop. Harry Stewart named the subsequent cut the Holland Tunnel, after the engineering marvel that had opened beneath the Hudson River just three years before. Rural electrification programs had made generators unnecessary. To accentuate the aesthetic qualities of the cave, the Stewarts needed only to tap into the power line that was erected along the new road.

Harry Stewart chose the name Hi-wa-may Caverns, referencing the highway responsible for its discovery and the month it was discovered in with a cryptic word play that looked and sounded somewhat Indian-like. Opening ceremonies on June 25, 1931, were an unself-conscious Renaissance union of reason and religion, featuring Ralph W. Stone's address on the "Antiquity of Cave Man" followed by a convocation and formal cave opening by Hartslog Valley's Rev. J. Madison Hare. A year later, the cave was up for sale.

Giving up on the confusing and easily mispronounced Hi-wa-may name in February 1932, Harry renamed the cave William Penn Caverns, a strong name that honored Pennsylvania's historic founder while also serving as a convenient highway location identifier. He even hung a photograph of the original 1763 property deed bearing the names of proprietors Thomas and Richard Penn in the office. What he did not expect was the persistent, annoying visitor question, "Where are the boats?" followed by the inevitable sigh of disappointment when they were told the boats were at Penn's Cave, not William Penn Caverns.

While looking to unload the cave, Harry diversified his holdings, building a restaurant and gas station on the fill located across Route 22 from the entrance door. This was the new show cave complement, providing food and fuel for passing motorists without the need for a sizable hotel. One of those motorists passing by was Myron C. Dunlavy, traveling between his Buffalo home and potential Virginia show caves. Myron drew a paycheck as a manager for the New York Telephone Company in Albion but had the heart of a showman. He had been involved with vaudeville, owned a theater, operated an amusement park, and was in the market for a cave. Having 500 feet of well-decorated passageways with satisfactory dimensions and a great location, William Penn Caverns adequately covered the commercial cave criteria. Myron leased the cave and restaurant in 1932, making the rounds through the banks in Huntingdon to pay off the outstanding debt accumulated by the Stewarts. He hired a manager to run the operation, and it proved successful

TICKET OFFICE & PARKING AREA
Lincoln Caverns
Huntingdon, Pennsylvania

This 1950s postcard shows the parking lot and ticket office constructed on fill dumped on the side of U.S. Route 22 opposite Lincoln Caverns. DEAN SNYDER

enough after five years that Myron sought financial backing from a couple of New York businessmen and bought the 40-acre cave property and underground rights for the rest of the Stewart farm. His first order of business was to change the name of the cave to that of his favorite president, Abraham Lincoln.

A fire consumed the restaurant in the Dunlavys' first year of ownership, but it was soon replaced by the new Lincoln Caverns Restaurant and ticket office. Later in October, Myron shoved a steel rod through a clay plug at the end of Pagoda Avenue and discovered a cavity beyond. Subsequent digging revealed a calcite-encrusted room containing live flies and two bats. Logically, the sealed room had to have at least a small opening to the outside world, but that didn't matter. It was a mystery as to how those critters got in there, and the Mystery Room it became when the chamber was added to the tour.

In September 1941, a teenage Myron Dunlavy Jr. made the greatest Lincoln Caverns discovery since the hole was opened eleven years before. Winter snows always seemed to melt first at the bottom of a small sinkhole on the hill above the cave. This suggested that a column of relatively warm air was rising from a fissure in the ground. Myron Jr. found this fissure by digging through the bottom of the sinkhole and entered a whole new world. The passage opened up after a tight crawl, then dropped down into a 16-foot-high chamber flanked by two thin columns. After an Easter Sunday service was held there, the chamber came to be known as the Chapel Room.

The sound of wind through the entrance caused Myron Jr. to christen the find Whisper Rocks. There was nearly as much cave in Whisper Rocks as there was down the hill at Lincoln, but a long-sought connection between the two needed to extend the tour was never found. Within three months of the discovery, the United States was at war, and like so many other show caves, Lincoln Caverns was shut down from 1942 to war's end in 1945. Further development would have to wait.

In the 1930 edition of *Pennsylvania Caves,* Ralph Stone claimed to have visited three caves in the vicinity of Williamson, a small Franklin County hamlet surrounded by limestone quarries. Two were deemed "commercially impracticable" and "uninteresting," but the third had potential. Stone reported that the cave had considerable dripstone, and was visited annually by boys from Mercersburg Academy. Although he lamented that the cave had been "despoiled of its best dripstone," he hopefully proclaimed that its development for "commercial exhibition could be done rather easily." By the printing of the 1932 edition, his challenge had been taken up.

One of the Natural Wonders of Pennsylvania
BAKER CAVERNS - Williamson, Pa.
11 Miles South of Chambersburg, Pa.

A combination ticket office and residence was constructed over the entrance to Baker Caverns in time for its 1932 opening. The door to the cave was on the opposite side of the house, beneath the porch. DEAN SNYDER

The cave was at the bottom of a collapsed sinkhole, a mere 30 feet from the Williamson-Upton Road. The discovery story claimed that John Coffy had broken into the cave in 1830 while quarrying building stone, and for much of its history, it was known as Coffey Cave. Quarrying would continue to play a major role in the life, and business death, of the cave. O. G. Edwards and M. L. Burgan, former guides at Maryland's Crystal Grottoes, leased the cave from J. E. Baker, a quarry operator who had recently purchased the property. When it opened on July 2, 1932, it bore the name of the landowner, Baker Caverns.

To bring this cave to life, Edwards and Burgan built a concrete stairway into the sink and through the ceiling of a large strike passage with a 10- to 15-foot ceiling. A large frame house was built over the sinkhole, with steps descending beneath the porch. The house functioned as the cave's gift shop and ticket office. Although the interior passageways were steeply sloped, a problem mitigated with the insertion of three more staircases, the cave geometry south of the entrance created a

The entrance stairway into Baker Caverns, and the passage north, to the right of the steps.

natural loop, leading visitors past a travertine bridge, rimstone ledges, soda straws, dripstones, and the cave's famous Umbrella, a flowstone canopy that had formed over cave clay that was subsequently eroded away.

It was the cave's north end that presented the greatest challenge. Breakdown blocked the main strike passage, restricting access to a parallel 150-foot crawlway with a maximum clearance of only 3 feet. Such a tube is more like the average tourist's nightmare than something people would be willing to pay money to experience. Once again, human ingenuity was relied on to showcase nature's subterranean splendor. A 20-foot-long concrete tunnel was driven through the collapse and into Echo Hall. The difficult access had protected Baker Caverns's north end from the effects of precommercial vandals. Stalagmites, a column blackened with manganese, and a white flowstone cascade decorated the passage, which led to a large room with a vaulted ceiling 20 feet high. Following the cave-naming tradition, Edwards and Burgan labeled this the Cathedral, which naturally contained a Pulpit and a flowstone Pipe Organ.

Failed Attempts at Creating Show Caves

Even though some natural grottoes seemed to have all the criteria needed for success as a show cave, attempts to commercialize them never panned out. In 1930, M. J. Wyrsich bought a Cumberland County farm that contained a well-known cave. It looked out over the Yellow Breeches floodplain a half mile north of Walnut Bottom. What the small cavern lacked in attributes, Wyrsich attempted to make up for in determination. He shoveled out the cave, piling the clay in heaps at the entrance. But the Depression continued to worsen, and by 1933, all work on the cave had ceased. A few years later, Yellow Breeches Creek overflowed its banks and redeposited Wyrsich's clay piles right back in the cave.

It was probably inevitable that Pennsylvania would get its own Mammoth Cave. This grandly labeled cave was first discovered as an innocuous, shallow crawlway on Billy Womer's Perry County farm near Elliottsburg. The outcropping of Silurian Tonoloway limestone was quarried for fertilizer lime, as was typical for karst-country farms in Pennsylvania. Then in 1914, Frank Leonard slithered into the hole and, illuminating it with a candle, found a walkable corridor. Four thousand feet of passage stretched off into the darkness. Leonard was convinced that he had found the cave he was looking for since his inspiring trip to Luray Caverns. Within a week, he had a twenty-year lease in which he promised to share equally any profits realized from the commercialization of the cave with Womer.

Frank and the occasional labor crew spent years digging out mud, building bridges, and opening passageways. The enlarged entrance was sealed with a steel door through which a handful of tours of what Leonard originally called Elliottsburg Caverns were led for 10 to 25 cents per person. Tourists delighted in leaving behind proof of their visit using a medium common to Pennsylvania caves—mud. Signatures were etched into muddy backroom floors, where tourists also fashioned their names and other figurines out of rolled and molded clay, leaving the personalized lumps affixed to walls and rocks.

At some point, a banner bearing the name Mammoth Caverns was suspended over the cave's access lane. The lease passed on to Bill Sheibley, who had accompanied Leonard on his first exploration of the cave and shared his desire to commercialize it. Sheibley named many cave features using references to state politics. The largest room of the cave was named the Supreme Court, with its seven large stalagmite columns, called the Justices of the Court, each named for a present incumbent. He christened another room the Department of the Interior, naming its central column after politician Harold L. Ickes.

Its name did not help Pennsylvania's Mammoth Cave achieve success, however. It was remotely located, muddy, and though dripstone was present, it was not abundant. Still undeveloped by 1942, the cave owners had missed their window of opportunity. The lease was not renewed, and interest waned. Sometime during the 1940s, a local quarry operator working the outcropping blasted a heaping load of overburden down over the entrance and sealed the cave.

7

Caves, Kids, and
Modern Mass Tourism

During the 1930s and 1940s, America's perception of its natural environments began to change. Mythically referenced, spiritual interpretations of nature once characterized by the sublime, the picturesque, and the beautiful were being supplanted by more scientific explanations. The interior tour circuits of all the show caves had long been enhanced by stories, myths, and legends, but these were now becoming out of sync with the trend toward modernization.

The miracles of the machine age—electric wizardry, modern medicine, airplanes, and automobiles—encapsulated the spirit of American progress, a feeling that was only enhanced by the deprivations of the Depression. Buck Rogers and the World's Fairs, Chicago's Century of Progress (1933–34), and New York's World of Tomorrow (1939–40) prepped the American populace for a post-Depression filled with wonder and prosperity predicated on the rationality of science and technology. In a radical shift away from traditional place-based cave references, Tennessee's Cherokee Caverns was renamed Atomic Caverns in the 1950s after the Atomic Energy Commission's nearby Oak Ridge National Laboratory. Although the name was short-lived, it represented the lengths to which tourist attractions were willing to go to embrace modernity. As a more nefarious by-product of the modern atomic age, many show caves, including Indian Echo, were certified and signed as official fallout shelters.

Sophisticated, modern Americans could live with both a rustically framed Grand Canyon and a wilderness-taming Hoover Dam, so long as they did not compete for the same scene. They were less likely to tolerate old-fashioned myth making in the face of scientific facts.

After fifteen years of depression and wartime restrictions, the economy was soaring on pent-up consumer demand and capital investments needed to retool and rebuild. The federal government subsidized housing, highways, and higher education. Postwar incomes rose, babies boomed, and the annual family vacation became an accepted summertime event. Each year, tens of thousands of middle-class Americans packed up the car and took to the road.

Wertz's Historic Indian Cave was one of the eleven Pennsylvania show caves to survive the Great Depression and World War II and realize the dawn of the greatest period of tourist expansion in American history. Hubby Wertz recognized that the new era required a new name for the cave and a new spirit of business cooperation. He organized the Pennsylvania Cave Men's Association in 1948 to unite the state's show cave operators under a banner of mutual assistance and coordination in matters related to the promotion and presentation of their scenic wonders. He also changed the name of his operation to Indian Caverns, recognizing that unaware tourists looking for standard show cave stalactites and stalagmites were mistakenly assuming that his cave was more a rockshelter with Indian artifacts, and taking their business to Lincoln Caverns. The new name emphasized both aspects of the attraction. The five hundred Indian artifacts displayed at the cave, and their association with the cave's history, were still a major part of the Indian Caverns experience.

Inevitably, this collection would come under the scrutiny of academics. Aside from the artifacts, the cave also displayed a rock tablet depicting "Indian picture writing" claimed to have been found in the Indian Council Room. The tablet was presented as the tombstone to a Mohawk chief buried in the cave. Etchings included a tepee with the flap open, implying that the chief's body was present but his spirit was gone. A turtle indicated the Mohawk tribe, and five strokes referred to its affiliation with the Iroquois confederation. A peace pipe suggested this to be a peaceful chief, and a semicircle symbolized heaven and earth.

Archeologists John Witthoft and Sam S. Farver visited the cave on October 10, 1950, as part of Witthoft's research on the validity of the cave as an important American Indian archeological site. Witthoft verified that twenty-three specimens and photographs from Indian Caverns had been sent to State Museum director Boyd P. Rothrock in 1929 and exhibited. In his estimation, however, the stone tablet was a newly carved fake. The artifacts displayed at the cave included some of local origin and others from places as far away as Arkansas, Michigan, Missouri, the Great Plains, and the American Southwest. Witthoft asserted that while the artifacts were genuine, most of the collection had probably passed through the relic trade rather than having been discovered at the cave.

The impact of Witthoft's findings on the public presentation of Indian Caverns was negligible. Apparently the traveling public did not read the *Pennsylvania Archaeologist,* or care about its assessment, and the colorful interpretation of the cave was passed down intact from father to son. Although certain named features and geologic facts have changed with the times, the core text still used to train the current generation of Indian Caverns tour guides was written by Lenore Wertz, Bear Wertz's mother, before World War II. The text preserved a different type of oral tradition, that of the cave itself and its presentation as a tourist attraction. Though academics found it intolerable, show cave tourists had come to accept a certain amount of ambiguity between the information and the entertainment received.

The baby boom ushered in a new era of mass auto tourism, so it was to be expected that show caves would be catering to kids in the 1950s. The stories were now reinterpreted with fewer Old World references to accommodate mid-twentieth-century children. The Indian angle played big in a postwar America increasingly obsessed with tales of the Old West. This meant less awestruck contemplation of the sublime, and more cowboys and Indians. Television and Hollywood movies, rather than Cooper, Longfellow, or even Shoemaker, provided the direct reference. Show cave gift shops stocked moccasins, rubber-tipped tomahawks, and toy tom-toms; at least three Pennsylvania caves sported

Teepees and totem poles—show cave visual shorthand for Indians. AUTHOR'S COLLECTION

tepees like the ones seen on TV; and cartoon brave Chief Kumsee made his appearance to promote Indian Echo Caverns.

Like the cave he would one day own, Edward Stover Swartz had suffered during the Great Depression. Forced out of a banking career in Marcus Hook, Pennsylvania, Ed returned home to Hummelstown and opened a service station on the square, a business later expanded into Swartz Service and Electric. Like Myron Dunlavy and Hubby Wertz, Ed Swartz had the showman's spirit needed to prevail along roadside America. Country-western music and comedy acts that he sponsored on a South Hanover Street lot drew such crowds that the events had to be moved to Blue Rock Park, on the banks of Swatara Creek, and then Clown Park on Chambers Hill.

People took notice—most importantly, the bank that held the papers to the bankrupt Indian Echo Cave. They suggested that Ed purchase the property and combine his entertainment show with the cave operation. Ed accepted their proposition and bought the slightly renamed Indian Echo Caverns in 1942. He developed a steep-sided hollow opening toward Swatara Creek on the north side of the property into Echo Dell, a natural amphitheater for shows. Country-western acts were a favorite at Echo Dell, which booked well-known performers from movies and radio, such as Roy Acuff of "Grand Ole Opry." Despite its initial success, attendance waned at Echo Dell immediately following the war. The final curtain was drawn in 1947, but by then the cavern sideshow had taken center stage.

The postwar popularity of Indian Echo Caverns supported a major capital improvement program that included a new souvenir and refreshment building, restrooms, playground, picnic pavilion to accommodate three hundred, and the limestone block entrance to the cave with the letters "I. E. C." embossed over the doorway in concrete. On July 16, 1961, Indian Echo Caverns received its largest single group ever, when 1,200 people arrived on an excursion train from Philadelphia that followed the Reading Railroad's Middletown and Hummelstown branch directly to the cave. This trip closed the book on train travel to Pennsylvania show caves.

Carloads of kids and parents led an upswing in attendance at the other show caves as well, where similar improvements were made. At Lost River Caverns, the Gilmans constructed a new entrance building against the wall of the old quarry in 1955, converting the exposed rock face into a jungle scene of tropical plants and animal mounts. The rest of the building was eventually filled with an antique gun collection and

ONYX CAVE

NEAR HAMBURG, PA.

a rock shop. At Indian Caverns, a second story was added to the cave-side gift shop in 1954, which lost its former adobe appearance beneath a modern facade of white stucco. At different times, Lincoln Caverns guests were treated to the somber presence of an Abraham Lincoln impersonator and the antics of two monkeys named Maggie and Jigs. A 1947 advertisement announced the adoption of curb service at the Lincoln Caverns Restaurant from 6:00 P.M. to 2:00 A.M. nightly.

Because the new highways often bypassed show cave locations, the entire business was more dependent on billboards than ever before. Railroad-era advertising had emphasized guidebooks and periodicals. The train knew the way; all the tourist had to do was decide to go. Now, however, show caves that had survived the Depression depended on an ever-expanding network of vividly hued, well-placed billboards to draw tourists. Dozens of signs were needed to plant the idea of a cave visit, and dozens more to lure potential visitors off the main highway and keep them from getting discouraged while trekking down back roads that under any other circumstance would be seen only if the travelers were lost. Bear Wertz spent a good portion of his business life seeking out new sign sites and maintaining the signs that were already up. At their peak, one thousand signs advertised the way to Indian Caverns, the farthest outpost being Fayetteville, North Carolina, where Bear's sister lived, 500 miles from the cave. Penn's Cave employed two hired hands to maintain their network of more than one hundred signs. While on the road, cave promoters also placed thousands of colorful brochures in racks throughout the state and into surrounding ones as another primary form of advertisement.

Through superlative-laden billboards and brochures, tourists came to recognize Penn's Cave by a simple, four-word declarative statement, "See it by Boat," to which a "World Famous" Indian Caverns billboard responded, "See it on Foot!" Woodward Cave became "The Big One," and Coral Caverns "Nature's Wonderland," similar to "Nature's Underground Wonderland" at Lost River, and Indian Echo where visitors could

view "nature's masterpiece of underground architecture." A Crystal Cave brochure promised a "dazzling arena of crystal magnificence," and a Lincoln Caverns brochure claimed it to be "PA's Most Beautiful." An Onyx Caverns brochure boldly pronounced the cave to be "one of the longest caverns in eastern Pennsylvania."

The cave business was brisk and continued to grow throughout the 1960s. Penn's Cave had broken its annual attendance record in 1949 and did so again in 1969. Indian Caverns had its best year in 1972. Success, however, was not assured. One freshly developed postwar show cave died nearly at birth, another did not even get that far, and two other established caverns followed them down.

Postwar Caves Lost and Found: Tytoona, Harlansburg, Baker, Alexander, Whisper Rocks, and Laurel

Myrtle L. Kiser bought the Sinking Valley Cave, located upstream from Arch Spring, in 1930. It was not until 1947, however, that the cave was ready to be shown. By then Kiser had erected a roadside ticket booth at the edge of the cave sink, constructed steps down to the gaping opening, and cleared a clay path about 400 feet to the back of the cave. After fabricating the name Tytoona Cave from the nearby towns of Tyrone and Altoona, Kiser was ready for business.

Tytoona has a dramatic discovery story reminiscent of the Mariposa Battalion's Indian pursuit that revealed Yosemite Valley in 1851. The Bedford Rangers reportedly chased a band of hostile Indians into the cave sometime during the 1750s. The Indians never came out, suggesting that they died in the cave, found another yet-to-be discovered opening, or simply eluded their would-be captors. Adding further drama, historical accounts frequently described the sump at the end of the cave as a swirling vortex that could swallow all that floated into it. Despite these fascinating stories, Tytoona was off the beaten path about a dozen miles southwest of Indian Caverns and never became successful as a show cave. The operation folded within the year.

A road-building crew cutting through a ledge of Pennsylvanian-age Vanport limestone for a new alignment of PA Route 108 west of Harlansburg relived the Lincoln Caverns discovery story. This time the road cut sliced through the center of a vast maze of intersecting passageways, revealing seven openings on both sides of the road. Roofed by a protecting layer of Kittanning sandstone not more than 30 feet below the surface, the cave was wet, muddy, and hopelessly confusing, with tight passages that seemed to wander on endlessly.

Before the first attempt to commercialize it, Tytoona Cave was known as Sinking Valley Cave. DEAN SNYDER

Harlansburg Cave, as it was soon called, attracted the immediate attention of amateur spelunkers, college science departments, and Challice Bruce, who leased the cave from property owner Anna Johnson, intending to commercialize it. Within a month, scientists from the Carnegie Museum pushed 3,600 feet into the darkness without finding an end. Expeditions went on for nine hours, finding only more cave. Bruce seemed to have plenty of cave to play with and began stringing wire while hired surveyors mapped the passageways. Unfortunately, the cave was not well decorated, most of the passages were claustrophobia inducing, and the thick, heavy mud seemed unconquerable. Bruce died in 1961, his dream unfulfilled. Although Harlansburg Cave was never developed, its 22,000 feet of mapped passage have pushed it to the top of the state's longest cave list. And still there is no end in sight.

A postcard dated August 28, 1954, began, "Dear Mabel, We were at Baker Caverns yesterday. It was very beautiful. If you haven't seen it, come down before November. They are going to close it." Baker Caverns was indeed closing, even though it was a successful operation.

Originally operating the cave on a 99-year lease, Martin L. Burgan purchased the property in 1942–43 after the death of landowner J. E. Baker. By 1954, however, Burgan was seventy-two and suffering heart problems. He sold the cave to Bethlehem Steel, which was assembling a 3,185-acre limestone reserve. Fortunately, the cave was not quarried away, but it was also never operated commercially again. In 1988, Beth-lehem Steel sold its holdings to a consortium of farmers who subdivided the land among themselves. Since then, the Baker Caverns property has been owned by Lee and Dean Myers.

Previously shuttered by Depression and flood, Alexander Caverns received a new resident manager, who reopened the cave in 1940. With wartime travel restrictions looming, the cave did only moderate business, but it was poised for impressive returns after the war. At least that is what manager Luther Kepler believed. The cave's owner had a different sense. When Kepler's lease expired in 1954, the cave farm was put up for sale. Kepler put in a bid but lost to Amish dairy farmer Mose Hostetler, who had absolutely no intention of showing the cave. The farm is now run by Mose's grandson Henry, who considers the long-remembered show cave something of a nuisance because of the people it still attracts even though it has not been open to the public for half a century.

Some tourist caves collapsed while others expanded. At Lincoln Caverns, Myron "Mike" Dunlavy Jr.'s Whisper Rocks discovery was being shoveled out and wired for light. As nature had neglected to provide a conduit between this upper grotto and the main cave, the Dunlavys were forced to bring tourists from Lincoln Caverns back out into the light of day, and troop them up the hill to a new entrance dug into the opposite end of the passage from Mike's discovery hole. Rather than detract from the attraction, the daylight link allowed it to be billed as two caves for the price of one. Whisper Rocks no longer whispered, probably due to the change in air circulation caused by the new opening, but the name was too evocative to give up. Inside, tourists were awed by a treasure trove of formations labeled in the time-honored way of show cave tradition. Visitors entered the high-ceilinged Ancient Tomb on their way to Diamond Cascade, a calcite crystal studded flowstone that was a larger version of the Purity Cascade seen down in the main cavern. Beyond the Keyhole, a matching white stalagmite-stalactite set were given the sobriquet King and Queen, and Twin Columns flanked the Chapel Room, one of them that could be viewed as a Cave Man with a Pole. In a nearby alcove, ceiling dripstone suspended over a mass of stalagmites was interpreted as a diminutive Cloud over the Giant's Castle. Whisper Rocks also contained its own melodious Pipe Organ. Just inside the door, like a foyer separated from the main house, the utilitarian Tool Room carried the casual name of its function, a place where tools were stored during the commercialization of the cave.

Whisper Rocks opened with advertising fanfare in 1961. A drought that same year lowered Lost River Cavern's Lost Lake to unprecedented levels, revealing a lost chamber studded with a wealth of speleothems.

The Gilmans christened the chamber the Queen's Room and contemplated its inclusion in the tour. The cave, however, was not going to give this treasure up easily, resealing the access with water when Lost Lake returned to its normal level. The Queen's Room was well photographed while accessible, and the images were framed and hung on the gift shop wall. The Queen's Room remained "lost," referenced on the tour but enjoyed only vicariously through the photographs, and on rare occasions by cavers when droughts cause a similar drop in the water table.

By far the biggest postwar addition to Pennsylvania's subterranean showplaces came with the commercialization of Delaney's Cave. It seems ironic that such a large cave with so long a history as a tourist curiosity, celebrated in novel and linked to local legend, would be the last cave commercialized. Although it was on the Victorian rail and ride circuit when tourists secured mounts and rode up Cave Hollow from the station at Fairchance, or along the ridge from one of the resorts, the cave was poorly located with respect to hard-surfaced early auto roads. The Cave Hollow trail was widened into a rough mountain road but never improved, and a decent ridgetop road running south from U.S. Route 40 (the National Road) was not constructed until the 1930s. Still, the cave was a popular outing and picnic place.

"Underground Chapel"

Tourists in the Chapel Room, flanked by Twin Columns, after Whisper Rocks was added to the Lincoln Caverns tour in 1961. DEAN SNYDER

Delaney's sprawled beneath hundreds of acres, and in order to effectively protect and control access to the cave, all of this land had to be assembled into a single property. Roy Cale, having grown up in the region, saw Delaney's Cave as a local landmark and jumped at the chance to own it when it came up for sale in 1926. He and his cousin Norman Cale, a Pittsburgh accountant, purchased the 40-acre tract that contained the cave entrance. They later purchased the adjacent tract with the help of additional partners, Roy's half-brother Charles Henry Cale and a friend, Wayne Jones.

Before initiating the dirty job of development, the Cales had Ralph "Buzz"

Bossart survey the cave. Buzz was a local caving enthusiast with a civil-engineering degree from Penn State, class of 1931. He had been exploring the cave since 1921, and he spent much of the 1930s working at the cave site, sometimes camping there for months at a time. Buzz and other friends and associates who came and went supported their meager lifestyle by charging cave visitors 10 cents to park in a lot they had hacked out at the top of the rough Cave Hollow road. By decade's end, a much better road had been completed by the state south along the ridge crest from a junction with U.S. Route 40 at Mount Summit Inn, making the cave more easily accessible by car.

The results of Buzz's survey showed that the Cales did not own all of the surface land above the cave, but they did own some land under which the cave wasn't. The Cales spent the next two decades buying and selling land on Chestnut Ridge, owning at one point more than 1,000 acres, but eventually whittling this down to the 429 acres needed to secure the

Norman Cale in the entrance to Laurel Caverns before it was developed, around 1961. DAVID CALE

cave. Their greatest concern had always been to outflank potential quarry operators from destroying the cave or its scenic ridgetop setting.

As time passed, interest in the cave waxed and waned. Roy Cale died in 1942, his passion for developing the cave having been passed to Norman, who eventually bought out all of the other investors and brought in his wife, Helen, as a partner. The Cales had missed the opportunity to open Delaney's during the show cave boom of the 1920s, but they were in a much better position to catch the wave when it came around again after World War II.

With a plan drawn up by Buzz Bossart to commercialize the upper maze part of the cave, Paul Gaskill, a local mining contractor, was hired to start moving dirt in 1961. The job was as huge as the cave itself. Laurel's long, steep passages were thought to be too much of a deterrent for most visitors, and tons of rock would have to be removed from the deep passage below the Dining Room in order to grade a walkable path. To minimize the amount of vertical climbing visitors would have to do and the amount of rock removed, initial development was limited to the upper Catacombs.

The cave's old Main Entrance was avoided because it did not connect directly with the maze. Instead, the small upper entry was opened with a bulldozer, providing access into the main strike passage. The opening was then resealed with a stone wall and door. The cave's extensive network of passageways was choked with sand. To provide a minimum 8-foot clearance, at least 5 feet of sand had to be removed from nearly every inch of passage. Gaskill erected a tramway to remove 500 pounds of sand per trip in a cart hoisted out to a hillside dump by a stationary engine.

Unlike Pennsylvania's other show cave development projects, which had numerous calcite formations but few passageways, Delaney's had few speleothems but a vast network of passageways. The tour circuit was mapped out through this maze to provide vistas of underground chambers, far-reaching conduits that stretched off into the darkness, and weird geologic forms shaped by the power of running water, all enhanced by both colored lights and sound.

The cave opened with a new name, Laurel Caverns. Norman's grandson David Cale suggested the name, dropping the long-standing reference to a family that had not been around for more than a century to adopt the name inspired by John Paxton's article of 1816, which called

The entrance to Laurel Caverns on opening day, July 1, 1964, showing the cave's first paying customer. DAVID CALE

it the Laurel Hill Cave. David was on hand to lead the first guided tour on July 1, 1964. The first family that went in just happened to have seen the newly erected billboards and wanted to visit a cave, not realizing it was opening day and they would be the inaugural tour group.

Tours were conducted through the sand maze to the precipice above Devil's Staircase, past the sculptured Pillar of Hercules, and then to the head of Grand Canyon Passage, where visitors were treated to a rousing sound and light show accompanied by the "Grand Canyon Suite." Laurel Caverns inherited the well-known names, legends, and rumors accumulated during Delaney's Cave's long history. The Devil's Staircase, the Dining Room with its table, chair and piano rock pile, Fat Man's Misery, the Ball Room, Post Office, Rainbow Canopy, and Sleepy Rock were already on K. A. Long's map of the cave in 1927. In fact, the known and named limits to the cave lay well beyond the upper maze to which the first tours were restricted. The old maps also located the Liberty Tubes, a short dual

David Cale's wife, Lillian, at the Pillar of Hercules. DAVID CALE

passageway in the upper maze given a modern reference to the Liberty Tunnels, which opened beneath Mount Washington to connect Pittsburgh with the South Hills suburbs in 1924. Similar to Lincoln Caverns's Holland Tunnel reference, this put Laurel squarely in Pittsburgh's sphere of influence.

More Laurel Caverns legends have been forgotten than have been fabricated for most other show caves. Indian tales are largely absent, but the cave has in times past been reported to contain a whirlpooling lake and to contain deep passages that link up with Virginia's Luray Caverns and even Mammoth Cave. Rumored Laurel Caverns treasure has included French brass cannons, train robbery loot, 115 tons of silver bars secreted away from invading British during the War of 1812, and a 1937 claim that local resident Clarence Higgenbotham found a pot of gold containing $30,000. This outlandish hoax attracted thousands of hopeful treasure hunters to the slopes of Chestnut Ridge.

Handing Over the Reins

Six of Pennsylvania's show caves became generational operations during the postwar boom years, passing from one generation to the next like the family farm. During that same period, corporate chains came to dominate the American roadside, but it's difficult to franchise a cave. They continue to be family run and owner operated.

Edwin and Marie Gilman's son Robert and his wife, Naomi, took over the reins at Lost River Caverns, a vocation they were destined to inherit after exchanging their wedding vows in the cave in 1949. Crystal Cave passed from J. Douglas Kaufman and Edwin L. DeLong to Doug S. Kaufman and Jim DeLong. Edward O. Swartz learned the ropes at Indian Echo from his father, Edward Stover Swartz; Edwin S. Bear Wertz took over the management of Indian Caverns from Hubby Wertz; and Lincoln Caverns passed from Myron Dunlavy Sr. to Myron Dunlavy Jr.

Second-generation Penn's Cave owner Bill Campbell and his wife, Sara, were married in 1938, and therefore were well-established cave operators by the postwar years when their daughter Jeanne was growing up. The Campbells lived at the hotel, so the cave and farm were home to Jeanne since back before she could even remember. She does, however, remember her father's dedication to the business and his adherence to the principles of tradition. Jeanne was free to accompany the tours, but as far as work went, her father saw the cave as no place for a woman. The realm of mud, rock, work boots, and boat motors, the cave was an extension of the farm, and tours were conducted by Bill or one of the farmhands whenever anyone showed up and pressed a bell at the ticket office near the cave entrance. Jeanne was tutored by her mother as a clerk in the gift shop, learning the trade through inventories, balanced cash drawers, account books, and customer relations. Bill was notorious for his unwavering tour presentations, which he recited to the word as his father had taught him.

In contrast to the generational operations, three other caves were sold and resold. Lewis and Hattie Snyder sold Onyx Cave to Gordon Frazer in 1957. Frazer ran the cave through the postwar glory years to his retirement in 1976 and was responsible for constructing its modern concrete entranceway. H. G. Whitmeyer had a similar tenure at Woodward Cave. Ollie Hosterman had passed from the show cave scene, and Whitmeyer operated the business from 1958 to 1971. Woodward was then sold to Henry and Dorothy Burd. Henry had worked for the Philadelphia Federal Reserve bank before bringing his family out of suburban New Jersey to start a new life as show cave entrepreneurs in the hills of central Pennsylvania.

Tour guides at what was once the exit from Coral Caverns. The 50-foot tunnel, bored in 1966, has functioned as the entrance and exit since the original entrance was sealed in 1985.

The "Wonderland" was dropped from Coral Caverns in 1966, when it was taken over by *Bedford Gazette* editor Hugo K. Frear and Edward McDevitt of Ed's Steakhouse. Frear and McDevitt built a new ticket office at the base of the hill and carried visitors up to the cave in a jeep tram outfitted to look like a train named the Dinosaur Express. They also reconfigured the tour, boring a 50-foot, I-beam-stabilized tunnel out the back of the cave and into the old north quarry, where through-routed cave trippers could reboard the Dinosaur Express for a ride back down to the parking lot. Although the Devonian rocks in which the cave was formed predated dinosaurs by nearly 200 million years, dinosaurs, like cowboys and Indians, were another frequently fictionalized feature exploited along the roadside because of their kid appeal.

The ownership of Laurel Caverns took a peculiar twist, being sold out of the Cale family, then gradually making its way back in. By the time Laurel Caverns opened, Norman Cale was seventy years old, and his wife, Helen, wanted a more peaceful retirement. Having invested more than three decades of effort, Norman and Helen sold the cave after only one open season. The new owners were Ned Nakles and Emmet Boyle Jr., who hired David Cale as cave manager in 1965. David was the persistent family link in the operation. When Nakles and Boyle considered leaving the business, David Cale found new buyers in Don and Eunice Shoemaker, owners of the nearby Mt. Summit Inn. The sale went through in 1972, and David was cut in for a quarter share. By then a new visitor center had been built around the entrance to Laurel Caverns, opening for the 1970 season. In 1986, David and his wife, Lilian, bought the cave.

If not labeled Ballrooms, large interior chambers are likely to be called Cathedral Rooms or Chapels. Five such rooms exist in Pennsylvania, and some of them have seen more than their share of weddings. Weddings have occurred in every one of Pennsylvania's currently operating show caves except Lincoln and Indian.

The earliest recorded Pennsylvania show cave wedding took place on October 15, 1919, in Crystal Cave. Philadelphia couple Marion Kurtz and Francis Finley had visited the cave the previous summer and decided that it was the perfect place to get married. A piano was carried into the cave, and a natural altar was decorated with flowers and ferns near the Frozen Fountain (now the Upside Down Ice Cream Cone). David Kohler made the most of the free publicity, and several hundred people showed up at the cave that day. The wedding was front-page news in Kutztown and Reading, and for years afterward Kohler sold postcards of the event. Despite the crowd-pleasing appeal of the wedding, the idea never caught on at Crystal Cave, and the next one did not occur until a couple of former cave guides got married there in the 1980s.

Lost River Caverns has turned matrimony into a regular cottage industry. Robert and Naomi Gilman's 1949 cave wedding was the first of nearly one hundred that have taken place there. No other cave comes close. To accommodate these blessed events, wall sconces for candles and an altar were set up in the Ball Room, which was renamed the Crystal Chapel.

Indian Echo also caters to the small cave wedding crowd, and maybe half a dozen marriages have taken place there over the last twenty years. Indian Echo's favorite tale of wedding romance is that of a little girl who, while on a school trip, tossed a coin in the Wishing Well and secretly wished to one day be married in the beautiful wonderland that surrounded her. Years later, her wish came true when she married a boy from her class who had tossed a coin into the Wishing Well on that same trip. The highlight of the wedding was when the newlyweds once again cast coins into the well, wishing for eternal marital bliss. The romance of weddings replaced the waning imagery of Old World myths in the reinterpretation of the Diamond Fairyland as the Wedding Chapel. The bridge now spans Wedding Lake, where visitors can view the elaborate Wedding Cake formation and Rustic Honeymoon Falls and the glistening, calcite crystal studded Honeymoon Ski Slope.

Michael Burd, the youngest son of Henry Burd, was married in Woodward Cave in 1974. Coral Caverns experienced its only wedding when Steve Hall was married there soon after purchasing the cave in 1984.

A few private weddings have taken place at Penn's Cave since the 1970s, the most memorable being a 1990 affair between a young couple who had met at the cave while working there. The ceremony was conducted after the bridal party emerged from the misty darkness of the cave by boat. Seven weddings have been held in the Chapel Room at Laurel Caverns, a chamber now outfitted with a dramatic colored light display that is synchronized to the "Hallelujah Chorus."

The Next Generation

The postwar boom ended somewhere between the Vietnam War and the turmoil in the Middle East. The second boom for caves came to an end as well, for multiple reasons.

A concern in the 1960s for highway beautification, particularly along the new interstates then under construction, led to legislation regulating billboards. Complex and inconsistent from state to state, these regulations adversely affected the show cave businesses, which drew much of its trade with billboards. Then, in the 1970s, theme parks like Walt Disney World and Six Flags opened, changing the meaning of the family vacation. With the Arab oil embargo of 1973, gasoline shortages curbed family day trips to nearby caves.

Beleaguered cave entrepreneurs who had started before the war were ready for retirement. It seemed like a good time to get out. After Gordon Frazer retired in 1976, Onyx Cave sat idle for two years. It was reopened by Lou Rizzo, and then resold in 1983, the last year it operated as a show cave. Frear and McDevitt sold Coral Caverns a year later.

But some people from the next generation were still optimistic. In 1967, Art Kiser bought Tytoona Cave from his father, Myrtle, for $1. Art was determined to do what his father couldn't—commercialize the cave. He regraded the paths; added steps, railings, and electric lights; and was ready to open under the name Indian River Caverns in July 1972. On June 21, the rainy remains of Hurricane Agnes parked itself over Pennsylvania and dumped as much as 19 inches over the next five days. The Tytoona fenster filled up with water bubbling from the cliff rise and pouring down the hillside from the surrounding fields, turning the sinkhole into a lake. The flood piled up a logjam at the back of the cave that is still there. In the debris were Art Kiser's wiring, railings, and step timbers. Indian River Caverns would never open.

Also preparing to open a Cave in 1972 were Henry and Dorothy Burd, who were getting Woodward ready for their first season as show

A large group poses in Woodward Cave, many cloaked in the cave's Indian blankets. DEAN SNYDER

cave proprietors when Agnes struck. Another sink cave, Woodward too was vulnerable. After days of steady rain on already soggy ground, Pine Creek overflowed the dike and rediscovered its old channel, flooding the gift shop and sending muddy water into the cave. Indian Echo, which normally sits 18 feet above Swatara Creek, was also flooded. The flooding did no permanent damage at either cave.

By now the interior layouts for every cave except Laurel were essentially set. Any future expansion of the cave business would have to take place on the surface. Crystal Cave went through a surface expansion program that began with the Dutch Hex Souvenir Barn (now the Fast Food Building) in 1968, followed by the Dutch Food Center (today's Ice Cream Parlor) in 1972. A miniature golf course and a new orientation building both opened in 1976.

By the end of the 1980s, most of Pennsylvania's show caves were being run by a whole new generation. This next generation brought a more scientific approach to understanding ecosystems and an increased emphasis on conservation and environmental sustainability, and these things began to influence how cave owners interpreted the caves and their formations. Cave science, conservation, education, and wild caving are all part of the new era of modern show caving. Plenty of imagination formations are still being shown, and the old legends are not entirely lost, but they are increasingly being presented alongside narratives highlighting natural science and development history. In nearly every case, the new owners have made significant capital investments to improve, expand, and diversify the business. Whereas previous generations saw themselves as cave discoverers, explorers, and developers, owners in this generation are more likely to view themselves as stewards, temporary caretakers of timeless and priceless natural wonders entrusted to them to be passed on for future generations.

A recent manifestation of cave stewardship is the commemoration of the past through memorials and museums that have begun to appear at the show caves. A commemorative wall of fame has emerged at Indian Caverns consisting of five bronze plaques preserving the memory of people, events, and interpretive perceptions.

Two of the plaques honor the cave's two owners. Harold A. "Hubby" Wertz Sr., and his son, Harold A. "Bear" Wertz Jr. Dedicated in 1997, Bear Wertz's plaque commemorates his 60 years of dedicated leadership. Bear ran the show at Indian Caverns until his death in January 2004. His grandson, Harold Aden Wertz IV, has since assumed command.

Like their father, siblings Robert, Charles, and Beverly Gilman grew up at Lost River Caverns. As with Penn's Cave's Jeanne Campbell, Beverly spent more time in and around the gift shop than in the cave. Married now as Beverly Rosewicz, she and her brother Bob have owned Lost River since 1989. Today most of the space in the entrance building is devoted to their rock shop and jewelry and lapidary supply house. In the Breakdown Room at the far end of the cave, visitors are treated to a fluorescent rock demonstration in which ultraviolet lights reveal the brilliant glow from specimens not from the cave itself, but from sources outside Pennsylvania. The Gilman Museum showcases big-game trophies, antique armor, and weaponry acquired by Beverly's father and grandfather.

Crystal Cave Corporation is into its third generation of Kaufmans and DeLongs. The Crystal Cave Museum opened with an Indian Trading Post in 1981. It is a storehouse of cave-related items that go back more than a century. Along with old postcards and brochures are the omnibus last used to transport visitors to the cave from the train station, 1876 bedroom furniture from the inn, the remains of the 1922 ice cream parlor, and a ticket machine from 1923.

Second-generation Edward O. Swartz took over Indian Echo Caverns in 1988. Gem Mill Junction was installed outside the gift shop a year later. Consisting of a wooden water trough where tourists sift through bags of dirt salted with gems, the gemstone sluice was a popular attraction added to show caves in the 1980s and 1990s.

The Burd brothers, Peter, Richard, and Michael, assumed control of Woodward Cave after the death of their father in 1987. That year they built a new visitor center with an expanded gift shop. Two years later, Woodward received its most famous visitor when Davy Jones of the

Posing at Penn's Cave's Giant Columns in this 1960 postcard view are proprietor Bill Campbell's daughter, and future proprietor, Jeanne and her husband, Russell Schleiden. PENN'S CAVE

Monkees showed up for a tour after having bought a horse farm in nearby Beavertown. His ticket and photograph are part of the Woodward Cave memorial display under glass in the gift shop. Davy Jones has been back to Woodward on other occasions, showing up with family and friends when they come to visit.

In 1964, a year after Bill Campbell took full ownership of Penn's Cave, his daughter Jeanne married Russell E. Schleiden, an Air Force man, avid sportsman, and future state game commissioner. Within two years of their 1968 return to the cave, Penn's Cave Airpark was constructed, and Russ was offering plane rides. Penn's Cave's diversification included trout fishing, camping, and guided snowmobile tours in the winter. Since 1982, however, they have operated the Penn's Cave Wildlife Park, featuring animals of North America. Boomer, the mountain lion, viewed on the descent to the cave, was the park's first acquisition. Jeanne assumed the presidency of Penn's Cave Corporation in 1983, and fourth-generation William Schleiden is now the vice president.

Myron and Marion Dunlavy's young daughter Patricia Ann appeared on her share of brochures and postcards for Lincoln Caverns. In 1977, now Ann Molosky, she became resident general manager and vice president of the company. Ann directed the rebuilding of the surface complex in the 1980s, including a new entrance for the cave. Ever since it was first commercialized, the Lincoln Caverns complex had been split by U.S. Route 22, with the parking lot, ticket office, gift shop, restaurant, and gas station all perched along a narrow shelf of fill along the west side of the highway, and the cave entrance through a hillside door on the east side. As highway traffic increased in volume and speed over the years, crossing the road was getting more difficult and dangerous. In addition, the plot offered no room to expand.

A much larger lot had been purchased on the east side of the road just north of the cave hill where the Moloskys lived. The site easily accommodated an expansive lot, new visitor center, meditation chapel, picnic pavilion, cave playground, and gem sluice. The only problem was that there was no easy access to the cave. Although the complex was on the right side of the road, cavebound tourists would still have to walk into the road cut along a narrow shoulder, with cars flying by only inches away. The solution was to bore into the cave through the back of the Mystery Room and seal off the original entrance. Opened in 1984, the new entrance is accessed by a peaceful sylvan stroll up the hill from the visitor center, a radical departure from the old approach.

Lincoln Caverns also hosts many school and scout trips, teaching kids about cave conservation, geology, bats, and other wildlife. To accommodate these programs, a learning center was added on to the visitor center in 1996, and a campground was established on Warrior Ridge in 2000. A popular annual event is the Ghosts and Goblins Haunted Cave Halloween Tour.

Coral Caverns was reinterpreted by two successive owners. Steve Hall moved from Baltimore to Bedford County in the late 1970s, when he purchased a farm there. He bought Coral Caverns in 1984 and was married in the cave a year later. Over the next two years, the Halls radically reoriented the property while Steve explored every crevice in his underground kingdom. They bought a new house on Main Street, and

The Lincoln Caverns complex moved to the cave side of U.S.Route 22 in the 1980s, necessitating a new entrance that now brings tours in through the Mystery Room.

then had it moved to the base of the cave hill. The Dinosaur Express was retired, and a new lot and gift shop/ticket office was constructed up the hill at the cave entrance, which became its exit. Coral Caverns's steep step descent was always a concern. One of the advantages Frear and McDevitt had realized by tunneling a new exit was that visitors no longer had to mount that long, slippery flight of stairs to get back out at the end of the tour. Steve Hall now sealed off the original entrance and its troublesome steps, using the exit as the entrance to a tour that doubled back on itself, going in as far as the base of the steps and then returning the same way. This completely reversed the tour from the way it was originally run, turning the steep steps into another cave feature rather than a conveyance.

Health problems forced Steve Hall to put the cave back up for sale in 1987. In 1992, it was purchased by Bill VanDeventer, an entrepreneur who initiated an extensive repair and restoration program at the cave. He built a house near the Hall house in 1998 that was soon home to his new wife, Kriss, her children, and Bill's parents.

Like many other show caves, Coral has a Cathedral Room, an Enchanted Forest, and a Painted Desert created through lighting effects, but the central signature feature has always been the Coral Reef Wall, interpreted relative to the historical geology of the cave. The current tour also incorporates a fair amount of Steve Hall history from the recent past, including the place where the Halls got married, the hole

Bill and Kriss VanDeventer and their sons continue the tradition of the family-owned and -operated show cave at Coral Caverns.

Steve went down to discover a room behind the stairs, and the 30-foot dome pit he descended to seek out more cave.

Although Laurel Caverns still has features from its past, David Cale's management has underscored modern innovations and cave science. Laurel Caverns has come up with some novel sound and light displays. The Chapel Room was converted into the Hallelujah Chorus Sound and Light Show Passage in 1991. A contest was held to come up with a lighting design for a passage between the top of the Grand Canyon and the Pillars of Hercules. The winning idea was a sound-activated corridor, named Vallanoren Passage after its young inventor. Visitors have to clap, yell, talk, sing, or make some other noise while passing through the corridor to keep the lights on.

Also in 1991, a meandering, 50-foot artificial tunnel was constructed from the visitor center to the predevelopment Main Entrance at the top of the Hall of the Mountain King. A flight of steps was built down the hall's steep slope. Since then, tours have gone down the Hall of the Mountain King and back up the paralleling Grand Canyon. In 1995, nearly 600 feet of passage were added to Laurel Caverns, already the biggest show cave in the state, when Cale Canyon was discovered as a parallel passage to the three connecting the upper Catacombs with the Dining Room. Although not on the tour, pristine Cale Canyon contains stalactites and other speleothems, implying that the Loyalhanna limestone cave's lack of dripstone is as much due to thoughtless souvenir hunters as to the high silica content of the rock.

Visitors can see Laurel Caverns by taking an accompanied exploring tour into the undeveloped parts of the cave as an alternative to the guided tour through the commercial part. Up until 1969, the bulk of the cave was beyond the reach of tourists. Because of their great length and cost of development, it was unlikely that the deeper passages would ever be added to the tour. That did not, however, stop people from wanting to see them. To accommodate this demand, Laurel Caverns began to offer wild caving to visitors providing their own lights.

Today Laurel Caverns offers accompanied High Adventure tours. Tourists don hardhats and carry flashlights or wear headlamps. Following the guide beyond the lighted path of the commercialized tour, adventuresome visitors crawl down through a crack in the ground, with only their own lights to show the way. For the next three hours, they walk, climb, crawl, and scramble through an underground jumble of massive boulder breakdown and sandy stream-cleared passage, with ceilings ranging from a high of 45 feet to as low as 3 feet. Some tight holes may be even lower. Over a mile of horizontal distance, visitors descend and reascend nearly 1,000 vertical feet, all of it underground.

After the steep, narrow passage from the Dining Room, the cave opens up into the Ballroom, where two underground streams converge. The stream followed is typically about as wide as a boot, sometimes two. It trickles beneath breakdown and over small, foot-size waterfall slots, the most noteworthy being a series of calcite-smoothed cataracts known as the Cascades. Deep in the bowels of the mountain, bus-size Sleepy Rock reclines in a side passage. Here High Adventure cavers are treated to a unique twist on "total darkness." Everyone is arranged with their left hands on the huge rock. Then all lights are quenched, and the group is invited to circumnavigate the boulder using touch alone. Although conducted with much hollering and good humor, the exercise is also an unsettling sample of what it would be like to be trapped in the cave without light.

Sleepy Rock was a noted stop for many early cavers, who then moved on to the Post Office, Laurel Caverns's writing room, where they smoked, chiseled, and painted their names onto the walls and ceiling. Marring the walls is forbidden today. Just beyond the Post Office, Millstream Passage intersects the main passage. It is named for its stream, described by 1816 cave explorer John Paxton as having a flow great enough to turn a mill wheel, a classic example of hyperbole common to the time period. The water in the Millstream could barely turn a hamster wheel.

Laurel Caverns's High Adventure wild caving and its more recent option of rappelling down Devil's Staircase are significant departures from how caves and other natural wonders have traditionally been experienced by tourists. This is nothing like show cave touring as it has come to be known since the 1920s. Oddly enough, it's a lot like cave touring as it was *before* the 1920s.

Other options for visitors to Laurel Caverns today are a twenty-five-minute surrey tram ride through the mountains, camping, panning for gemstones, and playing miniature golf in a simulated cave environment complete with the type of stalactites and stalagmites not found in the actual cave.

The Norman E. Cale Visitor Center honors the memory of David Cale's grandfather and pioneer developer at Laurel Caverns. Norman Cale died on his birthday, August 16, 1983. His wife, Helen, followed five years later. Their ashes are interred within a hillside memorial outside the visitor center, providing a tangible link to the human history scratched onto the surface of this timeless hole.

8

Other Rocky
Roadside Wonders

Profile Rocks

Similarly to cave formations, rock formations aboveground have also
been named for their resemblances to people, animals, or objects. The
difference between the cultural interpretation of surface geology and
that of subsurface geology is a matter of scale. In the confines of a cave,
every nook and knob can be scrutinized for imagined meaning. Out in
the great expanse of daylit landscape, however, Popeye has to be at least
the size of a house to warrant recognition worthy of a place name.

Profile rocks are the inverse of cave formations. The latter formed
underground due to the solubility of one of the weakest rocks, and the
former developed aboveground because of the resistance of some of the
strongest rocks. Tuscarora/Shawangunk quartzite, the rock that holds
up the ridges, accounts for a good portion of these features. Profile rocks
have also weathered from the Cambrian-age quartzites outcropping
along the anticlinal flanks of South Mountain. These profile rocks are
most associated with the Antietam and Weverton Formations.

As in caves, many formations were assigned religious or Indian references. Others were thought to resemble man-made structures or various animals.

High-seated rocks were often thought to resemble pulpits, castles, or
chimneys. Pennsylvania has at least six different Pulpit Rocks, and
Geyer and Bolles identified four Chimney Rocks and three Castle Rocks
in *Outstanding Geologic Features of Pennsylvania*.

A ridgetop jumble of exposed and weathered white quartzite caps the eastward-pointing Pinnacle of a Blue Mountain double-back in northernmost Berks County. One of the state's Pulpit Rocks stands high among the other boulders on the south-facing flank of the ridge. Dan's Pulpit rises from the same rock member on the north flank of the double-back in Schuylkill County. Another Tuscarora quartzite Pulpit stands above McConnellsburg on the rock's namesake Tuscarora Mountain. The Pulpit at Tuscarora Summit is well known among hang gliders, who use a launching platform at the site. Huntingdon County's Pulpit Rock is a spire of Devonian Ridgeley sandstone amid other rock towers and cliffs along the berm of the old road over Warrior Ridge, northwest of Huntingdon.

Separated by cliff recession along Sullivan County's Allegheny Front, Castle Rock stands as a stunning tower of Huntley Mountain conglomerate a mile down a jeep trail southeast from Eagles Mere. A second Castle Rock, held up by Bald Eagle conglomerate, rises above PA Route 880 just south of Ravensburg State Park in Clinton County. A third Castle Rock is just south of PA Route 3 in the Philadelphia suburb of Edgemont. This fortresslike pile of resistant rock is made up of an ancient Piedmont metamorphic rock known as enstatite. Its picturesque qualities and proximity to Philadelphia attracted developers, who used Castle Rock as the centerpiece in a housing development.

On the approach to Hollidaysburg, high up on Catfish Ridge to the south, Chimney Rocks, made of vertically tilted Tonoloway limestone, is a rank of grayish white towers standing among the trees. Another Chimney Rock, this one of Cambrian-age Chickies conglomerate, stands on the ridge a mile north of Hellam in York County.

Rock spires are common on the flanks of South Mountain. In addition to two more Chimney Rocks, the range has a Monument Rock, Sunset Rocks, and Pole Steeple. Monument Rock and one of the Chimney Rocks stand over Tumbling Run hollow, up from the Old Forge Ranger Station northeast of Waynesboro. They are part of the same outcrop of Weverton quartzite. Sunset Rocks (Weverton quartzite) and Pole Steeple (Harpers quartzite) are popular hiking destinations clustered around Pine Grove Furnace State Park. Pole Steeple is a fault scarp cliff of white rock overlooking Laurel Lake. The upthrown fault block was actually the one containing the valley that Pole Steeple rises above. Because of its former elevated location, the quartzite caprock was eroded more vigorously, exposing the weaker dolomites below, which were then quickly removed to a base level below the down-dropped Pole Steeple block still capped with resistant quartzite. The other Chimney Rocks are a lofty exposure of Antietam quartzite located northwest of Pine Grove Furnace along

High Mountain Road. Another formation, Lewis Rocks, named after the legendary nineteenth-century robber David Lewis, peaks along the ridge a few miles to the southwest. Including rock spires of Weverton quartzite and crevices formed by joint weathering and mass wasting, Lewis Rocks is accessible by an uphill hike through Dead Woman Hollow from PA Route 233 near the Adams-Cumberland County line.

To early agrarian place labelers, rocky, barren ground was frequently associated with the devil, for whom stony sites were often named. Combining the look of a pulpit with the rocky wasteland of the devil, Carbon County's Devil's Pulpit stands as a spire of Shawangunk quartzite on the west side of Lehigh Gap near Palmerton. The Lehigh River cuts through Blue Mountain at this location, exposing the outcropping of quartzite amid a talus scree of hillside boulders. Stony Ridge runs parallel to and immediately north of Blue Mountain. To northbound motorists exiting the Pennsylvania Turnpike's Lehigh Tunnel, this narrow spine of bare Ridgeley sandstone appears like the ruins of a massive wall constructed by some ancient civilization. It is known as the Devil's Wall. A similar feature of Pottsville conglomerate atop Sharp Mountain north of Swatara Gap, where I-81 crosses Blue Mountain, is called Chinese Wall.

Glen Onoko, Pa. Pulpit Rocks and Cascade

Guests at the nearby Wahnetah Hotel, the ladies in this postcard are enjoying a stroll through picturesque Glen Onoko to Pulpit Rocks (at left). Whether below ground or above, elaborately attired Victorian tourists needed level walkways, bridges, steps, and well-marked paths to experience nature.
AUTHOR'S COLLECTION

Sometimes the erosional differential in the outcropping caused the rocky surface to deteriorate at different rates, giving the formation the appearance of a face when viewed from the side. More resistant parts of the rock stand out or extend farther than less resistant parts. Resistant rocks, like sandstone, quartzite, and conglomerate, are likely to create cliff faces, while less resistant outcroppings, like shale, produce slopes. It is also common to have variable resistance in different parts of the same rock type. This all translates into the common occurrence of rocks that look like facial profiles, where alternating layers of resistance can appear as forehead (hard, cliff-forming rock), eye sockets (soft, recessive rocks), nose (hard rocks), mouth (soft rocks), chin (hard), and neck (soft). A prominent rocky nose coupled with the popular allusion to aboriginals at the time the features were named led to at least four such formations being labeled as Indians.

In addition to the classic chiseled profile, the towering mass of limy sandstone known as Indian Chief Rock has a curved top that sweeps back like a feathered warbonnet. The rocky profile stands just upstream from Williamsburg, at the entrance to the water gap carved by the Frankstown Branch of the Juniata River between Lock and Canoe Mountains.

Profile Rock juts out from a cliff face along PA Route 42 across the Susquehanna River from Catawissa. Its robust nose and prominent chin are nearly suspended over the roadway. In the early twentieth century, it was alternately known as the Indian Head. It is unknown when the residents of the upper Schuylkill Valley recognized an Indian profile in a large hillside boulder south of Pottsville, but a modern reaffirmation of its identity occurs periodically when the local Boy Scouts repaint the rock to accentuate its features. The painted block of Pocono sandstone overlooks PA Route 61 in the Schuylkill River water gap through Second Mountain.

Two cliff face Indian profiles are attributed to specific personalities. The more famous Indian Profile looks skyward from an outcropping of Shawangunk quartzite on Mount Tammany in the Delaware Water Gap. The profile is actually in New Jersey but cannot be seen unless you are across the river at a park pullout along PA Route 611. The profile is attributed to Chief Tammany, legendary friend of William Penn and canonized patron saint of patriots during the Revolution.

Farther west, another rocky profile looks east over the Susquehanna River from Blue Hill. It honors Chief Shikellamy, eighteenth-century Oneida ally when the

Shikellamy's Profile opposite Sunbury and Northumberland, Pa.

Chief Shikellamy's Profile overlooks the Susquehanna River at Sunbury.
AUTHOR'S COLLECTION

Colebrook's Sphinx-like Dinosaur Rock is made of the same Triassic diabase that outcrops in Gettysburg's Devil's Den.

upper Susquehanna Valley marked the frontier between the British colonies and the Iroquois nation. Blue Hill became Shikellamy State Park in 1960. Although the ongoing forces of erosion have taken their toll on the face, an observation deck still overlooks the floodwall in Sunbury.

Yet another such profile, down the Susquehanna at Half Falls, was named for Pennsylvania's most notorious antihero, Simon Girty. Born across the river in Halifax, Girty was raised by Senecas and fought with the Indians for the British on the frontier during the Revolution. Although assigned the identity of a local persona, these rocks hardly look like their namesake, unlike Washington's Profile in South Bethlehem's Sayre Park, which resembles the image seen on a quarter. Girty's Face was bypassed by the fast-moving, four-lane, divided U.S. Route 11-15, making the profile rock accessible only from the northbound lanes, with little to suggest that there is anything there to access.

A tall rock smack against an even taller rock appeared as an Indian Chair to unknown place name givers in two separate locations. One stands in the Brodhead Creek water gap through Godfrey Ridge just north of the Delaware Water Gap. The other rises from the flanks of Fulton County's Lowery Knob in the water gap Esther Run cut through Dickeys Mountain just east of Big Cove Tannery. Although separated by nearly 200 miles, the chairs' stratigraphic proximity is much closer. The Godfrey Ridge chair is Ridgeley sandstone, a resistant rock layer located just down the hill from the Tuscarora quartzite that holds up the Lowery Knob chair and the rest of Dickeys Mountain.

Although not named for Indians, Dial Rock was frequently described as an Indian sundial. Also known as Campbell's Ledge, the prominent fin of Pocono conglomerate is located within Lackawannock Gap where the Susquehanna River breaks into the Wyoming Valley near Pittston. According to legend, the Indians of the valley could tell when it was noon by watching the shadows on this south-facing ledge.

Animal formations abound in Pennsylvania caves, but out on the surface they are rarer. To be certain, Pennsylvania has no shortage of rock features named after animals, but they are more likely to be named for the creature that may have inhabited them rather than for the animals they happen to look like. On the list of animal look-alikes large enough to label is Turtle Rock, the rounded Burgoon sandstone mascot of Centre County's Black Moshannon State Park. In Lancaster County, a Furnace Hills ridgetop outcropping of quartz conglomerate 2 miles northwest of Brickerville has weathered into Eagle Rock. Dinosaur Rock, a heaping pile of spheroidal weathered diabase, is another Furnace Hills concoction located in the woods a mile south of Colebrook. A second Eagle Rock, weathered from Antietam quartzite, stands atop South Mountain up a constricted hollow named the Narrows, east from Mont Alto State Park. An Elephant Rock of Precambrian gneiss occupies a remote Northampton County hilltop a mile east of Raubsville.

Balanced Rocks

Balanced rocks have always been a favorite tourist attraction. There is something magically compelling about a giant boulder precariously perched as if the slightest breeze would topple it, yet standing firm against all manner of weather and mischief. There are at least a half dozen balanced rocks in Pennsylvania, dozens more nationwide, and countless snapshots of tourists posing as if to knock the rocks out of kilter, to no avail.

The classic balanced rock comes in one of two types: teetering or toddling. A teetering rock is a massive boulder balanced on the very edge of a cliff, commonly tilted toward the abyss like a seesaw. Toddling rocks are giant chunks of resistant capstone attached to relatively thin pedestals of rapidly eroding weaker rock. Truth be told, they're all doomed. Our first impression that they could topple at any instant is accurate, only the instant is measured in geologic time, over the course of centuries. The wind, water, and ice that have already eaten away

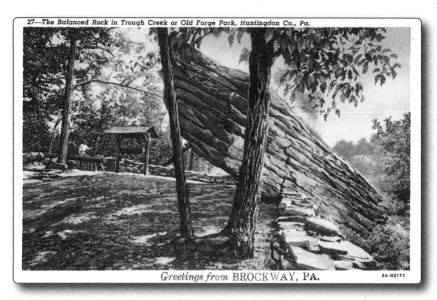

27—The Balanced Rock in Trough Creek or Old Forge Park, Huntingdon Co., Pa.

Greetings from BROCKWAY, PA.

SA-H2173

Nature balanced the rock, the Depression-era Civilian Conservation Corps provided the rustic landscaping, and the automobile brought the tourists.
AUTHOR'S COLLECTION

much of the cliff face or pedestal have only a little bit more to go to bring the rock down. That's the nature of erosion.

The balanced quartzite and conglomerate boulder at Sunset Rocks is teetering, securely resting on a base rock for the moment, but relentlessly attacked by forces of erosion that will inevitably send it careening down the slope. Trough Creek State Park's Balanced Rock is also teetering, a multiton mass of Pocono sandstone clinging to the edge of a cliff. The Balanced Rock at the edge of Pennsylvania's Grand Canyon is a toddling remnant of the receding cliff face left stranded on top of a weaker shale layer. Sullivan County's Ticklish Rock, an erosional remnant of Catskill sandstone, has been similarly isolated by the recession of the cliff face at the edge of the Allegheny Plateau.

Additional Balanced Rocks are found in Bedford County's Bald Knob State Park, at the edge of the Allegheny Front, and Gifford Pinchot State Park, south of York. The Pinchot Balanced Rock is a rounded boulder of Triassic diabase resting on two smaller pedestals. It is made from the same age, type of rock, and weathering process as Dinosaur Rock, 20 miles to the northeast. The spheroidal weathering that makes rounded rocks is controlled by a circular pattern of joints formed when the magma cooled and contracted.

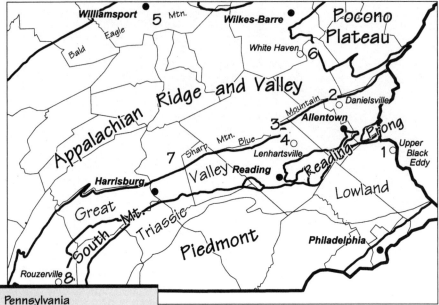

Boulder Fields

At the end of a long gravel drive through the woods of Hickory Run State Park, the trees break to a reveal a 60-acre plain of boulders devoid of all vegetation and life, with the exception of wandering tourists dwarfed by its mammoth scale. First-time visitors are frequently dumbfounded by the immensity of this alien landscape, a 400-foot-wide swath of boulders stretching off to the distant treeline a quarter mile away. Kids usually race right out onto the boulder field, scrambling over its irregular, rounded rock surface. The buff-colored sea of rocks has a pinkish hue to it and a surface that is not as level and homogeneous as it appears from the edge of the woods. It has a gentle slope that varies from 1 to 5 degrees. Boulders on the downhill side are smaller and more rounded than the angular blocks on the uphill side, which can reach lengths up to 25 feet, many of them upended like standing tablets. Boulders on the northern side of the field are made of sandstone; those toward the south are quartz conglomerate. Mysterious depressions out on the boulder field reveal that beneath the rocks are more rocks, up to 12 feet deep. Water can sometimes be heard trickling beneath the boulders. No one leaves unimpressed.

The Hickory Run Boulder Field is confounding because the processes that created it no longer exist in Pennsylvania, though they continue to be active far to the north in places like northern Canada and Alaska. It is a twenty-thousand-year-old echo from the prehistoric past, when Pennsylvania was gripped by an arctic climate that allowed 1,000-foot-thick lobes of glacial ice to push into the northeastern and northwestern corners of the future state. The boulder field was not deposited by glaciers, but formed in a periglacial—or near glacier—environment south and west of the terminal moraine, the low ridge of dirt and rock that marks the southernmost extent of glaciation. It shares its cold climate genesis with other rocky wonders all over the state, including several other boulder fields, dozens of quartzite talus slopes that interrupt the forests along the flanks of many ridges, and numerous rock cities.

A combination of coincidental occurrences caused the largest boulder field to form at Hickory Run, where the prerequisite cold climate, plentiful water supply, and hard rock outcrops all existed. The boulder field sits high up on the Hickory Run drainage basin, on the westernmost extension of the Pocono Plateau. This accounts for its low gradient. The Devonian Catskill sandstone and conglomerate that cap the plateau outcrop less than a mile upstream. The Champlain-Hudson Lobe of the Wisconsin ice sheet—a continental glacier stretching north to the Arctic Circle and as far west as the Great Plains—came to a grinding halt

Many first-time visitors to the Hickory Run Boulder Field are astounded by its immense proportions.

a mere mile to the north and east. All that was not buried in ice was tundra, a vast treeless environment with plenty of bare rock.

The exposed and fractured ledges of sandstone and conglomerate were attacked relentlessly by frost wedging. Water seeped into joints and cracks when summer daytime temperatures rose above 32 degrees, then crystallized into expanding ice wedges during nighttime freezes. Shattered blocks of rock tumbled to the base of the outcrop, accumulating as talus. While frost wedging created more talus, frost heaving carried the talus downslope. The ground and everything on it heaved upward, perpendicular to the slope, with each freeze but moved straight downward under the force of gravity with each thaw, shifting dirt, stone, and boulders slightly downhill with each cycle. Creep is a slow process, although more rock is moved faster when the entire mass-wasting event takes place over permafrost. At a certain depth, the ground in a polar climate never thaws. The weather just doesn't stay warm enough long enough. When the ground above the permafrost thaws, the water has no place to go, making a soupy, muddy mess that slowly slips downhill over the frozen subsurface in a process known as solifluction.

Rocks feeding into the boulder field from the north were quarried out of a sandstone layer tinged red with iron oxide; those from the east came from an outcrop of quartz-studded conglomerate. Rocks toward the toe of the boulder field traveled farther, experiencing a longer period of mechanical weathering that reduced their size and rounded their formerly sharp edges.

The polar climate assured that countless freeze-thaw cycles would occur over thousands of years. The nearby glacier provided plenty of water, and the outcrop contained an inexhaustible supply of rock. As the climate warmed at the end of the ice age, the retreating glacier sent torrents of meltwater over the boulder field, washing away the sand and silt, leaving behind larger cobbles and the biggest boulders. The headwaters of Hickory Run still flow beneath a boulder field that has been stationary since the retreat of the glaciers. Forests returned with the warming humid climate, encroaching onto the boulder field over a layer of humus deposited as accumulating leaf litter. Thus, the boulder field now is not only fairly static, but actually shrinking as more of it gets covered by forest.

The pits and depressions commonly found out on the boulder field, some deep enough to reach water, are caused by a more recent erosive process: humans. Curious tourists have been moving rocks on the boulder field since the early twentieth century. Some engaged in scientific study, measuring field depth, rock size, or hydrology. Others made stone mounds and pits for the same reason beachgoers make sand castles.

Unlike the majestic Delaware Water Gap, Hickory Run Boulder Field was underappreciated during the early years of tourism. Pocono Mountain resorts did not reach this remote western section of the plateau until well into the twentieth century. Plagued by thin, rocky soils and a short growing season, and mantled with deep forests, the plateau was passed over by agrarian settlers, who saddled the region with the barren title "Shades of Death" before moving on. The entire plateau was timbered over, then abandoned to flood and fire, which ravaged the region into the twentieth century. Allentown millionaire Harry C. Trexler bought the tract in 1918 to establish a state park. The region was reseeded and rearranged along the lines of recreation by the Civilian Conservation Corps during the 1930s and established as Hickory Run State Park in 1945. A year later, Split Rock Resort opened just to the northeast near a large, 25-foot-high outcrop of Catskill sandstone cleaved in two by a 5- to 6-foot gash.

There are other, lesser boulder fields in the vicinity of Hickory Run, including one on the opposite side of the drainage divide to the east near Big Boulder Ski Resort. South of the Pocono Plateau, three boulder fields are arrayed along the flanks of Blue Mountain: one in Little Gap, and two in the zigzagging double-back at the northern tip of Berks County. All three originate with the Shawangunk quartzite that outcrops at the top of the ridge. Like Hickory Run, they are the result of frost wedging, ground heave creep, and solifluction in a periglacial environment, and they have been largely stationary since the retreat of the Wisconsin ice sheet. Although their genesis is similar, boulder fields differ from the rocky talus slopes common to Shawangunk/Tuscarora quartzite ridges because of their low gradients and linear arrangement.

The Little Gap boulder field on the mountain just north of Danielsville is known as the Devil's Potato Patch. The aptly named River of Rocks is a long, narrow boulder field that occupies the head of Eckville Valley down from the Hawk Mountain Sanctuary. The Shawangunk quartzite ridge from which the boulders were drawn wraps around the hollow on three sides, forming a natural amphitheater. The same ridgetop outcrop is offset by the Eckville Fault and doubles back to the west from the Pinnacle. The white rock exposure from the Pinnacle to Pulpit Rock is the source ledge for the Blue Rocks Boulder Field, which extends down the slope to the south. River of Rocks and Blue Rocks actually rest on Martinsburg shale, which outcrops beneath and downslope from the Shawangunk quartzite. Rocks like these deposited downslope by some mass-wasting event are known as boulder colluvium.

River of Rocks and Blue Rocks have attracted tourists for over a century. The base of Blue Rocks was easily accessed from the Reading Railroad depot in Lenhartsville, the next stop north of the Virginville station serving Crystal Cave. During the 1930s, the Appalachian Trail was carved out along the crest of Blue Mountain above both boulder fields, and the Hawk Mountain Sanctuary was established as a safe haven and popular viewing platform for migratory hawks and eagles following the Great Valley flyway.

Farther west in Dauphin County, Blue Mountain's Silurian Shawangunk quartzite turns into Tuscarora quartzite. A synclinal basin parallels Blue Mountain to the north, causing the upturned rocks to get progressively younger as the synclinal axis is approached. Continuing north from the axis, the same upturned rocks are crossed again in reverse order, getting progressively older. Devonian shales and siltstones underlie the valley immediately north of Blue Mountain, then Second Mountain's ridge of Mississippian-age Pocono sandstone, followed by a narrow valley of Mauch Chunk red beds bordered to the north by the Pennsylvanian-age Pottsville conglomerate that holds up Sharp Mountain. A narrow valley of Llewellyn coals and shales—the southwest extension of the Lower Anthracite Field—sits along the synclinal axis, paralleled to the north by Pottsville conglomerate doubling back as Stony Mountain. Mauch Chunk shales return to the surface north of Stony Mountain in Clark Valley, then the Pocono sandstone of Peters Mountains, and the Devonian rocks beyond.

Cupped in the remote, narrow synclinal valley between Sharp and Stony Mountains is another head-of-hollow boulder field, surrounded on three sides by the double-backing ridge of Pottsville conglomerate. The Pennsylvanian Pottsville conglomerate is younger than the Silurian Tuscarora/Shawangunk quartzite by more than 100 million years. The Silurian sands eroded off the Taconian Mountains, which were reduced to plains and replaced by the Acadian Mountains, thrown up in the continental collision between Europe and North America before the erosion of this latter range provided the sands and gravels that went into the Pottsville conglomerate. Despite the unimaginably long time interval separating their origins, both rock layers are essentially made up of the same base material, which acted the same way when exposed to the periglacial climate of the last ice age. Blocks of Pottsville conglomerate were ice-wedged from the outcropping and deposited through mass wasting on the Llewellyn shales below, creating a boulder field 120 feet wide and 3,500 feet long that was ultimately interpreted by transplanted European Christians as the Devil's Race Course.

Sixty miles farther north, the Silurian Tuscarora quartzite outcrops again along the crest of Bald Eagle Mountain. Here, another boulder field formed at the same time and by the same process as the rest. The boulder field is in a gap long used as a shortcut to get to Williamsport from the lower Susquehanna Valley and now occupied by U.S. Route 15. Iron oxide in the rock causes many of the boulders to cast a pinkish to purple hue, leading early settlers to label this mountaintop piece of bad farmland the Devil's Turnip Patch.

Pennsylvania's South Mountain extension of the Blue Ridge is a physiographic province onto itself. In addition to its Cambrian quartzite profile rocks, it has a periglacial boulder field made from the same stratum. Weverton quartzite supports the South Mountain crest followed by the Appalachian Trail near the Maryland border. It is also the source rock for another boulder field labeled the Devil's Racecourse, which runs parallel to the ridge in the east cast shadow of Buzzards Roost. The Devil's Racecourse is just north of PA Route 16, on the mountain between Rouzerville and Blue Ridge Summit. The sound of trickling water beneath the boulder field belongs to the southward-flowing Devils Run.

The rocks in some boulder fields have the extraordinary ability to resonate like a bell when struck. Pennsylvania has several such boulder fields, the most noteworthy of which is in Ringing Rocks County Park, between Revere and Upper Black Eddy in Bucks County. Located within the Newark Basin Traissic lowland, the boulders of Ringing Rocks were frost-wedged out of a diabase sill. The igneous source rock originated as magma forced between the partings of red shales and sandstones deposited in a fault bound graben during the breakup of Pangaea that created the Atlantic Ocean basin. The diabase is loaded with plagioclase and pyroxene, two minerals that give the rock its dark color. In the old days, it was known as trap rock. Ringing Rocks sits at the edge of the Piedmont plateau and is drained by a run that tumbles over the escarpment to the nearby Delaware River.

For more than a century, visitors have been coming to Ringing Rocks to rap boulders in search of a tone not unlike that of a blacksmith's hammer against an iron anvil. The diabase does contain iron, but the resonance is more likely caused by the absorption of water into the outer surface of the rock, which converts the pyroxene into montmorillonite, a mineral common to clay. The montmorillonite swells at the molecular level, pulling the rock surface taut and allowing the crystals to resonate. The process does not uniformly affect all the rocks. Some rocks ring, but others do not. Like suspended bells, the best ringers are those perched on other rocks rather than rooted into the ground. The easiest way to find good ringers is to look for the nick marks where others have whacked them before.

Different rocks resonate at different pitches. This was a fact recognized by Dr. J. J. Ott in 1890, when he searched the boulder field for

Clever musicians have held rock concerts at Buck's county's Ringing Rocks Boulder Field by finding and playing stones with different tonal qualities.

rocks with just the right pitches to assemble an octave scale. Backed by a brass band, Ott played his rock music for the Buckwampum Historical Society. Many others have since followed in Ott's footstep, drawn to Ringing Rocks to conduct their own rock concerts.

Potholes

It somehow seems appropriate that Pennsylvania would have the world's largest pothole. Rather than proof of poor road maintenance, however, the pothole is more evidence from the state's glacial past. Potholes commonly form at the base of waterfalls, where turbulent water traps stones in swirling eddies that abrade a hole in the rocky streambed. For one of the higher Pocono falls, potholes 6 inches in diameter and 2 feet deep would not be unusual. The abrasive grindstones eventually wear away but are inevitably replaced by others that fall into the hole.

Truly massive potholes, on the order of 3 feet wide and 6 feet deep, can be found drilled into the hard metamorphic and igneous rocks of the lower Susquehanna River. Here the holes became so large that their grindstones broke through the walls into adjacent holes, resulting in a weird rocky landscape of curved forms and smooth surfaces surrounded by water. A 6-foot partial pothole is located along the shore of the river downstream from Holtwood Dam, but the greatest concentration of these features is at Conewago Falls, downstream from Three Mile Island. They are only visible during low water.

Conewago Falls is where the Susquehanna River cuts across the relatively resistant outcrop of Triassic diabase that extends between Lebanon County's Dinosaur Rock and Gettysburg. The current volume of the Susquehanna, however, could not account for potholes of this magnitude. They are the legacy of glacial meltwater that poured down the valley from the retreating Wisconsin ice sheet twenty thousand years ago, swelling the river many times its present size.

As big as the Susquehanna partial potholes are, they do not compare to the Archbald Pothole, a naturally excavated hole 38 feet deep with a surface opening 42 feet by 24 feet, a world record holder as far as potholes go. A pothole this large would require a Niagara-size waterfall 200 feet high, but this hole is curiously located in the middle of a broad valley where no such cliff exists. The pothole went unnoticed until 1884, when the *bottom* of it was discovered first. That year, underground coal miners working a seam beneath the Lackawanna Valley near Archbald dug into a mysterious column of rounded cobbles. In excavating the loose rock, they found the column extended 40 feet up to the surface through the shale and sandstone that rested on the coal seam.

Nothing remains of the waterfall's cliff, because it had literally melted away. The Archbald Pothole was drilled out by the swirling water and grindstones of an icebound river that flowed over or entirely within the Wisconsin glacier, before falling into a deep crevasse that extended down to a ground-level plunge pool. The water then flowed beneath the glacier to its terminal outlet. As the glacier retreated, the ephemeral ice crevasse collapsed, and the meltwater swept sand and cobblestones into the hole, filling it to the brim. The climate warmed and forests returned to the valley, camouflaging the pothole until miners dug into it thousands of years later.

Rock Cities

The cold climate of continental glaciation attacked the upended edges of resistant quartzite, conglomerate, and sandstone in the Appalachian ridges of central and eastern Pennsylvania. The combination of geology, geomorphology, and climate favored the formation of boulder fields and talus slopes throughout the region. These features, however, are not as prevalent in the dissected plateaus of western and northern Pennsylvania, where the geologic stratigraphy is more horizontal and rocks tend to outcrop in hillside ledges. Nonetheless, the Pleistocene glaciers were just as close, and frost wedging attacked the outcrops just as vigorously, resulting in periglacial rock cities.

Rock cities consist of great rectangular blocks of massive ledge stone eroded out of hillside perches and separated from one another by narrow, streetlike corridors. In places the blocks are tilted against each other, creating short tectonic caves, balanced rocks, natural bridges, and other interesting features that give the cities detail and texture. The strata most commonly associated with rock cities is the Pennsylvanian-age Pottsville Group. This massive layer of sandstone and conglomerate underlies the state's most productive coal seams. It outcrops as the upturned, ridge-forming edges of the anthracite fields in northeastern Pennsylvania and the exposed capstone on western Pennsylvania plateaus where the overlying bituminous coal seams have been eroded away. Over a dozen different rock cities have formed in Pottsville rocks, far more than any other rock type in the state.

The intense folding of the Pottsville Group in the anthracite fields has tilted and fractured the rocks, creating closely spaced joints that are more likely to erode into boulder fields and talus slopes. In western Pennsylvania, the same rock stratum has been uplifted without the extreme deformation, so that joints are widely spaced and outcrops are less severely dipped. These thick sandstones and conglomerates tend to rest on weaker shales that erode out faster when exposed, leaving the resistant outcrop unsupported and vulnerable to frost wedging and root wedging along the joints. If the massive sandstone-conglomerate layer is at the top of a slope, the joint-separated blocks will slowly move downhill under the force of gravity, widening the "streets" that make up the rock city.

Rock cities, natural features that mimic the rectilinearity of human landscapes, have long enchanted tourists. Pennsylvania rock cities are not as well known and more modest in scale and presentation than some found in other states, but were formed in the same way. Remoteness kept tourists from visiting them until the rise of state parks, forests, and recreational hiking. A concentration of rock cities stand in and around Allegheny National Forest, where the plateau caprock is Pottsville conglomerate, a hard, quartz-pebble-studded rock colloquially known as pudding stone. This same stratum makes up Olean's Rock City Park and New York's Panama Rocks.

Jakes Rocks overlooks the Allegheny Reservoir and is easily accessed from a national forest road south of PA Route 59. Warren Rocks is on the road to Scandia, 7 miles northeast of Warren. A number of rock cities line up on the drainage divide between Little Brokenstraw Creek and Mathews Run, north of U.S. Route 6 in western Warren County. The largest of these is Pikes Rocks, located up the hill 2 miles east of Wrightsville. Nuttles Rocks are a mile south along the same ridge. Baker Rocks is a stiff hike up onto the ridge north of Garland. The Devil's Den is a rock city developed in Mississippian Shenango sandstone on the ridge south of Smethport.

Farther south, Seneca Rocks is a Pottsville conglomerate rock city overlooking the Clarion River valley in Cook Forest State Park. It is one of the numerous Pennsylvania rock cities that have recently become more well known because of being in or near a state park. On the ridge-running drainage divide to the south, Seneca Rocks has a counterpart in Beartown Rocks, 4 miles east of Sigel off Pine Run Road.

Wolf Rocks is perched on the eastern rim of Linn Run Gorge, which is dissected into the western flank of Laurel Ridge. The Pottsville sandstone rock city is about a mile southeast of Linn Run State Park in Westmoreland County. In Somerset County, Mount Davis, highest point in the state at 3,213 feet above sea level, is underlain by Pottsville conglomerate. Not a stand-alone peak, Mount Davis is a high point along the crest of Negro Mountain. The white, pebbly conglomerate outcrops just north of the high-point lookout tower in a tight rock city known as Baughman Rocks. The narrow, 1-foot corridors between many of the blocks suggest that they have not yet separated much in their downhill creep. The formation gets its name from Henry Baughman, who beat his youngest son, August, with a stick in anger aroused by the frustration of searching for some lost cows. Thinking he had killed August, Henry hid the body among the rocks. On the testimony of his eldest son, Henry was convicted of second-degree murder, even though the rocks were searched and the body of his son was never found. Vought Rocks is a similar tightly set rock city a few miles farther north along Negro Mountain.

Far to the east in Sullivan County, Pottsville conglomerate outcrops again in the Labyrinth, located up the hill to the south from the Canyon Vista Overlook. Famous for its waterfalls, nearby Ricketts Glen State Park has the Midway Crevasse rock city, formed in Pocono sandstone on the hilltop bluff between Glen Leigh and Ganoga Glen.

Pennsylvania's most historic rock city jumble is the Devil's Den at Gettysburg, a stony citadel that protected Confederate troops in their attempt to take Little Round Top. It is generally assumed that the Devil's Den received its name from the hellish carnage that took place there in July 1863. In actuality, as yet another untillable outcrop, it was given this label years before the battle.

Unique among Pennsylvania's rock cities, Devil's Den is a pile of rounded boulders and blocks separated into passages, crevices, and

Spheroidal weathering of Triassic diabase created the nations most historic rock city: Gettysburg's Devil's Den.

short tectonic caves. It was created by both downhill creep toward Plum Run and the spheroidal weathering of Triassic diabase. This is the same igneous intrusive vein that shows up as Balanced Rock in Governor Pinchot State Park, crosses the Susquehanna River at Conewago Falls, and is heaped up to form Dinosaur Rock in Lebanon County.

When most other rock cities were known only to hunters and loggers, White Rocks, a massive ledge of Loyalhanna limestone atop Chestnut Ridge near Uniontown, achieved infamy with the May 12, 1810, murder of eighteen-year-old Polly Williams. Polly was allegedly thrown from the cliff by a suitor who lured her there with the ruse that they were on their way to the justice of the peace to be wed. Philip Rogers was tried for the crime but was not convicted because the evidence was circumstantial. The story was nonetheless sensationalized in the media, became the subject of poems and ballads, and then was fictionalized by local writer Ashbell F. Hill in 1865, under the title *The White Rocks; or, The Robber's Den.*

As often happens with blockbuster movies today, the story's setting became a well-known tourist attraction. Local guides took visitors on a circuit of places in the book, including Delaney's Cave—future Laurel Caverns—which set the scene for a chilling chapter in which the main character, called Philip Kirke, was lost underground. The highlight of the tour was a visit to White Rocks, some miles south along the ridge from

Delaney's Cave. Today the story has been all but forgotten. The gray rocks still stand upon the sylvan ridge but are visited only by those willing to undertake a forty-five-minute hike into the mountains and know where to look and what to look for.

Farther north along the crest of Chestnut Ridge, halfway between the Dunbar-Ohiopyle Road and the Youghiogheny River water gap, Elk Rock picked up some of the notoriety given to picturesque mountain locations in Fayette County resulting from the fame of White Rocks. Elk Rock is a beefy ledge of Allegheny sandstone (stratigraphically located above the Pottsville Group) standing amid an

When the story of Polly Williams faded, so did the tourist appeal of White Rocks, which stands on the slopes of Chestnut Ridge unchanged by the drop in notoriety.
AUTHOR'S COLLECTION

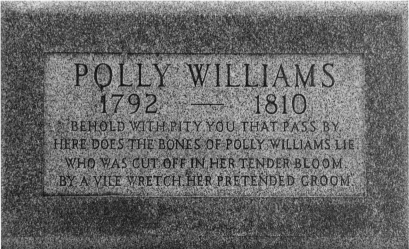

Polly Williams's previous headstone was chipped away by souvenir hunters. A more recent headstone marks her grave in White Rocks Church Cemetery north of Fairchance.

array of lesser erosional remnants cleaved from the larger block along vertical joints. Like White Rocks, Elk Rock is remotely located in deep forest and visited only by nature lovers willing to hike into the mountains to see it.

Having a long tradition as a local tourist attraction, Bilger's Rocks has become even more popular in recent years. This impressive rock city is about 5 miles north of Grampian and 2 miles east of U.S. Route 219 in Clearfield County. It was formed in the massive Homewood member of the Pottsville Group, a sandstone bed 20 to 25 feet thick overlying a thinner layer of shale. Although root wedging is evident, frost wedging in a periglacial climate accounts for most of its joint separations, which have cast adrift a rank of large, shed-size blocks that have slowly moved eastward downslope toward nearby Bilger Run. Many of the even larger, uphill western blocks are still attached to the outcropping. This causes the overall "street" pattern to be characterized by parallel north-south passages that are generally broader on the downhill east side of the rock city, and narrower toward the west. Intersecting cross-passages get wider to the east but funnel down into impenetrable cracks to the west. Some blocks are tilted, and others support natural bridge slabs that span the passageways. In places, the narrow defiles are entirely roofed over, presenting themselves as tectonic caves. The entire site is thoroughly wooded.

The rock city honors the original German settler Jacob Bilger, who owned the rocks as part of the property on which he homesteaded. In Clearfield County's conversion from agrarian frontier to industrial frontier, Bilger's descendants lost the land to a sheriff sale, where it was picked up by J. H. France Refractories. Stone quarrying, brick making, and coal mining were profitable pursuits in Clearfield County beginning in the late nineteenth century. Although mines and quarries were found throughout the area, Bilger's Rocks was not disturbed. Quite the contrary, its picturesque nature caused it to be a local outing destination for workers employed in the county's mineral industries and their families.

Bilger's Rocks had a ready-made network of picturesque paths that acquired the traditional appellations, some of which survived through oral tradition to the present day. The main passage into the rock city from the road eventually leads to a large, rectangular room bound by six 20-foot-high blocks separated by three narrow, parallel corridors that intersect the room at right angles. This is the rock city's central square, and it carries the name Devil's Dining Room. The far passage to the left narrows as it proceeds westward, passing a perpendicular passage to the right that ducks beneath an overhanging rock. This

Following an old farm-culture custom of naming barren, rocky land for the devil, the largest room at Bilger's Rocks is known as the Devil's Dining Room. A narrow crevice to the left leads to the Devil's Dungeon and the Devil's Kitchen.

gloomy, semidarkened passage is known as the Devil's Dungeon. The next passage parallel to and west of the dungeon is a smaller replica of the Devil's Dining Room, labeled consistently with the theme as the Devil's Kitchen.

The Ice Cave is a dark tunnel paralleling the main passage to the west. Water that collects on the floor of the southern entrance and freezes during the winter can occasionally still be seen in June, depending on the weather. The ice is shaded from the sun, protected by cold air drainage, and located at an elevation of 1,700, feet just 10 miles from the eastern Continental Divide. In short, summer is sometimes long in coming to Bilger's Rocks.

Like wild caves and other rocky wonders in the early days of tourism, Bilger's Rocks was a natural no-man's land where the average tourist trip included the contemplative pleasure of leaving behind an immortal mark. Since the open-air attraction did not require lanterns or candles, the inscription tool of choice was the chisel. Etched into the rocks are plenty of examples of "historic" graffiti.

Over the years, Bilger's Rocks became less visited by tourists and more of a youth hangout and party spot plagued by spray-paint graffiti

The most elaborate etching at Bilger's Rocks is John W. Larson's map of the world, finished in 1921 and captioned The World is Looking to Us, *his impression of the country's international role following World War I.*

and litter. In 1988, the nonprofit Bilger's Rocks Association was formed to restore the rocks to their natural beauty. Two years later, the association purchased the 173-acre property with state and local grants, and fund-raiser events.

Cold Air Cave

A talus slope of loose rock and boulders covers the base of both Mounts Tammany and Minsi on opposite sides of the river in the Delaware Water Gap. The rock was brought down from the Shawangunk layer over centuries of freeze-thaw action during the last glacial period. It is not unusual that the heaving, frost wedging, and movement of pitched boulder fields such as these creates openings among the rocks that can be entered as caves. One such talus cave in the base of Mount Minsi at the southern entrance to the Gap gained notoriety as Cold Air Cave.

The July 10, 1873, *Philadelphia Inquirer* reported that the cave was discovered around 1870 by a Mr. Frear, who was cutting timber on 100 acres of land he had just purchased on the south slope of Mount Minsi. After removing some rocks from around the opening, Frear was astonished to feel a rush of cold air that chilled him thoroughly and did not abate. In the sensationalistic writing style of the time, the newspaper reported that the interior of the cave contained a lead bar, a gun barrel, and bones—possibly human. It also stated that Frear's dog went into the cave, no more than 70 feet deep, and was never seen again. The article concluded with the declaration that the cave was "one of the greatest curiosities in the world."

Frear intended to excavate a passageway into the cave and erect a building over the entrance to accommodate visitors, but he died before he could put these plans into motion. The opportunity passed to Charles Nightingale, who developed Cold Air Cave in the first decade of the twentieth century and hired Mrs. Philip Sigafuss to run it. By 1907, a rustic cabin was built on the site to dispense hot dogs, ice cream, soda, and buttermilk to tourists, who could enter the cave through a connecting stone-walled passageway. The original cave tour, short as it was, used lanterns to illuminate the interior, but eventually electric lights were strung. Myrtle Williams and her son-in-law Arthur Cox succeeded Mrs. Sigafuss after her death in 1918. An open-air lunch pavilion was attached around 1920, and then the entire business was reconstructed to include a gift shop, restaurant, and gasoline pumps. Its location directly on the main road through the Delaware Water Gap, which became the route of the Stroudsburg, Water Gap, and Portland Railway's electric interurban line in 1911, helped make Cold Air Cave profitable. Only a short, inexpen-

This 1931 postcard shows the Cold Air Cave operation at its peak, with more ancillary activities—gas, food, souvenirs—than natural attraction. Today, only the natural attraction remains: the cave and a massive talus slope of Shawangunk quartzite and conglomerate. DEAN SNYDER

sive trolley ride separated Cold Air Cave from all of the Delaware Water Gap resorts. The streetcar arrived around the same time as its ultimate successor, the automobile, which forced the abandonment of the Water Gap line in 1926.

Cold Air Cave's big attraction was advertised as its constant temperature of 38 degrees, maintained on even the hottest of days. This mystified as well as refreshed summertime tourists traveling before the invention of air-conditioning. During the winter, cold air penetrates the mountain slope above the cave, where it is stored within the talus under an insulating blanket of rock, soil, and vegetation. The warm air rising at the base of the mountain in the summer draws the cold

Left: *Cold Air Cave at Delaware Water Gap.* Below: *Once an A-list natural attraction in northern Pennsylvania, the Coudersport ice Mine has faded from the tourist map.*

air down through the talus and out the mouth of the cave. Some such caves also baffled visitors with their ability to produce ice in the summer while remaining dry in the winter. If the cold-air draft was less than 32 degrees, it would cause any water trickling through the cave to freeze in the summertime, creating an ice cave.

Although seemingly contradictory, the occurrence is quite natural. Cold air will not drain through the ice cave until warmer weather causes the air at the mouth of the cave to rise, creating a low-pressure draft. This is also the time when spring meltwater and increased rainfall make more water available to freeze. Ice caves start producing ice in the spring, and then the ice gradually diminishes over the course of the summer, as the warming ground heats the air trapped within it.

The air temperature at Cold Air Cave was never low enough to freeze water, however, probably because of the shallow depth of its wintertime storage within a south-facing talus slope that would warm quickly in the summer. Recent studies have even brought into question whether it could even maintain a temperature as low as 38 degrees. It was nonetheless cool enough on a hot summer day to allow tourists to *believe* that it was 38 degrees.

Cold Air Cave still opens toward Route 611, the old Lackawanna Trail, at the southern entrance to the Delaware Water Gap. The attraction, gas station, and gift shop were closed by 1952, and soon afterward the building was destroyed by a fire of suspicious origin. Stone walls and steps still lead to a gaping hole among graffiti-marred rocks suggesting that *something* used to be here. The curious can still crawl into the darkness a short way, but no sign or marker explains why the air feels chilled.

Ice Mines

On a crisp, brilliant blue October afternoon I drove along U.S. Route 6 in search of what was once the most well-known natural tourist attraction west of Pennsylvania's Grand Canyon. Roadside billboards, postcards, brochures, and booklets once extolled the wonders of the Coudersport Ice Mine. The paraphernalia is all gone now. The billboards have been pulled down, and the paper products scattered to the winds to surface in the occasional antique shop. Like a closed show cave, however, I suspected the feature itself must still exist. Just about anybody who has lived in Potter County for more than twenty years remembers it, as well as many others around the country who visited this "wonderful freak of nature" when it was in its prime. Theories abound: that it was destroyed when the mountain above it was logged, or that it stopped producing ice after the hole was enlarged, or that it was "torn down." How could an attraction go from renowned to rumor over the course of a single generation? South of Sweden Valley, a chained-off driveway leads up a hill. Discarded on the ground to the side of the drive was an old sign blanketed with a freshly fallen layer of leaves. Two black-lettered words peeked out from beneath the golden leaf litter: Ice Mine.

Although not immediately obvious by name or appearance, the formation of state's boulder fields, rock cities, and even profile rocks was hastened along by the influences of an ice climate. It seems oddly ironic, then, that Pennsylvania's ice mines, also known as *glacieres* or devil's ice boxes, have nothing to do with glaciers. Like more intense versions of the Delaware Water Gap's Cold Air Cave, ice mines are sinks that capture trapped winter air as it drains beneath a mountain slope during the summer. If the draining air temperature is less than 32 degrees, any water that collects in the mine will freeze. What makes the natural phenomenon such a compelling attraction is that the ice begins to form in the spring and lasts into summer. A hundred years ago, telling tourists sweltering in 90-degree summer heat that they could be taken to a chilly hole in the ground rimmed with giant icicles was mystifying enough to induce them to pay for the privilege of seeing it. Thus Ice Mine was born as a tourist attraction.

Ice mines rely on an uphill slope where cold air can be stored in the winter. Beneath the soil on the forested, north-facing slope above the Coudersport Ice Mine is a zone of broken Devonian Lock Haven shale that traps cold winter air that settles on the mountainside. The frigid air maintains its temperature due to the insulating effects of the soil, vegetation, and frequent blankets of snow, which tend to stay around for prolonged periods of time because of the slope aspect. Just like at Cold Air Cave, the chilled air is heavy, creating localized high pressure that prevents the air from draining out. When the ground is warmed at the base of the mountain in the spring, the rising warm air allows the cold air stored in the rubble beneath the slope to drain out the bottom. Tectonic caves, excavations, or depressions that collect dripping water at the bottom of the slope will start to produce ice as the cold air drains out in the spring. As warming outside temperatures gradually penetrate the hill slope by midsummer, the draining cold air warms above freezing, and the ice begins to melt. By September, as the cold season nears, the ice is usually gone. The entire process, however, is variable depending on the weather. Any water in the ice mine would freeze in the winter, but the drier, colder weather causes less liquid water to be available at that time of the year.

Pennsylvania's other well-known ice mine is in Huntingdon County's Trough Creek State Park. The geology and geomorphology are different, but the process is essentially the same. This ice mine is located within the Great Trough Creek water gap, at the base of a talus slope made of Mississippian Pocono sandstone and conglomerate boulders frost-wedged from the crest of Terrace Mountain. The hole at the base of the slope is a cavelike tunnel that is generally thought to have been initially excavated by prospectors in search of iron ore to feed the nearby Paradise Furnace, which was built in 1827. After realizing its warm-weather ice-making ability, local residents enlarged the tunnel and used it as a natural refrigerator. The iron industry failed by midcentury, and the mountains were stripped of their timber with the arrival of the Juniata and Southern Railroad in 1913. The railroad grade passed directly in front of the ice mine, which was preserved by local residents, who laid up a stone wall and constructed steps down to the mine from track level. The CCC (Civilian Conservation Corps) reseeded the slopes; developed trails, including one past Rainbow Falls and up to Balanced Rock; and converted the old railroad line into an access road. In 1936, Trough Creek State Park was created, with the Ice Mine as one of its natural attractions.

Although not an actual mine, the Coudersport glaciere was also discovered and initially opened by metal prospectors. The tale retold to tourists was that a Cattaraugus Indian came to Coudersport in 1894 with a piece of silver ore tied in a handkerchief. The Indian was silent as to where or how he got the specimen, but witnesses saw him go into the woods near Sweden Valley. The incident touched off a minor prospecting craze around Sweden Valley that swept up John Dodd, owner of the hillside tract south of the village. Dodd employed William O'Neil to search the mountain with a magic divining rod. When the rod took a sudden dip, the two men tore into the earth, encountering a layer of ice 2 feet into their shaft, but no silver.

The ice was an unexpected find, but since it was early spring, its occurrence was not recognized as significant. When O'Neil returned later that summer, there was even *more* ice in the hole. Undeterred from his mining mission, O'Neil dug a 10- by 12-foot shaft 32 feet deep. Although he turned up not one speck of silver, he had unwittingly created the perfect ice mine. Each spring thereafter, ice would form in O'Neil's pit, building massive frozen tapestries along the walls that extended down into the hole as tapered icicles. As the weather warmed, more ice was made. When the neighbors started coming around to get a look at the strange site, John Dodd realized that the hole contained riches other than the ones he had previously prospected for.

By spring of 1901, Dodd had opened the Ice Mine up as a tourist attraction. He built a boardwalk connecting the road to the mine and sold the experience of feeling winter in the summer for a dime, in addition to ice cream and sandwiches, which he dispensed from a tent erected near the hole. By 1907, Dodd had trenched through the hillside intersecting the shaft. A viewing platform was built around the hole, into which a 17-foot-long ladder descended. Dodd constructed an entrance building in front of the trench and extended a wooden wall from the building around the hole. Visitors entered through a door and were escorted to the ice box viewing platform, where they could feel the chill of 32-degree air, see their own breath as if it were a brisk January day, and witness a curtain of ice clinging to the hillside wall and down into the hole. For a more intimate view, visitors could climb down a ladder to be surrounded by icicles 20 feet long and the size of tree branches.

Dodd did a modest business. Mother Nature provided him with a first-rate attraction—especially for 10 cents—in a terrible location. Coudersport was 5 miles away, and though it was the largest town in the county, it barely had 2,000 people. The nearest railroads were branch lines to nowhere without through-routed passengers that could have made up a potential tourist base. Most Ice Mine patrons were locals and visitors drawn into the region for other reasons. One of these visitors was Professor M. L. Kelly, a teacher from Mount Vernon, Ohio, who was enamored enough with the Ice Mine to purchase it and the 25 acres it sat on in 1915.

Kelly immediately raised the gate fee to 50 cents, a price that was maintained until 1965; made capital improvements; and began an advertising campaign to increase the Ice Mine's notoriety. This included postcard mailings, advertising, and published literature, which necessitated the writing of the official discovery story, history, and explanations of the phenomenon in prose that was descriptive and sensational enough to make people want to come see the site. Therein lies the blurry boundary between fact and fiction. Is it purely coincidental that the Ice Mine's discovery story, like those of many show caves, involved Indians and lost treasure?

Kelly also took out ads in the *Automobile Blue Book,* the most popular regional road atlas of the day. The automobile, just becoming popular when Kelly took over, ensured the future success of the Ice Mine. While peripheral to the rail network, the Ice Mine sat at the intersection of the old Jersey Shore Turnpike (PA Route 44), the main road to the more populous south-central and southeastern parts of the state, and the Roosevelt Highway (U.S. Route 6), the main east-west trunk route across

ENTRANCE 10 ICE MINE, COUDERSPORT, PA.   5A607

The Ice Mine in 1935; a registry book stands to the left of the entrance door.
AUTHOR'S COLLECTION

northern Pennsylvania. After popularizing the Ice Mine, Kelly sold it to William A. Shear in 1921. Shear continued to improve and promote the Ice Mine, maintaining the attraction through its most prosperous years.

Although the Ice Mine was a man-made hole, it was packaged, presented, and operated in a fashion not unlike that of a show cave. In 1938, Shear enhanced the picturesque qualities of the site by constructing a new stone entrance and a Swiss chalet–like refreshment and souvenir stand. The property was meticulously maintained and decorated with flowers, a tradition carried on by his son Thomas. The Shears also maintained a network of billboards guiding tourists to the attraction.

Early visitors were baffled by a hole that made ice as the weather warmed and lost ice when the warm weather started to cool, and the Ice Mine proprietors played up this bizarre quality by presenting the attraction as a genuine roadside oddity. Like their show cave counterparts in the nineteenth century, Ice Mine owners encouraged scientific scrutiny of the attraction, and then converted the studies into promotional material. In addition to numerous newspaper articles, the Ice Mine was written up in *Literary Digest* (1913), *Popular Science Monthly* (1913), *Scientific American* (1916), and even *Ripley's Believe It or Not*. Glaciere expert Edwin Swift Balch visited the Ice Mine in 1921 and presented his findings before the American Philosophical Society. Arctic explorer Vilhjalmur Stefansson inspected the Ice Mine in 1922 in preparation for a lecture delivered before an audience at Coudersport's Coit-Alber Chautauqua. A parade of university professors came and went, leaving behind pages of scientific descriptions of the Ice Mine that essentially outlined the current understanding of the phenomenon.

The business was flagging by the 1980s. William Shear had passed the attraction on to his children, Tom, Grace, and Dorothy in 1960. Tom and his wife, Maxine, managed the Ice Mine until Tom's death in 1987, when Maxine and her two sisters-in-law sold the property to Ernie Mosch. Times had changed, and the thrill had gone out of standing in an ice-covered hole sipping lemonade in July, even if it was somewhat unusual.

Ernie Mosch, a Potter County native looking for a retirement activity, ran the Ice Mine until the note was paid off. Age, illness, and dwindling receipts caused Ernie to shut the attraction down in 1990. When I arrived more than a dozen years later, the Ice Mine parking lot was being used to store building materials and other assorted flotsam. The quaint gift shop, however, still stood like a realistic rendering of an old linen postcard. Ernie was living there alone as, by his own definition, somewhat of a recluse. He enjoyed the solitude of the mountain, loved the Ice Mine, and busied himself with numerous writing projects and other pur-

Ernie Mosch within the Ice Mine. At its spring peak, icicles cover the walls and hang well below the platform Ernie is standing on.

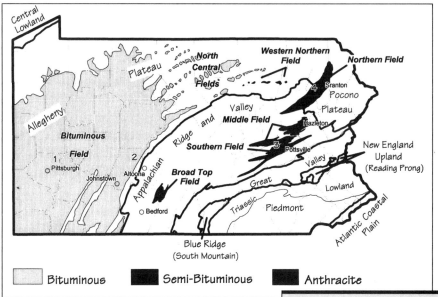

Bituminous   Semi-Bituminous   Anthracite

suits. Ernie had done extensive research on the Ice Mine and was interested in one day turning it into a nonprofit glaciere nature education center. He shared with me much of what he knew about the Ice Mine's history and geology and took me on a tour. Being October, it was the wrong season for ice, but he assured me that the ice still returns every spring.

Pennsylvania Coal Fields
1. Tour-Ed Coal Mine (Tarentum)
2. Seldom Seen Coal Mine (St. Boniface)
3. Ashland Pioneer Tunnel (Ashland)
4. Lackawanna Coal Mine (Scranton)

Tourist Coal Mines

Coal mines that offer tours to the public are another way to explore the subterranean geology of Pennsylvania. These mines are akin to show caves in that they lie underground and have been manipulated by humans but for completely different purposes. Their interpretation and public presentation also differ. Coal mines are man-made, utilitarian spaces, expected to be seen only by the industrial laborers employed to work in them. Most of the coal mine guides are retired miners who present this underworld setting as a workspace, usually from a historic point of view. The focus of the tours is not contemplation of geologic wonders or recreation in a natural setting. Instead, the coal mine tourist is presented with a window into the work lives of those who toiled underground.

Pennsylvania has four tourist coal mines, all nonprofit operations. Seldom Seen Coal Mine and Tour-Ed Mine are in the bituminous fields, and the Ashland Pioneer Tunnel and Lackawanna Coal Mine are in the anthracite fields. They all have surface museums that include mining artifacts, maps, photographs, and equipment.

The coal seams in both the anthracite and the bituminous fields are of a similar age and lie above the Pottsville sandstone and conglomerate that mark the base of the Pennsylvanian rocks.

Seldom Seen Coal Mine

Seldom Seen was opened in 1902 by the Miller Run Coal Company, which first got at the coal from an entry on the other side of the hill to the west. Most of the product was sold as steam coal for power plants and was shipped out on the Hasting's branch of the Pennsylvania Railroad. The mine advanced eastward toward the intersecting slope of Chest Creek Valley, where the current portal was opened in 1933, when the mine was sold to the Chest Creek Coal Company. By then the mine had advanced so far to the east that it was more expedient to take the coal out through a new opening overlooking Chest Creek than to carry it back through the mine to the west. Coal coming out of the new portal was transported to a loading tipple on the railroad along Chest Creek by way of an inclined plane that descended 260 feet to the valley floor. The deep mine closed

The Seldom Seen mine motor returns to the surface with another load of tourists. SELDOM SEEN COAL MINE

in the 1960s, and the entire hilltop was stripped off to get at the pillars left behind in the Lower Freeport and Upper Kittanning seams that lie above the deep mine. The postwar development of giant draglines and stripping shovels made this type of surface mining profitable, since it allowed the overburden to be completely removed and the coal to be dug out with a lot fewer miners.

After the deep mine shut down in 1963, E. J. Haluska bought it to operate as a tourist attraction. He reopened the operation as the Seldom Seen Valley Mine, the first commercial mine in the state designed to extract a revenue from tourists rather than coal. Gas rationing brought on by the Arab oil embargo of 1973 led to fewer visitations, scaring Haluska out of the show mine business. A number of operators ran the mine in succession, presiding over an attraction with dwindling patronage. Mine equipment and parts were sold off, the incline was dismantled for salvage, and reinvestment ceased. In 1990, the mine closed.

A small group of Cambria County historians, former miners, and concerned citizens dedicated to preserving local mining heritage acquired a $75,000 community and economic development grant to assist in reopening the Seldom Seen mine as a nonprofit operation. In 1993, they were successful. The attraction was restored as the Seldom Seen Tourist Coal Mine, and none too soon. The closed mine had almost been sealed for good due to progressive deterioration. Today Seldom Seen depends on volunteers, and uses admission fees to maintain this important piece of Pennsylvania heritage. A good part of its annual operating budget comes from the popular haunted mine tours conducted every October.

Seldom Seen is a textbook example of a western Pennsylvania room and pillar drift mine. Many of the nearly horizontal bituminous coal seams were intersected by streams cutting down into the Allegheny Plateau, exposing the coal outcrops in the valley hillsides. A drift is a horizontal tunnel driven back into coal seam from the hillside outcrop. The Seldom Seen portal is in the western hillside of Chest Creek Valley, a couple miles east of Hastings and just off PA Route 36. The coal vein that outcrops here is the 4-foot-thick Lower Kittanning, or B Seam. From deepest (oldest) to shallowest (youngest), the profitable coal seams of the Pennsylvanian Allegheny Formation include the Brookville/Clarion, Lower Kittanning, Upper Kittanning, Lower Freeport, and Upper Freeport, more commonly known by miners as A, B, C, D, and E. Thirty to 50 feet of rock separate each of these seams. The Lower Kittanning was mined below Seldom Seen and the Lower Freeport above Seldom Seen, creating three tiers of mines. The Upper Freeport and any younger coal seams were eroded completely away at this location eons ago.

Within the mine, passages called entries are driven parallel to the main gangway every 30 to 60 feet, depending on conditions. Crosscuts are made perpendicular to the entries, causing the mine to develop as a rectilinear grid of underground passages bordering pillars of coal. As the mine advances through the seam, coal is removed from the passages, or rooms, but left in pillars to support the roof. As much as 60 percent of the coal in any panel, a certain predetermined area to be mined out, may be left to hold up the roof. In the final stage, a crew works from the back of the mine toward the portal, removing the coal in every other, every third, or maybe every two of three pillars, depending on the roof conditions, allowing the ceiling to subside in their wake.

Known as "robbing the pillars," this last stage is the most dangerous, but it is also the most profitable if more pillars can be mined out than anticipated. The operators base their estimated profit on how much coal can be removed. Every additional pillar mined beyond the ones they had anticipated is pure profit. A 30-by-60-foot pillar 4 feet thick may contain 300 tons of coal. At $50 per ton, the pillar represents $1,500. If thirty pillars are left behind to support the panel roof, the operator has to write off $45,000 worth of coal as unrecoverable. The economic pressure to dig this money out can have dire consequences. Each pillar removed transfers the weight of the roof to the remaining pillars. If too many are taken, the supporting pillars can literally explode under the weight of the roof, touching off a catastrophic cave-in.

Tourists at Seldom Seen are taken into and out of the mine using the same battery-powered man-trip motors that once carried miners to and from the working face. Once deep within the hillside, visitors disembark for a guided hike around one of the pillars. Guides demonstrate with mining equipment positioned along the path to explain how the coal is cut, shot, shoveled, and removed from the mine. The dark, damp, and gloomy underground environment is not presented as picturesque, but more as a potentially frightful workplace endured by the stout of heart. Like their show cave counterparts, every mine tour includes a period of "total darkness." Rather than being a scary novelty, however, tourists recognize total mine darkness as a working condition, usually accentuated when the guide finally lights a feeble headlamp. Rather than the enveloping silence of a cave, the darkness of a coal mine roared with the sounds of cutting machinery, continuous miners, shaking and banging pan lines, and conveyor belts that carried the coal from the face and into waiting cars. And this is an *improvement.* Formerly the base of the seam at the working face was undercut with a pick. Holes were bored into the top of the seam and packed with dynamite. The coal was shot downward into a heaping mound of shattered lumps that were laboriously shoveled into a car to be transferred out of the mine. The emotional response experienced by coal mine tourists is not an overwhelming reverence for sublime nature and the powers responsible for it, but a renewed respect for the people who created and worked in this seemingly unnatural environment.

Tour-Ed Mine

Twenty miles up the Allegheny River from Pittsburgh, another bituminous coal tourist mine overlooks the Tarentum exit of Route 28. The Tour-Ed Mine has a commercial history that goes back to 1859. Allegheny Valley iron smelters recognized the value of the high-grade coal that outcropped in the hillsides and began mining the Upper Freeport seam for coke. Coke is coal cooked in an oven to burn off impurities, increasing its heating value, and strengthening its structure. Strong enough to support a heat of ore and hot enough to smelt out the iron, coke is primarily used as a blast furnace fuel. Tour-Ed's predecessor came to be known as the Avenue Mine, which was operated by the Leechburg Coal Company for Allegheny Steel of nearby Brackenridge. At its peak, the Avenue Mine stretched underground for 7 miles and had eleven active workplaces and ten different entrances. In 1964, the mine was purchased by Ira Wood and run by the Wood Coal Company. That same year, surface mining began to strip the overburden off the hilltops to remove the coal left as pillars in the deep mine.

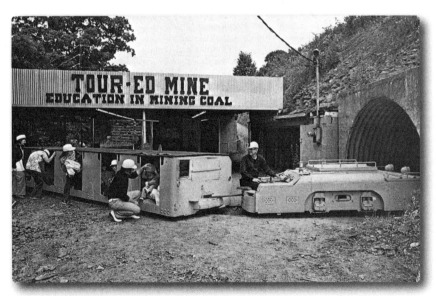

The Tour-Ed mine motor prepares to enter the drift with an inbound load of tourists. AUTHOR'S COLLECTION

The Avenue Mine shut down in 1969. Ira and Frances Wood reopened it a year later as the private, nonprofit Tour-Ed Coal Mine for the purpose of preserving mining heritage.

Like Seldom Seen, Tour-Ed is a room and pillar drift mine. Tourists are taken underground by tracked mine motor, and then guided around a standing pillar 40 feet wide by 60 feet long. There is a chronological arrangement to Tour-Ed's underground mining museum. Each stop around the block contains vintage equipment that emphasizes a different era of mining technology. The first stop is devoted to hand-pick mining, common before the Civil War. Next comes late-nineteenth-century punch mining, using a pneumatic drill. The guide, a former miner, demonstrates a shaker conveyor and loader from the 1930s and 1940s, and finally the continuous miners used since the 1950s. Mining and loading 8 tons of coal, work that once took an antebellum hand-pick miner a day to complete, can now be done in forty-five seconds.

For the comfort of tourists, the passageways are about 6 feet high, but the coal seam is just a bit over 3 feet thick. An active operation never would have extracted 3 feet of worthless rock just so the miners could stand up while they worked. When the mine was running in operation, the headroom was no greater than the thickness of the seam, approximately the clearance beneath the average desk. Equipment operators reclined on low-slung continuous miners. Before that, men crawled or duck-walked to the face and frequently spent an eight-hour shift swinging a pick and hefting a shovel while lying on their sides, sometimes in water.

Besides the mine, visitors can tour Mine Village, a collection of buildings representing a company store, barber shop, miner's home, blacksmith shop, and log cabin. It even has one of only two surviving original 1940 Pennsylvania Turnpike tollbooths. The other is at the Smithsonian.

Ashland Pioneer Tunnel

The first tourist coal mine in the anthracite region was opened in Ashland in 1962. The Ashland Pioneer Tunnel is a hillside mine on the southern edge of the borough. Visitors load into railcars, which are pulled underground by a mine motor. Although it has the appearance of a drift, the passage is actually a tunnel. A drift extends into the seam and roughly parallel to the geology, whereas a tunnel cuts across the geology, providing access to multiple seams. A horizontal tunnel can do this in the folded anthracite fields because the coal seams, like the rest of the rock, are steeply pitched. This presented a challenge for anthracite miners, who had to dig coal from seams tilted, as in the case of Pioneer Tunnel, as much as 50 degrees off the horizontal.

The man-trip cars carry visitors through the belly of the mountain, the portal receding as a distant point of light in the gathering darkness. No timbers hold up the rock roof, which is sound, but wooden cribbing surrounds the tunnel at every coal seam: Orchard, Primrose, Holmes, Mammoth, Seven Foot, Big Buck Mountain (#1), and Little Buck Mountain (#2). The tunnel intersects with parallel gangways that were driven west through the coal veins. Each seam intersects the gangway at a 50-degree angle, so that the left wall and floor of the gangway are the exposed faces of a vein that extends up and to the left, and down and to the right. The gangway's slanted ceiling is the seam's top rock.

Using the pillar and breast method, anthracite miners dug up into the left wall coal face, excavating a tilted, bottle-shaped chamber called a battery. The neck of the battery acted like a coal chute into the gangway. Anthracite miners had to do everything their bituminous counterparts did—set the timbers, cut the coal base, drill the top for dynamite charges, and shoot the coal—but at a steeply pitched angle that prevented them from using continuous miners and other equipment designed for horizontal seams. As a result, anthracite deep mines had much higher labor costs that nailed the coffin once the industry was killed by a loss of markets. The most effective way to mechanize the anthracite mines was to strip the coal out from the surface outcrops, a method that accounts for most of the production today.

Once the miner shot the coal, the shattered lumps careened down the slope of the battery and into the chute, which was closed on the gangway side by a wooden door. Removing the door gravity-fed the coal into awaiting cars. Miners always dug up into the seam so that gravity could assist them in loading the coal. The blast-shattered coal, however, frequently jammed in the chute and had to be laboriously dug out.

After the 1,250-foot mine train trip to the back of the Pioneer Tunnel, tourists are walked into the Seven Foot and Big Buck gangways. A manway dug as an emergency exit extends 400 feet up through the Big Buck to the surface—one long climb. Equally harrowing is the manway's downcast side, slanting into the deep darkness to a level 300 feet below, and then another level 300 feet below that. The seams outcrop to the east in Mahanoy Gap, sandwiched within the tilted rock strata that extend from the hilltop down to the banks of Mahanoy Creek. This is where the mine was first opened in 1911, at the water-level outcrop of the Big Buck seam near the Reading Railroad tracks that ran through the gap.

The railroads controlled most of the coal production in the anthracite fields, and the Reading Railroad in particular dominated much of the fields in which Pioneer Tunnel lies. Its subsidiary, the Philadelphia and Reading Coal and Iron Company, opened the Mahanoy Gap mine, naming it after the Bancroft Colliery, which stood nearby. The old Pioneer Colliery, for which the tunnel was later named, was located just up the tracks.

A colliery is a coal-processing plant built near the head of a mine and centered on the breaker, a towering structure where the coal is cleaned, screened, and sorted. Using the preexisting Bancroft Colliery to process the coal, the Reading drove gangways into the Big Buck on three different levels and worked the seam westward for 3,400 feet. An inclined plane was constructed to carry coal from the upper two levels down to the water-level breaker. Tunnels were driven north from all three gangways to access the other seams, especially the Mammoth. True to its name, the Mammoth vein at this location is 50 feet thick in three shale-parted splits.

In 1925, the Reading opened a surface mine to strip coal from the Mammoth seam's hilltop outcrop. Two years later, another strip mine began digging coal from the 14-foot-thick Primrose outcrop. Realizing the area around the top-level Big Buck portal was needed for strip-mine spoil piles, the Reading extended Pioneer Tunnel from the Mammoth vein to a new portal on the north side of the hill. Track was then laid around the outside of the hill to the top of the inclined plane. Once out of the Pioneer Tunnel, coal could be taken to the plane in longer trains pulled by powerful little engines known as "steam lokies."

The Bancroft Mine played out in 1931 and was closed. The underground workings lay sealed up and undisturbed for the next thirty years. By the end of the 1950s, it was becoming clear that the anthracite region's economic engine was passing into history. Coal towns scrambled to find any economic means to fill the big hole left by mining. In the case of Ashland, Borough Manager Emil R. Ermert suggested that the town reopen the Pioneer Tunnel as a tourist attraction.

After digging through the entrance cave-in used to seal the mine, the tunnel was found to be in stable condition, with the exception of collapses at the Primrose and Mammoth seams. To help get the mine restored and running, the newly founded Ashland Community Enterprises secured a $44,000 federal loan from the Area Rehabilitation Administration. In 1962, the Pioneer Tunnel opened for walk-in tours that went back to the Orchard seam, where a demonstration battery had been mined. Two steam lokies rescued from a Wilkes-Barre junkyard were restored to offer train rides along the rebuilt track leading from the mine to the foundations of the long-demolished inclined plane. Within the mine, the coal seam cave-in debris was removed, and new track was laid the length of the tunnel for mine motor trips to the Buck Mountain seams. Since this time, the Pioneer Tunnel and Steam Lokie have been successfully run with proceeds from the gate. In 1992, the nonprofit operation welcomed its millionth visitor.

Lackawanna Coal Mine

The entrance of the Lackawanna Coal Mine at Scranton's McDade Park overlooks the city from a western hillside. Deep inside, the gangway is roomy, the batteries are huge, and the mine looks as if it continues on forever. The tour seems to only scratch the undersurface.

When the Continental Mine was first opened in 1860, coal was removed from a 528-foot-deep shaft located 2 miles out in the valley. The shaft intersected a half dozen seams that were mined in all directions. The field's syncline is so broad that the coal seams at the axis are lying nearly flat, accommodating a room and pillar method more commonly used in the bituminous fields. In 1904, the 457 miners removed 246,561 tons of coal. Even as late as 1964, more than a century after its inauguration, 51,872 tons came out of the mine.

Early in the twentieth century, the mine entrance was relocated to the hillside so that anthracite could more effectively be removed from the western slant of the syncline. Today tourists enter the mine through this same portal by descending Slope #190. Unlike a horizontal drift or a vertical shaft, a slope cuts into the ground at a steep angle. Lackawanna's 1,300-foot-long, 25-degree slope drops 300 feet into the Clark vein gangway. Empty cars were winched down and loaded ones hoisted up using a cable and stationary engine. Once out of the mine, loaded coal cars were cut loose and shunted onto a side track that led to the tipple.

Looking east aross the Lackawanna valley, the portal to Slope 190 is left, and the coal tipple is in the center distance.

The mine passed through a number of different owners, including the Glen Alden Coal Company, which ran it into the 1930s, and the Moffat Coal Company, which operated the mine until its final day in 1966. By then the anthracite outcrops along both sides of the valley were being intensively strip-mined. The area around the abandoned slope was an uninviting lunar landscape of gob piles, stripping holes, and cast-off mine equipment.

In the late 1970s, the county began a long-term program to convert this postindustrial liability into a community asset. The relandscaped strip mine is now the 200-acre McDade Park. Its chief attraction opened in 1985, when the restored Slope #190 carried its first group of tourists into the newly christened Lackawanna Coal Mine.

Lackawanna visitors ride in on man-trip cars, then are led south through the gangway. Empty batteries, or chambers, as they are called in this mine, extend up and to the right. Visitors can also look down and to the left into the mined chambers of the next lower level. The mine operated on four different levels, all but the tourist level now flooded. Water was a constant concern at Lackawanna, where 8 to 10 tons of water had to be pumped out for every ton of coal mined. The pumping stopped with the mining, allowing the unchecked water table to envelop the lower three-quarters of the mine.

A rock tunnel leads west from the Clark vein gangway to intersect the underlying seams. Tourists are led back through the 15-inch-thick Dunmore #1 to the more profitable 3-foot Dunmore #2. Amazingly, the Dunmore #1 was mined, requiring workers to excavate chambers from a slanted slot not much wider than their shoulders. A "roll" in the vein, a kink caused by faulting, was also mined out, leaving a high, cathedral-like ceiling in this part of the mine. The peg shanty where miners hung their numbered tags at the beginning of each workday so that the fire boss could tell who was in the mine still stands back near Dunmore #2.

Although inactive for more than three decades, Lackawanna presents the appearance of a mine that was closed yesterday. Underground structures and equipment are still down there, and the dioramalike scenes set up to explain each step in the mining process are further enhanced with the use of mannequins dressed like miners. A dimly lit miner is frozen in a perpetual crawl. A door boy sits on eternal watch to clear the way for coal cars that never come. Equipment operators stare blankly at rock walls. A mechanical hand wriggles its fingers to be pulled from the debris of a simulated cave-in. The effect causes this underground museum to resemble an amusement park dark ride, but one that graphically illustrates the human cost of converting coal into warmth on a winter day.

9

Confessions of a Flashlight Spelunker

I felt well prepared when I showed up for my first real spelunking trip wearing a pair of sneakers, a T-shirt, and jeans, and armed with a 99-cent flashlight. Outfitted against the inky blackness with my flickering yellow beam, I crawled into the hole alone, and not another person on the planet knew where I was. In my mind, I was Lewis *and* Clark. In reality, I was an accident waiting to happen.

A little light goes a long way in a cave; even a match throws off a broad and comforting glow in total darkness. Once adjusted to moving within the artificial orb of my flashlight beam, I gained the confidence to proceed beyond the twilight zone of semidarkness created by daylight filtering through the opening. The reassuring glow of my little flashlight drove me deeper into the cave. The sense of discovery in such an extreme environment was both exhilarating and scary, like an amusement park thrill ride. That feeling turned to sheer terror the instant my flashlight failed, plunging me into an utterly disorienting blackness. The light had lasted just long enough to ensure that I was completely entombed. It was kind of funny, in a horrific sort of way, how fast my mind pointed out every mistake I had made now that I was helpless to do anything about it. I made my life dependent on a 99-cent flashlight? What was I thinking? I was already cold and wet. Why didn't I grab my jacket? No one knows I'm trapped in here! Instinctively, I did an about-face to feel my way back out, and whacked my head against a rock I was certain was not there when I came in. Panic-stricken, I rapped my flashlight against the wall, and it flickered back to life. I scrambled back through the passage as quickly as possible. I'd never seen anything so welcome as that patch of light filtering in through the opening.

Randy Schaetzl and Kevin Patrick at Schofer's Cave in 1989.

While I rested in the safety of daylight, the cave seemed ominously detached from my plight. It remained as it had for eons, a silent hole in the rock unable to care whether I lived or died. It would take in the experienced and the foolish alike on their own accord, and regardless of the gravity of their situations, no warning sirens would sound and no authorities would be summoned. In the aftermath of any unexpected tragedy, the cave would remain unchanged and unmoved, and the event unrecorded as a warning to the next ill-prepared visitor. This was no amusement park.

I don't know what it is about caves that cause people to act so irrationally. Maybe we take light too much for granted. Maybe for many of us, our only experience with caves is in well-lit tourist operations. Maybe our everyday lives are so well protected and safe that we associate that anxious, panicky feeling with the fun-loving thrill of a horror movie rather than as the sign of imminent danger it was intended to be. And our minds are so quick to forget trauma. Having survived my brief brush with danger, I felt all the more invincible. I was back a week later with two other friends. No longer Lewis and Clark, I was Daniel Boone leading others to my great discovery, a feeling equally exhilarating. I was a little wiser, but not much. I wore a jacket, and my little band of spelunkers had *three* 99-cent flashlights. Two failed. We slithered out on the beam of the third.

When I finally met up with my first group of well-equipped cavers, I discovered they had a name for people like me: spelunkers. I never saw a lone caver underground. There are always at least two, usually three to five. They wear heavy-treaded boots, layered clothing, and helmets, typically with headlamps. Extra lights and water bottles hang from their belts, and their pockets bulge with concentrated food bars. They have left word with others who are not in the cave about where they are and when they expect to return. They come to the cave armed with maps of its interior, possibly drawn by themselves over dozens of supervised mapping expeditions. They take nothing but photographs (and other people's trash) and leave nothing but footprints. They are organized into local grottoes recognized by the National Speleological Society, and anyone is welcomed to join.

My first wild caving experience was in Schofer Cave, located a couple miles northwest of Kutztown in Berks County. Like nearby Crystal and Onyx, Schofer is in the Hamburg Klippe of the Ordovician Martinsburg Formation. Cavers would refer to Schofer as a "beginners cave." It is easy to access, being a few dozen feet from the road. It is not too big or complex, lowering the chance of getting hopelessly lost, and with the exception of a couple crawl-under points, much of the cave can be seen while walking upright. It is also on state game lands, precluding the need to seek permission.

Local noncaving students from Kutztown University would call it a "party cave." Half of the times I was ever in Schofer for more than three hours, a party showed up. College coeds would noisily assault the cave with hollers and drunken laughter, drag in cases of beer, and set up a party in the Big Room with a handful of candles and a couple flashlights. Partiers are always more eager to take beer into the cave than to carry empties out. During one party, the repeated sound of beer bottles smashing on the rocks—that some unsuspecting caver would inevitably crawl over—caused me to get religion. As irresponsible as my early caving days were, I never exhibited this type of careless behavior or inflicted this level of environmental damage, and I wanted only to distance myself from these other spelunkers.

The next wild cave I came to experience was Westmoreland County's Bear Cave. Having first visited the most popular wild cave in eastern Pennsylvania, I had unknowingly joined a trip to the most well-known wild cave in western Pennsylvania. This time, however, the expedition was bit more organized. Consisting of about a dozen college students, the trip was run by members of the Loyalhanna Grotto. The forty-five-minute hike up Chestnut Ridge keeps casual cave parties to a minimum, but like any open cave, Bear attracts its share of unthinking visitors. Loyalhanna Grotto members have spent countless hours removing graffiti from the Garden of the Gods, the breakdown chamber that has acted as the cave's traditional writing room. The private property is now patrolled, and cavers who do not obtain a permit first run the risk of being prosecuted as trespassers.

Outfitted with helmets and multiple light sources, the group entered Bear Cave through a stream sink. The water trickled into the dark distance of Appian Way while we turned into a side passage. As daylight receded and the walls closed in, I was struck with a claustrophobic cave queasiness that faded with my acclimation to the alien underworld. It was replaced by the sense of exhilaration that comes with the exploration of the unknown, even if the unknown has been known for quite some time. The group went where countless other Bear Cave visitors had gone before: Serpent's Sanctum, Garden of the Gods, Table Rocks, Propeller Pass, Coffin Rock, and the Keyhole. Past cavers now long dead had visited these same places and handed their names down through the ages without the use of signs.

I cannot help but think that part of the attraction of going underground is that soul-lifting sense of renewal experienced when you at last see daylight again.

After entering Sand Cave, Kentucky, on the morning of January 30, 1925, Floyd Collins would never again experience the joys of daylight. Collins got trapped in a tight passage while searching for a back way into Mammoth Cave, touching off a rescue attempt that turned into a national media circus. The rescue attracted thousands of tourists, but could not save Collin, who was pronounced dead 18 days into the ordeal. The Floyd Collins affair hangs like a specter over every cave rescue that has occurred since.

In the wake of a well-publicized rescue, especially one involving serious injury or death, well-meaning but misguided authorities may decide to blast the offending cave shut to prevent future accidents. Such knee-jerk reactions come from the latent perception of caves as dangerous nuisances that may now harbor something more frightening than robbers, wild animals, or suspicious hermits—legal liability.

Laurel Caverns was reported to have been sealed by concerned citizens as early as 1802, after two guys from Smithton got lost in the cave. They were found embracing each other in the dark, resigned to await death. The cave did not stay sealed for long. Having overseen wild caving trips through its undeveloped section for more than thirty years, the Laurel Caverns staff is familiar with the nature of cave injuries and rescues. Although relatively infrequent, most injuries occur in the Millstream Passage, at the farthest point from the entrance where inexperienced cavers may be tired, anxious to get back out, and likely to make mistakes. It may take 8 to 12 hours to get a stretcher-bound caver from the Millstream Passage to Uniontown Hospital.

Within a month of Harlansburg Cave's 1950 discovery, a rescue mission was being mounted to retrieve three flashlight spelunkers who lost their way when their lights failed in the subterranean maze. It took a bloodhound, a mile of wire for illumination, and eleven hours to find them 2,000 feet from the entrance. A week later, the sheriff officially closed the cave, but unblocked openings still beckoned. Another well-publicized rescue in 1966 precipitated a more determined attempt to seal the entrances with poured cement. The road cut that had opened the cave, however, sliced across several passages, making its total closure difficult. Access points still admitted entry until 2003, when they were gated.

A 1983 rescue at Lemon Hole Cave in Westmoreland County sparked recommendations to fill it in or blast it shut for the public's safety. Like nearby Bear Cave, Lemon Hole is a large Loyalhanna limestone cavern remotely set within the forested slopes of Chestnut Ridge. Although Lemon Hole had been open to cavers for more than a century without incident, most county residents had never heard of it until the day the media reported that one hundred fireman, coal miners, and emergency medical personnel were converging on a mountain cave to rescue a man trapped underground. The victim was rescued, having sustained a broken arm and shoulder. Lemon Hole was not sealed in the aftermath, and once the press stopped writing about it, the cave returned to benign obscurity.

Carolyn Trimarchi and Liz Ann Okey explore Bear Cave.

Proprietor Tom Metzgar at the entrance to Bear Cave.

If there was ever a cave susceptible to a Floyd Collins haunting, it was Schofer's. On August 15, 1980, seven Kutztown students were having a cave party when their lights failed sometime after 3:30 in the morning. Around dawn, friends not in the cave called the state police, who entered the Big Room and led the party to safety. In November 1988, Kutztown volunteer firefighters extricated a man caught in the cave's Corkscrew by chiseling away a piece of the rock that held him captive. On October 21, 1990, Kutztown firemen were again called to remove a girl who had broken her ankle after slipping from a rock in the Big Room. On December 19, 1992, a Boy Scout suffered serious injuries after falling from the cliff above the cave entrance, requiring an emergency evacuation to Lehigh Valley Hospital. The Pennsylvania Game Commission finally gated Schofer Cave in 1994. All requests to enter the cave have been denied.

Gating has become the popular solution for protecting a cave as natural habitat that can accommodate exploration and recreation, while also protecting irresponsible cavers from themselves. The heavy steel barriers allow animal access—primarily bats, wood rats, and invertebrates—but can still be opened depending on the willingness of those who keep the keys.

Even the secrets of cold, dark, watery sumps are open for scrutiny with the recent merger of caving and scuba diving. In 1965, cave divers began to challenge the two-thirds-mile-long subterranean water passage that connects Tytoona Cave and Arch Spring. Divers plumbed the Log Jam sump at the back of the cave, entering an air-filled room covered in calcite formations after forty feet. The sump on the downstream side of this room was also explored to reveal another room. The third sump proved to be too long for the air tank, and was aborted. Although 600 feet were added to Tytoona, 2,500 feet of unexplored passage still existed between the third sump and the resurgence at Arch Spring. Cave diving in Pennsylvania is a dangerous affair. The water is frigid, and visibility is usually near zero. A diver's ability to get back through a passage clouded with fine silt stirred up on the inbound trip may depend entirely on the grasp of a guideline carried into the water.

Fading Show Caves

When a show cave closes, time and nature slowly disintegrate its former place identity. Cave souvenirs are scattered and lost, electric wires corrode, wooden planking rots, discovery stories fade, and metal railings rust. Watery clay rises to absorb graveled walkways, and only the most obvious signature formations hold their names for a time. Then they, too, give them up before a caving generation without memory or record of previous identities.

Onyx Cave had been closed for twenty years when owner Janice Eshleman invited me in for a tour. Although it had been a long time since the last paying tourist passed through Gordon Frazer's concrete bunkerlike entrance, the cave had been well maintained, and most of the lights were in working order. We carried flashlights anyway.

Armed with an old Onyx Cave tour guide instruction manual, we tried to make sense of the cave. The Fallen Giant stalactite was easy enough to find, as was the Elephant's Head. But the Lady of the Nile, Inverted Hornet's Nest, Turkey's Head, and George Washington's Beet had already receded into the walls of the cave from whence they came, hidden in plain sight. Possible Human Remains still remained.

No tour guide manuals were available when I entered Baker Caverns with Curtis Meyers, his wife, Colleen, and a group of their friends and relatives. Curtis and Colleen were renting the house above the cave but had lived there only two years. The cave had been closed to the public for nearly half a century. We each had to carry our own light. The wiring was rusted through and bulbs were long burned out, but the lighting fixtures remained, trained on objects that no longer had names.

Baker Caverns was a well-orchestrated show cave. The concrete steps and walkways, railings, platforms, and light fixtures still suggest the tourist trail and define where groups were to stand in order to see certain visually accented formations. The tourist path went clockwise around the southern loop first, before returning past the entrance steps and through the tunnel to the Cathedral Hall in the north end. Railings and viewing platforms encouraged visitors to look through windowlike apertures to see picturesque dripstone vistas whose interpretive meanings are now lost.

The arrangement of the whole cave was like a beautifully illustrated storybook in which the text had been erased, or a visually stunning movie without sound.

Deep within the Cathedral, the group spontaneously burst into a rendition of "How Great Thou Art." The music reverberated through the passageways, where the acoustics really are like that of a cathedral. It seemed both curious and natural that the group should suddenly do that, and I asked Curtis and Colleen if it had ever happened before. They said, all the time.

Bedford County's Hipple Cave had a brief commercial life of about a dozen years and then closed down, possibly as early as 1940. Peggy Sell, who has owned the property with her husband Richard since 1973, was kind enough to escort me to the top of the knoll, and then allowed me to wander about inside the cave for as long as I wanted. Hipple is like an archeological ruin. A concrete pad that once supported the cave's electric generator lies just outside the opening. A huge breakdown boulder that apparently dropped since the cave's closing rests halfway down the steps. With each step down from the boulder, the cave stream gurgled louder, cascading out from beneath a rock shelf and over a small dam. The bridge over the stream was long gone, but a concrete walkway could be discerned beneath an accumulated layer of mud.

Deep in the cave, the 10-foot-high Palm Tree Column and the Pillar of Salt stalagmite still retained their regal appearance after decades in the tourist-neglected darkness.

Beyond the Palm Tree, I continued to follow the main strike passage along the stream. A small spot of light from the stream rise beyond the back of the cave filtered into the darkness of the last chamber. Graffiti-covered walls revealed Hipple's writing room.

I sat down and turned off my lamp, comfortably ensconced in the near total darkness of the cave, and listened to the buried water rushing on to the day-lighted spring. The meaningless names of tourists who had been there before me festooned the walls and ceiling. They came and went, like me and the water. And the cave stayed, weathering this brief encounter with human place identity with the nonchalant indifference of a rock that has been around for 450 million years, and is likely to be around for a few hundred million more.

Pennsylvania Show Caves

Cave: Coral Caverns
Address: PO Box 100, Manns Choice, PA 15550
Web site: www.coralcaverns.com
Telephone: (814) 623-6882
Hours: 10 A.M. to 5 P.M. May–June, open weekends only;
  July–August, open seven days a week; September–October,
  open weekends only; November–April, closed
Discovery circumstance: Limestone quarrying
Discovery year: 1928
Years of commercial operation: Since 1932
Geology: Devonian Helderberg limestone
Former names: Wonderland Coral Caverns

Cave: Crystal Cave
Address: 963 Crystal Cave Road, Kutztown, PA, 19530-9141
Web site: www.crystalcavepa.com
Telephone: (610) 683-6765
Hours: 9 A.M. to 5 P.M. March–May and September–November, daily;
  9 A.M. to 6 P.M. June–August, daily; December–February, closed
Admission fee: $8.50 adults; $5 children 4–11; children age 3 and
  under, free
Discovery circumstance: Limestone quarrying
Discovery year: 1871
Years of commercial operation: Since 1872
Geology: Ordovician Hamburg Klippe limestone

Cave: Indian Caverns
Address: Indian Trail, Spruce Creek, PA 16683
Web site: www.indiancaverns.com
Telephone: (814) 623-7578
Hours: 10 A.M. to 4 P.M. May, September, October, daily; 10 A.M. to 6 P.M. June–August, daily; November–April, closed
Admission fee: $9 adults; $4.50 children 6–12; children 5 and under, free
Discovery circumstance: Natural opening
Years of commercial operation: Since 1929
Geology: Ordovician Nealmont/Benner limestone
Former names: Franklinville Cave, Franklin Cave, Historic Indian Cave

Cave: Indian Echo Caverns
Address: 368 Middletown Rd. PO Box 188, Hummelstown, PA 17036
Web site: www.indianechocaverns.com
Telephone: (717) 566-8131
Hours: 9 A.M. to 6 P.M. June–August, daily; 10 A.M. to 4 P.M. September–May, daily
Admission fee: $10 adults; $8 senior citizens; $5 children 3–11; children under 3, free
Discovery circumstance: Natural opening
Years of commercial operation: 1929–1930s; Since 1942
Geology: Ordovician Beekmantown Group Epler limestone
Former names: Grotto on the Swatara/Swatara Cave, Hummelstown Cave, Echo Cave

Cave: Laurel Caverns
Address: 200 Caverns Park Rd., Farmington, PA 15437
Web site: www.laurelcaverns.com
Telephone: (724) 438-3003; 800-515-4150
Hours: 9 A.M. to 5 P.M. May–October, daily; 9 A.M. to 5 P.M. November and March–April, weekends only; December–February, closed
Admission fee: $11.25 adults; $5.50 children 2–12; children under 2, free
Discovery circumstance: Natural opening
Years of commercial operation: Since 1964
Geology: Mississippian Loyalhanna limestone
Former names: Delaney's Cave, Laurel Hill Cave

Cave: Lincoln Caverns
Address: R.R. 1 Box 280, Huntingdon, PA 16652
Web site: www.lincolncaverns.com
Telephone: (814) 643-0268
Hours: 9 A.M. to 4 P.M. March–May, daily; 9 A.M. to 5 P.M. June,
  daily; 9 A.M. to 6 P.M. July–August, daily; 11 A.M. to 3 P.M.
  September–November, daily and weekends in December;
  January–February, closed
Admission fee: $9.50 adults; $8.50 senior citizens; $5.50 children
  4–12; children 3 and under, free
Discovery circumstance: Road building
Discovery year: 1930
Years of commercial operation: Since 1931
Geology: Devonian Helderberg limestone
Former names: Hi-way-may Caverns, William Penn Caverns

Cave: Lost River Caverns
Address: Durham St. PO Box M, Hellertown, PA 18055
Web site: www.lostcave.com
Telephone: (610) 838-8767
Hours: 9 A.M. to 6 P.M. June–August, daily; 9 A.M. to 5 P.M.
  September–May, daily
Admission fee: $8 adults; $4 children 3–12; children under 3, free
Discovery circumstance: Limestone quarrying
Discovery year: 1883
Years of commercial operation: Since 1930
Geology: Cambrian Leithsville limestone
Former names: Rentzheimer's Cave, Lost Cave

Cave: Penn's Cave
Address: 222 Penn's Cave Road, Centre Hall, PA 16828
Web site: www.pennscave.com
Telephone: (814) 364-1664
Hours: 11 A.M. to 4 P.M. February 15–May and December, week-
  ends only; 9 A.M. to 7 P.M. June–August, daily; 9 A.M. to 5 P.M.
  September–November, daily; closed January–February 14
Admission fee: $11.25 adults; $10.25 senior citizens; $5.50 children
  2–12; children under 2, free
Discovery circumstance: Natural opening
Years of commercial operation: Since 1885
Geology: Ordovician Nealmont/Benner limestone
Former names: Long's Cave

Cave: Woodward Cave
Address: Route 45, P.O. Box 175, Woodward, PA 16882
Web site: www.woodwardcave.com
Telephone: (814) 349-9800
Hours: 10 A.M. to 4 P.M. April–May 15 and September, daily; 9 A.M.
to 6 P.M. May 16–August, daily; 10 A.M. to 4 P.M. by appointment
October and March, weekends; November–February, closed
Admission fee: $10.50 adults; $5 children 2–12; children under
2, free
Discovery circumstance: Natural opening
Years of commercial operation: Since 1926
Geology: Ordovician Nealmont/Benner limestone
Former names: Red Panther's Cave

Tourist Coal Mines

Mine: Seldom Seen Coal Mine
Address: P.O. Box 83, Patton, PA 16668
Web site: www.seldomseenmine.com
Telephone: (814) 247-6305; (814) 674-8939
Hours: 11 A.M. to 5 P.M. June, weekends; 11 A.M. to 5 P.M.
July–August, Thursday–Sunday; 3 P.M. to 9 P.M. around Halloween
for haunted mine tour, weekends
Admission fee: $6 adults; $3.50 children 12 and under
Mine type: Bituminous coal. Drift into room and pillar workings
Coal mine operating years: 1902–1963
Tourist mine operating years: 1963–1990; since 1993
Geology: Pennsylvanian Allegheny Formation; Kittanning and
Freeport seams

Mine: Tour-Ed Mine
Address: 748 Bull Creek Road, Tarentum, PA 15084
Web site: www.tour-edmine.com
Telephone: (724) 224-4720
Hours: 1 P.M. to 4 P.M. June–August, daily (closed Tuesdays); 1 P.M.
to 4 P.M. September–October, Friday–Sunday
Admission fee: $7 adults; $4 children 12 and under
Mine type: Bituminous coal. Drift into room and pillar workings
Coal mine operating years: 1859–1969
Tourist mine operating years: Since 1970
Geology: Pennsylvanian Allegheny Formation; Upper Freeport seam

Mine: Ashland Pioneer Tunnel
Address: 19th & Oak Streets, Ashland, PA 17921
Web site: www.pioneertunnel.com
Telephone: (570) 875-3850
Hours: 10 A.M. to 5 P.M. June–August, daily; 10 A.M. to 6 P.M. May
    and September–October, weekends; 11 A.M., 12:30 P.M. and
    2 P.M. tours, April–May and September–October, Monday–Friday
Admission fee: Coal Mine: $7.50 adults; $5 children 12 and under
                Train Ride: $5.50 adults; $4 children 12 and under
Mine type: Anthracite coal. Tunnel into breast and pillar workings
Coal mine operating years: 1911–1931
Tourist mine operating years: Since 1962
Geology: Pennsylvanian Llewellyn Formation; numerous seams

Mine: Lackawanna Coal Mine
Address: Bald Mountain Road, McDade Park, Scranton, PA 18504
Web site: www.thevisitorscenter.com/mine
Telephone: 800-238-7245
Hours: 10 A.M. to 4:30 P.M. April–November, daily
Admission fee: $6 adults; $5.75 senior citizens; $4 children 3–12;
    children under 3, free
Mine type: Anthracite coal. Slope into breast and pillar workings
Coal mine operating years: 1860–1966
Tourist mine operating years: Since 1985
Geology: Pennsylvanian Llewellyn Formation; numerous seams

Closed Show Caves

Cave: Alexander Caverns
County: Mifflin
Discovery circumstance: Natural opening
Years of commercial operation: 1929–1936; 1940–1954
Geology: Ordovician Nealmont/Benner limestone

Cave: Baker Caverns
County: Franklin
Discovery circumstance: Limestone quarrying
Discovery year: 1830
Years of commercial operation: 1932–1954
Geology: Ordovician Chambersburg limestone

Cave: Cold Air Cave
County: Northampton
Discovery circumstance: Timbering
Discovery year: c. 1870
Years of commercial operation: c. 1905–c. 1952
Geology: Silurian Shawangunk quartzite

Cave: Hipple Cave
County: Bedford
Discovery circumstance: Natural opening
Years of commercial operation: 1928–c. 1940
Geology: Ordovician Nealmont/Benner limestone

Cave: Onyx Cave
County: Berks
Discovery circumstance: Limestone quarrying
Discovery year: 1872
Years of commercial operation: 1923–1930s, 1930s–1976;
    1978–1983
Geology: Ordovician Hamburg Klippe limestone
Former names: Luckenbill Cave, Mengel Cave

Cave: Seawra Cave
County: Mifflin
Discovery circumstance: Skunk hunting
    (retold as treasure hunting)
Discovery year: 1925
Years of commercial operation: 1928–1938
Geology: Devonian Helderberg limestone

Cave: Tytoona Cave
County: Blair
Discovery circumstance: Natural opening
Years of commercial operation: 1947
Geology: Ordovician Hatter limestone
Former names: Arch Spring Cave, Sinking Valley Cave,
    Indian River Caverns

Cave: Veiled Lady Cave
County: Centre
Dicovery circumstance: Natural opening
Years of commercial operation: 1930–1933
Geology: Ordovician Nealmont/Benner limestone

BIBLIOGRAPHY

"A Tremendous Cave." *Weekly Ithacan,* August 30, 1878.

"A Wonderful Cave." *Philadelphia Inquirer,* July 10, 1873.

Appleton's General Guide to the United States and Canada. New York: Appleton and Co., 1897.

Arnold, Larry E. "The Pennsylvania Triangle." *UFO Report* 6, no. 4 (October 1978).

Aron, Cindy S. *Working at Play: A History of Vacations in the United States.* Oxford: Oxford University Press, 1999.

Barnsley, E. R. "Dragon Cave." In *Pennsylvania Caves,* edited by Ralph W. Stone. Topographic and Geological Survey Bulletin G3. Harrisburg: Commonwealth of Pennsylvania, 1932.

Barrick, Mac E. "Lewis the Robber in Life and Legend." *Pennsylvania Folk Life* (August 1967).

Bates, Samuel P. *Our Country and Its People: A Historical and Mineral Record of Crawford County, Pennsylvania.* W. A. Fergusson and Company, 1899.

Bayard, Samuel. "English-Language Folk Culture in Pennsylvania." *Pennsylvania Folklife 10,* no. 2 (1959).

Beaver, Frederick L., James N. J. Henwood, and John G. Muncie. "The Road to Resorts: Transportation and Tourism in Monroe County." *Pennsylvania Heritage* (Fall 1984).

Bellefonte *Democratic Watchman,* July 11, 1930.

"Berks Historians' Underground Trip." *Reading Eagle,* October 28, 1906.

Blake, Peter. *God's Own Junkyard: The Planned Deterioration of America's Landscape.* New York: Holt, Rhinehart and Winston, 1964.

Bowen, Eli. *The Pictorial Sketch-Book of Pennsylvania*. Philadelphia: W. White Smith, 1854.

Brandt, Francis Burke. *The Wissahickon Valley: Within the City of Philadelphia*. Philadelphia: Corn Exchange National Bank, 1927.

Bronner, Simon J. *Popularizing Pennsylvania: Henry W. Shoemaker and the Progressive Uses of Folklore and History*. University Park: Pennsylvania State University Press, 1996.

Bullitt, Alexander Clark. *Rambles in the Mammoth Cave during the Year 1844*. Louisville: Morton and Griswold, 1845.

Burnet, Thomas. *The Theory of the Earth: Containing an Account of the Origin of the Earth, and of All the General Changes Which It Hath Already Undergone, or Is to Undergo, Till the Consumption of All Things*. Vol. 1. London: W. Kettilby, 1684.

Butko, Brian A. *The Lincoln Highway: Pennsylvania Traveler's Guide*. 2nd ed., Mechanicsburg, PA: Stackpole Books, 2002.

Cale, David. *From Ocean Floor to Mountain Top: The Geological Story of Laurel Caverns*. Laurel Caverns publication, 1983.

Chew, Paul A. *Masterworks of George Hetzel: A Centennial Exhibition*. Johnstown, PA: Johnstown Flood Museum, 1999.

Clymer, Virgil H. *Story of Howe Caverns*. Cobleskill, NY: Howe Caverns, 1937.

Conwill, Joseph D. "The Wissahickon Valley: To a Wilderness Returned." *Pennsylvania Heritage* (Summer 1986).

Courbon, Paul, Claudet Chabert, Peter Bosted, and Karen Lindsley. *Atlas of the Great Caves of the World*. St. Louis: Cave Books, 1989.

Crupi, Corrie. *The Pagoda—Skyline Drive: An Illustrated History of Reading's Mountaintop Landmarks*. Berks County, PA: the Historical Society Press, 1998.

Cullen, George. *Mountain and Lake Resorts*. New York: Lackawanna Railroad, 1911.

Cupper, Dan. *Our Priceless Heritage: Pennsylvania State Parks: 1893–1993*. Harrisburg, PA: Pennsylvania Department of Environmental Resources, 1993.

Custed, Elizabeth. *Rose and Elza*. 1882.

Czmor, Garrett. "Tytoona Cave Preserve: A New NSS Cave Preserve." *National Speleological Society News* 58, no. 12 (December 2000).

Damon, Paul. *History of Laurel Caverns of Fayette County, Pennsylvania*. Spelean History Series 2. Altoona, PA: Speece Productions, 1976.

Damon, Paul H., ed. *Caving in America: The Story of the National Speleological Society, 1941–1991*. Huntsville, AL: National Speleological Society, 1991.

Davies, Pete. *American Road: The Story of an Epic Transcontinental Journey at the Dawn of the Motor Age.* New York: Henry Holt and Company, 2002.

Dayton, Gordon O., and William B. White. "Seawra Cave." In *The Caves of Mifflin County, Pennsylvania,* edited by Gordon O. Dayton, William B. White, and Elizabeth L. White. Mid-Appalachian Region of the National Speleological Society, Bulletin 12, July 1981.

Dayton, Gordon O., and William B. White, eds. *The Caves of Centre County, Pennsylvania.* Mid-Appalachian Region of the National Speleological Society, Bulletin 11, February 1979.

Demars, Stanford E. "Romanticism and American National Parks," *Journal of Cultural Geography* 11, no. 1 (Fall/Winter 1990).

DePaepe, Duane. *Gunpowder from Mammoth Cave: The Saga of Saltpetre Mining before and during the War of 1812.* Hays, KY: Cave Pearl Press, 1985.

DiCiccio, Carmen. *Coal and Coke in Pennsylvania.* Harrisburg, PA: Pennsylvania Historical and Museum Commission, 1996.

Eavenson, H. N. *The First Century and a Quarter of American Coal Industry.* Pittsburgh, 1942.

Ellis, Franklin, ed. *History of Fayette County, Pennsylvania, with Biographical Sketches of Many of its Pioneers and Prominent Men.* Philadelphia: L. H. Everts & Co., 1882.

Ermert, Emil R. *Story of Pioneer Tunnel.* Ashland, PA: Pioneer Tunnel, 1994.

Evening Press, Latrobe, PA. October 1, 1883.

Fabos, Julius Gy., Gordon T. Milde, and V. Michael Weinmayr. *Frederick Law Olmsted, Sr.: Founder of Landscape Architecture in America.* Cambridge: University of Massachusetts Press, 1968.

Fawley, Philip J., and Kenneth M. Long. "Harlansburg Cave: The Longest Cave in Pennsylvania." *Journal of Cave and Karst Studies* 59, no. 3 (December 1997).

Frank Leslie's Illustrated Newspaper, June 27, 1889.

Freedman, Sally A. *Delaware Water Gap, the Stroudsburgs and the Poconos.* Images of America Series. Dover, NH: Arcadia Publishing, 1995.

Fryer, Benjamin A. "Rare Allegheny Cave Rats Discovered by Reading Man." *Reading Eagle,* June 20, 1931.

Gay, Peter. *Great Ages of Man: Age of Enlightenment.* New York: Time Incorporated, 1966.

Geyer, R. Allen, and William H. Bolles. *Outstanding Geological Features of Pennsylvania,* Part 2. Environmental Geology Report 7. Harrisburg: Pennsylvania Geological Survey, 1987.

Geyer, Alan R., and William H. Bolles. *Outstanding Scenic Geologic Features of Pennsylvania,* Parts 1 & 2. Harrisburg, PA: Topographic and Geologic Survey, 1978 & 1987.

Good, Albert H. *Park and Recreation Structures.* U.S. Department of the Interior, National Park Service, 1938.

Gordon, Thomas F. *A Gazetteer of the State of Pennsylvania.* Philadelphia: T. Belknap, 1832.

Gottlieb, Steven. *Television's Greatest Hits.* Vol. 2, *TeeVee Toons Trivia Booklet.* New York: TeeVee Toons, 1986.

Hall, C. E. *Field Notes in Delaware County.* Pennsylvania Geological Survey, 2nd ser., Report C5, 1885.

Hartwell, Richard H. *Indian Echo Caverns: A History.* Hummelstown, PA: Indian Echo Caverns, 1990.

Hays, Rev. Clifford E. "The Paradise Falls Lutheran Association." In *History of Monroe County, Pennsylvania,* edited by Robert Brown Keller. Stroudsburg, PA: Monroe Publishing, 1927.

Heath, Duncan, and Judy Boreham. *Introducing Romanticism.* New York: Totem Books, 2000.

Henn, William F. *The Story of the River Road: Life along the Delaware from Bushkill to Milford, Pike County, Pennsylvania.* William F. Henn, 1975.

Henry W. Shoemaker. "Red Panther's Funeral Pyre. *Centre Hall Reporter,* August 19, 1926.

Hill, Ashbell F. *The White Rocks; or, The Robber's Den.* Morgantown, WV: Morgantown Printing and Binding, 1925.

History of Skytop. Canadensis, PA: Skytop Lodge, 2000.

Homan, Wayne E. *The Story of Famous Crystal Cave and the Kutztown Area of Pennsylvania.* Kutztown, PA: Crystal Cave Company, 1966.

Hovey, H. C. *One Hundred Miles in Mammoth Cave—In 1880.* Reprint. Silverthorne, CO: Vistabooks, 2000.

Hovey, Horace C. *Celebrated American Caves.* Cincinnati: Clarke, 1882.

Ibberson, Dale, ed. *The Caves of Perry County.* Mid-Appalachian Region of the National Speleological Society, Bulletin 13, 1983.

"Ice Mine." *Coudersport Journal,* January 19, 1916.

"In Abe Holland's Cave," *Pennsylvania Argus,* January 2, 1895.

Jensen, Oliver. *The American Heritage History of Railroads in America.* New York: American Heritage Publishing, 1975.

Johnson, Kenneth A. "Origins of Tourism in the Catskill Mountains." *Journal of Cultural Geography* 11, no. 1 (Fall/Winter 1990).

Jones, Calvin. "Description of Wier's Cave." *American Farmer* (November 23, 1821).

Kranzel, Rich. "The Doan Outlaw Caves." *Bucks County Diviner* 18, no. 2 (October 1997).

Kranzel, Rich. "Merkle Cave, Bucks County." In *Caves of Berks County, Pennsylvania,* edited by Michael Mostardi and Joe Durant. Mid-Appalachian Region of the National Speleological Society, Bulletin 18, 1991.

Kruse, Carol. "Celebrating the CCC's 70th Anniversary." *Ancient Times Park News.* Flagstaff Area National Monuments, National Park Service, 2003.

Lewie, Chris J. *Two Generations on the Allegheny Portage Railroad.* Shippensburg, PA: Burd Street Press, 2001.

"Life of Amos Wilson, The Pennsylvania Hermit." Reprint, Indian Echo Cave: Hummelstown, PA, 1945.

Lowenthal, David, and Hugh C. Prince. "English Landscape Tastes." *Geographical Review* (April 1965).

Mathews, Alfred. *History of Wayne, Pike and Monroe Counties, Pennsylvania.* Philadelphia: R. T. Peck and Co., 1886.

McFarland, J. Horace, and Robert B. McFarland. *Eagles Mere and The Sullivan Highlands.* Harrisburg, PA: J. Horace McFarland Company, 1944.

McGlade, William G. *Pennsylvania Trail of Geology: Archbald Pothole.* Harrisburg, PA: Bureau of Topographic and Geologic Survey, n.d.

Meehan, William E. "The Mountain Lakes of the State." *Report of the State Commissioners of Fisheries,* 1896.

Meloy, Harold. "Introduction to the Reprinted Edition." In Alexander Clark Bullitt, *Rambles in the Mammoth Cave during the Year 1844.* 1845. Reprint, St Louis: Cave Books, 1985.

Merrill, Lynn L. *The Romance of Victorian Natural History.* New York: Oxford University Press, 1989.

Metzgar, Tom. "Cave History Recorded by Andrew J. Waychoff." *Loyalhanna Troglodyte* 12, no. 2 (1998).

Metzgar, Tom, and Kim Opatka-Metzgar. "Bear Cave" In *Caves of Westmoreland County,* edited by Kim Opatka-Metzgar. Mid-Appalachian Region and the Loyalhanna Grotto of the National Speleological Society, Bulletin 20, 1996.

Milford Dispatch, April 14, 1898.

Milford Herald, October 3, 1865.

Miller, Donald L., and Richard E. Sharpless. *The Kingdom of Coal: Work, Enterprise, and Ethnic Communities in the Mine Fields.* Philadelphia: University of Pennsylvania Press, 1985.

Minks, Louise. *The Hudson River School.* New York: Knickerbocker Press, 1998.

Mintz, Leigh W. *Historical Geology: The Science of a Dynamic Earth.* 3rd ed. Columbus, OH: Charles Merrill Publishing, 1981.

Monk, Samuel H. *The Sublime: A Study of Critical Theories in 18th Century England.* Ann Arbor, MI: 1960.

Montgomery, Morton L. *Historical and Biographical Annals of Berks County, Pennsylvania.* J. H. Beers and Company, 1909.

Montgomery, Morton L. *History of Berks County, Pennsylvania.* Chicago: J. H. Beers and Company, 1909.

Moore, George W., and G. Nicholas Sullivan. *Speleology: The Study of Caves.* St. Louis, MO: Cave Books, 1978.

Mumma, Laura Sickel. "Eagles Mere: Of Cottages and Kings." *Pennsylvania Heritage* (Summer 1986).

Murray, Robert K., and Roger W. Brucker. *Trapped! The Story of Floyd Collins.* Lexington, KY: University Press of Kentucky, 1982.

Nagy, B. "Durham Cave Number 1 and 2." In *Caves of Southeastern Pennsylvania,* edited by J. R. Reich Jr., General Geology Report 65. Harrisburg: Pennsylvania Geological Survey, 4th ser., 1974.

New York Times, June 14, 1908.

Opatka-Metzgar, Kim, ed. *Caves of Westmoreland County.* Mid-Appalachian Region and the Loyalhanna Grotto of the National Speleological Society, Bulletin 20, 1996.

Ostrander, Stephen J. *Great Natural Areas in Eastern Pennsylvania.* Mechanicsburg, PA: Stackpole Books, 1996.

Palmer, Tim. *Youghiogheny: Appalachian River.* Pittsburgh: University of Pittsburgh Press, 1984.

Penn's Cave: All Water Cavern. Centre Hall, PA: Penn's Cave, 1998.

Pennsylvania Argus, October 4, 1839.

Pennsylvania Railroad. *Summer Excursion Routes.* Philadelphia: Pennsylvania Railroad Passenger Department, 1883.

"Philadelphia Pair Wedded Underground." *Reading Eagle,* October 15, 1919.

Platt, Franklin. *Special Report on the Coke Manufacture of the Youghiogheny River Valley in Fayette and Westmoreland Counties.* Pennsylvania Geological Survey, 2nd ser., 1876.

Pulling, Anne Francis. *Around Cresson and the Alleghenies.* Images of America Series. Dover, NH: Arcadia, 1997.

Reading Times & Dispatch, May 23, 1872.

Reed, Diane B. "The Magic of Mount Gretna: An Interview with Jack Bitner." *Pennsylvania Heritage* (Spring 1992).

Rock City Souvenir Book. Chattanooga, TN: See Rock City, 2003.

Robbins, Peggy. "William Penn's Colony of Cave People." *Pennsylvania Heritage* (Summer 1987).

Rupp, Daniel I. *History of Northampton, Lehigh, Monroe, Carbon, and Schuylkill Counties.* Harrisburg, PA: 1845.

"Samuel D. F. Kohler." *Kutztown Patriot,* August 22, 1908.

Schmidlapp, Christina M. "Pittsburgh's Park of the Century," *Pennsylvania Heritage* (Spring 1986).

Sears, John F. *Sacred Places: American Tourism in the Nineteenth Century.* Amherst: University of Massachusetts Press, 1989.

Seymour, Tres. *Mammoth Cave National Park: A History.* Washington, D.C.: Eastern National, 1997.

Shank, William H. *Three Hundred Years with the Pennsylvania Traveler.* York, PA: American Canal and Transportation Center, 1976.

Shaw, Trevor R. *History of Cave Science: The Exploration and Study of Limestone Caves, to 1900.* Sydney, Australia: Sydney Speleological Society, 1992.

Shoemaker, Henry W. *Juniata Memories.* N.p.: J. J. McVey Publishers, 1916.

Shoemaker, Henry W. *Pennsylvania Mountain Stories.* Reading, PA: Bright Printing Company, 1907.

Shoemaker, Henry W. "The Legend of Penn's Cave." *Penn's Grandest Cavern: The History, Legends, Photos and Description of Penn's Cave in Centre County, Pennsylvania,* 8th ed. Centre Hall, PA: Penn's Cave, 1971.

Shoemaker, Henry W. *Wild Life in Western Pennsylvania.* New York: Composite Printing Company, 1903.

Shultz, Charles H., ed. *The Geology of Pennsylvania.* Harrisburg, PA: Pennsylvania Geological Society and Pittsburgh Geological Society, 1999.

Shultz, Jim. "Veiled Lady Cave." *Nittany Grotto News* 17, no. 4 (March–April 1969).

Slingerland, Rudy, and K. P. Furlong. *Geodynamic and Geomorphic Evolution of the Permo-Triassic Appalachian Mountains.* In Gardner, T. W., and Sevon, W. D., eds. *Appalachian Geomorphology.* Amsterdam: Elsevier, 1989.

Smeltzer, Bernard L. "Caves of Dauphin County" and "Caves of Southern Cumberland Valley." In *Mid-Appalachian Region,* edited by William B. White. Mid-Appalachian Region of the National Speleological Society, Bulletin 6, October 1964.

Smeltzer, Bernard L. "Crystal Cave" (1985) and "Onyx Cave" (1984). In *Caves of Berks County, Pennsylvania,* edited by Michael Mostardi and Joe Durant. Mid-Appalachian Region of the National Speleological Society, Bulletin 18, December 1991.

Smith, Margaret, and Nedra Patrick. *History of Monroe County, Pennsylvania, 1725–1976.* East Stroudsburg, PA: Pocono Hospital Auxiliary, 1876.

Smith, Helen, and George Swetnam. *A Guidebook to Western Pennsylvania.* 2nd ed. Pittsburgh: University of Pittsburgh Press, 1991.

Smith, Frederick, W. *Skytop: An Adventure.* Skytop, PA: Skytop Club, 1963.

Snyder, Dean H. *The Caves of Northampton County, Pennsylvania.* Mid-Appalachian Region of the National Speleological Society, Bulletin 16, 1989.

Snyder, Dean H. *The Hidden Green Diamond: A History of Caves in Berks County, Pennsylvania.* Self-published, 2000.

Soule, Gary K. "A Historical Perspective: Seawra Cave." *Wisconsin Speleologist* 15, no. 1 (1977).

Stellmack, J. A. "Goss Cave." In *The Caves of Mifflin County, Pennsylvania,* edited by Gordon O. Dayton, William B. White, and Elizabeth L. White. Mid-Appalachian Region of the National Speleological Society, Bulletin 12, July 1981.

Stone, Ralph W. *Caves of Pennsylvania.* Bulletin 15. N.p.: National Speleological Society, 1953.

Stone, Ralph W. *Pennsylvania Caves.* Pennsylvania Geological Survey, 4th ser. Bulletin G-3. Harrisburg: Topographic and Geologic Survey, 1930, 1932.

Strother, David Hunter (pseud. Porte Crayon). *Virginia Illustrated: Containing a Visit to the Virginian Canaan, and the Adventures of Porte Crayon and His Cousins.* New York: Harper, 1871.

Summer Excursion Routes: Pennsylvania Railroad Company. Philadelphia, PA: Pennsylvania Railroad, 1883.

Swetnam, George. *Pennsylvania Transportation.* Gettysburg, PA: Pennsylvania Historical Association, 1968.

Taylor, Kirk R., John H. Ganter, William B. White, and Elizabeth L. White. *Caves of Bedford County, Pennsylvania.* Mid-Appalachian Region of the National Speleological Society, Bulletin 19, 1993.

Templeton, David. "Seldom Seen: Meadowcroft still ignites controversy over settlers." *Washington Sunday,* October 15, 2000.

The History of Ruby Falls. Chattanooga, TN: Lookout Mountain Caverns, c. 1846.

"The Robber's Cave: Lewis, the Notorious Robber." *Indiana Weekly Register* 3, no. 11, n.s. (September 5, 1854).

The Wonderful Ice Mine. Coudersport Ice Mine, c. 1940.

Thoreau, Henry D. *Walden; or, Life in the Woods.* Boston: Ticknor and Fields, 1854.

Topfer, Kurt A. "The Anthracite Aristocracy Takes to the Mountains." *Pennsylvania Heritage* (Summer 1994).

Torsell, Daniel V. "The Anatomy of a Defunct Commercial Cave." *Nittany Grotto News* 27, no. 1 (Fall 1979).

Trego, Charles B. *A Geography of Pennsylvania.* Philadelphia: Edward C. Biddle, 1843.

Trowbridge, J. T. *Cudjo's Cave.* Boston: Lothrop, Lee and Shepard Company, 1863.

Tyson, Carroll B. *The Poconos.* Philadelphia: Innes and Sons, 1929.

Van Diver, Bradford B. *Roadside Geology of Pennsylvania.* Missoula, MT: Mountain Press Publishing, 1990.

Walthier, Sally. *The Story of Bushkill Falls.* Stroudsburg, PA: D. Hannan Associates, 1992.

Wertz, Harold A. *Pennsylvania's Historic Indian Cave.* Franklinville, PA: Historic Indian Cave, 1931.

Wheeland, Keith D. "Seawra Cave: Fact and Fiction." *Nittany Grotto News* 49, no. 1 (September 2003).

White, William B. "Alexander Caverns." In *The Caves of Mifflin County, Pennsylvania,* edited by Gordon O. Dayton, William B. White, and Elizabeth L. White. Mid-Appalachian Region of the National Speleological Society, Bulletin 12, July 1981.

White, William B. "Woodward Cave." In *The Caves of Centre County, Pennsylvania,* edited by Gordon O. Dayton and William B. White. Mid-Appalachian Region of the National Speleological Society, Bulletin 11, February 1979.

White, William B., and Elizabeth L. White. "Caves." In *The Geology of Pennsylvania,* edited by Charles H. Shultz. Pennsylvania Geological Survey and Pittsburgh Geological Society, 1999.

White, William, ed. Mid-Appalachian Region of the National Speleological Society, *Bulletin 6,* 1964.

White, William B., ed. *Geology and Biology of Pennsylvania Caves.* General Geology Report 66. Harrisburg: Pennsylvania Geological Survey, 4th ser., 1976.

Williams, Harold A. *The Western Maryland Railway Story: A Chronicle of the First Century, 1852–1952.* Baltimore: Western Maryland Railway, 1952.

Wilshusen, J. Peter. *Geology of the Appalachian Trail in Pennsylvania.* Harrisburg: Pennsylvania Geological Survey, 4th ser., 1983.

Wilson, Martin W. *Delaware Water Gap: A Treasury of Times Past.* Delaware Water Gap, PA: Antoine Dutot School and Museum, 1993.

Witthoft, John. "Historic Indian Caverns." *Pennsylvania Archaeologist,* vol. xxi, no. 1-2, January–June (1951).

"Writes News from Sacony Corner." *Kutztown Patriot,* May 22, 1924.

INDEX